Advancement
of
Women

Advancement of Women

A Bahá'í Perspective

Janet A. Khan
and
Peter J. Khan

Bahá'í Publishing Trust
Wilmette, Illinois

Bahá'í Publishing Trust, Wilmette, Illinois 60091-2844
Copyright © 1998 by Janet A. Khan and Peter J. Khan
All rights reserved. Published 1998
Printed in the United States of America

01   00   99   98   4   3   2   1

Library of Congress Cataloging-in-Publication Data

Khan, Janet A. (Janet Adrienne), 1940–
    Advancement of women : a Bahá'í perspective / by Janet A. Khan
and Peter J. Khan.
        p.   cm.
    Includes bibliographical references and index.
    ISBN 0-87743-269-4 (hardcover).
— ISBN 0-87743-271-6 (softcover)
    1.   Women in the Bahai Faith. 2.   Women's rights—Religious
aspects—Bahai Faith. 3.   Bahai faith—Doctrines. I. Khan, Peter. II.
Bahá'í Publishing Trust. III. Title.
BP370.K48   1998
297.9'3178344—dc21   97-50297
                                                                CIP

Design by Suni D. Hannan
Cover photo by Susan Davis

Contents

Preface   ix

Chapter 1: The Transformation of Human Society

The Equality of Men and Women 5
The Teachings of Bahá'u'lláh 6
   A Statement of Principles 6
   The Bahá'í Administrative Order 7
   The Use of Power 11
The Process of Change 11

Chapter 2: Defining Equality

The Significance of Equality 19
A Brief Historical Survey 19
   Attitudes toward Women in Antiquity 20
   Teachings of the Manifestations of God 23
   Religious Practice 27
Bahá'í Teachings on Equality 36
   A Spiritual and Social Principle 37
   The Education of Girls and Women 40
   The Participation of Women in the World at Large 44

Contents

Complementarity, Not Uniformity 46
The Bahá'í Approach to Implementation 49
  Creating the Psychological Climate for Change 49
  Designing the Future 51
  Methodology 52
The Present Day 53

Chapter 3: Family Dynamics and Peace

The Family as Matrix 61
Traditional Family Values and Warfare 63
  The Patriarchal Family 63
  The Transmission of Attitudes to the Wider Society 70
Bahá'í Family Values and Peace 74
  The Bahá'í Family 74
    The Role of Parents 76
    Collaboration, Cooperation, and Encouragement 79
    Decision-Making 81
  The Bahá'í Family's Contribution to Creating Peace 87
    Changing Attitudes 88
    Teaching the Skill of Consultation 89
    Fostering Women's Development and Participation 90

Chapter 4: Women and Bahá'í Law

Equality and Law 97
The Nature of Bahá'í Law 98
Women and the Laws of Personal Conduct 102
  Devotional Practices 102
  Sexual Conduct 105
  Marriage and Divorce 111
Financial Rights 118
Service on Bahá'í Institutions 120
The Application of Bahá'í Law 134

**Chapter 5: Implementing Equality: The Ministries of
  Bahá'u'lláh and 'Abdu'l-Bahá**

Belief and Practice 139
The Actions of Bahá'u'lláh 140

His Teachings 140
His Guidance and Encouragement to Women 142
Examples from His Personal Relationships 145
Ásíyih Khánum 146
Bahíyyih Khánum 148
Other Bahá'í Women 149
The Role of 'Abdu'l-Bahá 152
The Exemplar of the Bahá'í Faith 153
Authoritative Interpreter 162
Timeliness 162
Enlarging the Context 163
Challenging Stereotypic Thinking 167
Use of Analogy 167
Use of Rhetorical Questions 167
Use of the Direct Challenge 168
Use of Examples from History 169
Use of Contemporary Examples 171
Assigning Responsibilities 172
Ethel Rosenberg 172
Corinne True 173
Agnes Parsons 176
Ella Cooper and Helen Goodall 177
Lua Getsinger 178
Agnes Alexander and Martha Root 178
Providing Encouragement 180
Promoting the Enlightenment of Women 183
Fostering Intellectual Development 191
The Power of Example 194

Chapter 6: Implementing Equality: The Role of Shoghi Effendi
and the Universal House of Justice

The Formative Age of the Bahá'í Dispensation 201
The Role of Shoghi Effendi 203
Interpreting the Teachings 204
Developing the Administrative Order 205
Fostering the Advancement of Women 212

Contents

International Assignments to Women 216
Effie Baker 216
Keith Ransom-Kehler 217
Martha Root 221
Amelia E. Collins 223
The Role of the Universal House of Justice 225
Elucidating the Teachings 226
Advancing the Process of Implementation 228
Fostering Women's Participation in
Bahá'í Administration 235
The Office for the Advancement of Women 240
Promoting the Social and Economic Development
of Women 249
Education 251
Health Care 255
Attitudinal Change 258
Significance of the Examples 261

Chapter 7: Practicing Equality

The Moral Imperative 267
Translating the Bahá'í Teachings into Practice 268
The Spiritual Dimension 269
Individual Conduct 271
Interaction with Society 277
Applying the Principle of Equality of the Sexes 283
At the Individual Level 283
Within Marriage and Family 287
Within the Community 291
Facing the Future with Confidence 294

Appendix: *Two Wings of A Bird: The Equality of Women*   299
and Men, a statement by the National Spiritual
Assembly of the Bahá'ís of the United States

Notes   307

Bibliography   333

Index   339

Preface

Our purpose in writing this book has been to present our understanding of the contribution of the Bahá'í Faith to the advancement of women and the implementation of the principle of the equality of the sexes. Our expectation is that the book will be principally of interest to those seeking a deeper understanding of this vital element of the Bahá'í teachings, many of whom will already have some knowledge of this religion, its principles, and its form of organization. Nevertheless we have included, as the first chapter, a brief summary of those aspects of the Bahá'í Faith that bear directly on the themes addressed in the subsequent material.

We write as Bahá'ís, seeking to explore the principle of equality of men and women set out in the Bahá'í teachings and to trace the measures taken progressively over many decades to implement this principle throughout the globe. Our special interest in this subject is long-standing and has been heightened by our travels in recent years. In these journeys we have observed the critical need for the emancipation of women from the barriers that impede their progress in many diverse cultural settings and have witnessed the strenuous endeavors of Bahá'í communities all over the world to foster this process of the advancement of women.

This book had its origin in an invitation to Janet to participate in a Bahá'í women's conference in Bophuthatswana, South
Africa, in 1992. The materials prepared for presentation on that
occasion formed the basis for the studies we have both carried
out into this subject subsequently. In the clarification of our
thinking, we have benefited greatly from discussions with many
other Bahá'ís and from study of their articles and talks. We are
deeply grateful to them and hope that our book will provide a
further stimulus to the discourse within the Bahá'í community
and among its friends and inquirers on this vital aspect of the
Bahá'í Faith.

JANET A. KHAN
PETER J. KHAN
JULY 1997

1

The Transformation
of Human Society

The utterance of God is a lamp, whose light is these words: Ye are the fruits of one tree, and the leaves of one branch. Deal ye one with another with the utmost love and harmony, with friendliness and fellowship. . . . So powerful is the light of unity that it can illuminate the whole earth.

—Bahá'u'lláh

THE EQUALITY OF MEN AND WOMEN

To promulgate and implement the principle of the equality of the sexes throughout the world is one of the fundamental aims of the Bahá'í Faith. This objective is an integral element of the Bahá'í endeavor, in all parts of the planet, to foster adherence to justice as an enduring foundation for the unity of humankind and the development of an ever-advancing world civilization.

From a Bahá'í perspective the role of religion is to bring about true liberty for the individual. This is accomplished through commitment to principles of belief which, when translated into practice, enable all to free themselves from the barriers impeding their spiritual development and thus to achieve their ordained purpose in life. Not only does this lead to liberty in its fullest sense, but it is also the means by which true happiness may be attained. The Bahá'í Faith is thus a religion of freedom and happiness, specifying that these ends are attained through observance of the laws prescribed by Bahá'u'lláh (1817–1892), the Founder of the Faith, and through self-discipline and restraint in curbing those elements of human nature that inhibit the flourishing of its spiritual elements.

The Bahá'í teachings can be considered appropriately from a historical perspective which encompasses the coming of Messengers, or Manifestations, of God at periodic intervals in various parts of the world over the span of thousands of years. Bahá'ís believe that each of these Manifestations of God gave teachings appropriate to the needs of the age in which He appeared, providing the inspiration and values for the advance of civilization and moving humanity forward toward a promised time of world unity, the emancipation of all peoples, and the inauguration of world civilization. Full expression of the equality of men and women is an integral and indispensable component of that stage in the spiritual and social evolution of humanity.

Central to Bahá'í belief is the acceptance of the claim of its Founder, Bahá'u'lláh, to be the Manifestation of God Who is the Promised One of all the preceding religious Dispensations, Whose purpose is to provide the means for spiritual reinvigoration and for the establishment of the long-anticipated time of freedom, equality, and unity. This book is devoted to an exploration of one aspect of His teachings, that of the equality of the sexes. However, the significance of this principle and the means for its implementation can only be assessed adequately within the context of the Bahá'í teachings as a whole.

THE TEACHINGS OF BAHÁ'U'LLÁH

The means set out in the Bahá'í teachings for attaining the ideals described above, and particularly the equality of the sexes, can best be appreciated by considering three closely related elements that are discussed in turn below.

A Statement of Principles

The Bahá'í teachings include principles that are directed to all aspects of human thought and conduct. They rest on the foundation of the spiritual transformation of the individual, which is accomplished through the renewal of one's relationship with the Creator and with the Manifestation of God for this age. Fundamental to Bahá'í life are the devotional practices of prayer, daily reading of the Word of God, observance of an annual period of fasting, and the unceasing striving to internalize those spiritual values that have formed the intrinsic core of all religions in their authentic form.

The principles of the Bahá'í Faith include not only precepts addressed to the individual, but also those that aim at social change and transformation. To a Bahá'í, the ideal spiritual life does not conform to the traditional model of an individual engaged in solitary spiritual disciplines, remote from interaction with other people and removed from the transactions of social life. Rather, the Bahá'í teachings direct attention to the interactive relationship between individual and social development, calling for a holistic approach in which the actions of the individual and of the social organism mutually reinforce each other and give rise to evolutionary change. This is discussed in greater detail in chapter 7.

Thus the Bahá'í approach to the equality of the sexes cannot be reduced naively to the creation of a group of well-meaning individuals who seek to bring about attainment of this condition simply by repeatedly asserting its necessity and importance. It is embedded in a complex of intimately related principles that include such matters as the religious obligation of all Bahá'ís to strive to eradicate prejudice from their thinking, the commitment to all forms of education for both males and females, the exaltation of unity based on justice and adherence to principle, the recognition of the value of intellectual and scientific activity as an approach to truth-seeking that is complementary to that of authentic religion, and the emphasis placed on enhancing means of communication between people of diverse backgrounds, languages, and cultures.

THE BAHÁ'Í ADMINISTRATIVE ORDER

It is depressingly familiar to all students of history that endeavors to attain high ideals and noble objectives are almost invariably doomed to ultimate failure as a consequence of an eventual loss of motivation, the inability to overcome deeply entrenched barriers of traditional thought and habit, the power of vested interests, and division and disunity among those who had initially united themselves in the pursuit of these goals.

A unique feature of the Bahá'í teachings is the provision that Bahá'u'lláh has made for perpetuating the unity and integrity of the Bahá'í community as it continues striving to implement these teachings over the centuries. In contrast to the religions that originated in distant times, succession of authority and the form of organization in the Bahá'í Faith are explicitly specified in writing by the Manifestation of God in His Book of the Covenant and in related passages of His writings. Such specific provisions assure unity in these vital aspects of Bahá'í community life, since deviation from such explicit prescription can only be accomplished by the self-contradictory rejection by a Bahá'í of a portion of the authentic writings of the Founder of the religion.

The Covenant of Bahá'u'lláh provides for the appointment of His eldest son, 'Abdu'l-Bahá (1844–1921), as His successor in authority as the Head of the Faith and Center of the Covenant, with well-defined functions that include authoritative exposition of the Bahá'í teachings. The reader will find Him referred to as "the Master" in some passages from the Bahá'í writings that are quoted in this book; "the Master" is a term used in recognition of His authority as an exponent of the Bahá'í teachings. In His Will and Testament 'Abdu'l-Bahá continued this pattern of explicit written provisions concerning authority by formally ordaining the institutions of the Bahá'í Administrative Order, to which reference had hitherto been made in the writings of Bahá'u'lláh.

The Bahá'í Administrative Order has as its principal institutions the Guardianship and the Universal House of Justice. Shoghi Effendi (1897–1957), the eldest grandson of 'Abdu'l-Bahá, was appointed by Him as Guardian of the Bahá'í Faith and performed the prescribed functions—which included that of authentic interpretation—from the passing of 'Abdu'l-Bahá in 1921 until his own death in 1957. The Universal House of

Justice, which was first elected in 1963 by delegates who had themselves been elected from National Bahá'í communities throughout the world, and which renews its membership by election every five years, is now the Head of the Bahá'í Faith. Included within its clearly prescribed functions are the authority to enact laws and ordinances that are not expressly set out in the Bahá'í writings and the authority to elucidate questions that are obscure in the teachings of Bahá'u'lláh.

The Bahá'í Administrative Order, functioning under the direction of the Universal House of Justice, consists, on the one hand, of elected National and Local Spiritual Assemblies, which are scattered over the entire length and breadth of the planet and which guide and coordinate the activities of the Bahá'í community. The Administrative Order also includes, on the other hand, eminent and devoted believers designated as Hands of the Cause of God, Counselors, Auxiliary Board members and their assistants, all of whom are appointed to provide a vital counseling and advisory function to the Spiritual Assemblies and to the believers generally under the guidance of an International Teaching Center.

A detailed exposition of the Bahá'í Administrative Order is far beyond the purposes of this book. However, certain features are of particular relevance to the theme of the achievement of equality of the sexes. There is no priesthood in the Bahá'í Faith and no ecclesiastical structure, thus removing that element of religious organization which has traditionally been associated with the suppression of women. Entirely absent also are any means by which the views and assumptions of individual Bahá'ís can be incorporated into the body of Bahá'í belief, since authoritative interpretation and legislation are restricted to those institutions ordained by Bahá'u'lláh and clarified by 'Abdu'l-Bahá. The process apparent in religious history, by which the freedom accorded to women by the Founder of each religion was gradually abridged or abrogated by dominant individuals or vested interests in later years, is prevented from taking root in the Bahá'í community, through the provisions of the Covenant, as described in chapter 7. The true purpose of religion is, as stated above, to liberate the human spirit and to foster initiative, freedom of thought, and creativity; the Bahá'í Administrative Order, by imposing sharp and precisely defined limits on authoritative interpretation, provides the freedom for the individual to practice these virtues and to express his or her individual interpretation and understanding of the teachings of this religion. Thus intellectual vitality is stimulated, cultural diversity is fostered, and legitimate rights of self-expression are safeguarded.

An administrative system that relies entirely on the goodness of people and which has no provision to protect itself against malicious or ambitious elements within its community will surely be vulnerable to disruption and distortion. The Bahá'í Administrative Order has carefully designed safeguards that have successfully preserved its integrity and unity after more than a century of attempts to divide it and pervert its aims; these are discussed in detail in books that analyze this Order. There is no legitimate means by which any individual can seize power or claim authority; the men and women who serve on the Faith's consultative National and Local Spiritual Assemblies perform functions in guiding the affairs of the community that cannot be assumed by any individual. Their endeavors, under the supervision of the Universal House of Justice, ensure that the Bahá'í community remains committed unequivocally to the pursuit of its exalted objectives, including the establishment of the practice of the equality of the sexes.

THE USE OF POWER

Power is indispensable to the accomplishment of all endeavors. A variety of forms are employed in the world today as individuals strive to have their views and aims accepted by the mass of the people—forms ranging from the power of persuasion to the coercive exercise of physical, economic, or military power, and including within this spectrum the power of large-scale financial resources and the power of influential persons.

The Bahá'í Faith is not oblivious to the need for power to accomplish its objectives of the transformation of individuals and of human society through the spread and implementation of its teachings. However, its approach to the use of power is radically different from the means listed above. It places its reliance on the mysterious spiritual powers of inspiration and motivation that are associated with accepting Bahá'u'lláh's claim to be the Manifestation of God for this age and with the individual believer's sincere and persistent striving to put into practice the teachings he or she has espoused. Without the assurance of this power, the Bahá'í teachings would be doomed to remain no more than an impractical dream and the followers of this Faith to be but well-meaning idealists vainly pursuing an unrealistic goal. With access to this spiritual power, change does occur, barriers are demolished, and dreams are translated into living reality.

THE PROCESS OF CHANGE

The Bahá'í Faith is a religion of change and regards all human beings as having the true purpose of participating in an ever-advancing civilization. Through the liberation of the human spirit and the practice of unified cooperation, the creative powers of humanity may be given full expression and may promote beneficial change and the enrichment of the life of all people.

The historical process over a period of thousands of years has brought humanity to the present condition in which freedom, equality, and unity are both feasible and necessary as a consequence of the social, educational, and technological condition to which the world has advanced. One element of this condition is that the facilities now available to women for their emancipation and self-development are unprecedented.

The advance of this growing process has also given rise to a counterreaction that seeks to preserve the obsolescent outlook of earlier times and is resistant to change and innovation. The tumultuous present-day scene can thus be represented in terms of the simultaneous operation of processes of growth and decline. The tension between these two processes produces the antagonism and clashes of peoples, the fanatic extremism of the disoriented and the insecure, the breakdown of the social fabric, and the determination of conservative groups to resist the emancipation of women and the consequent changes in employment, in education, and in the dynamics of the family.

The Bahá'í teachings give direction and focus to the growing process and are designed to accelerate its momentum and hasten the attainment of its objectives, upon which foundation an ever-advancing world civilization will be constructed. As the growing process continues to develop, the appropriateness and relevance of the Bahá'í teachings becomes more clearly evident to the unbiased observer, and the necessity of these teachings to produce harmony within and between individuals becomes more apparent.

At this point in its development the worldwide Bahá'í community represents a steadily growing mass of people committed to the expression of all of the Bahá'í teachings, including those which pertain to the equality of the sexes. The Bahá'í community does not claim to have attained to the full expression of these precepts, and it is not difficult to notice examples of inadequacy in the practice of these teachings, most especially in cultural settings where age-old traditions have reinforced discrimination against women. It does, however, claim a consistent and unified commitment on the part of its administrative institutions to the implementation of these teachings, the result of which is a steady and relentless advance toward this exalted goal. Thus the Bahá'í community looks to the future with confidence that it will accomplish its objective to bring about equality of the sexes and that the liberation of women will be an essential component of the transformation of human society and the advance of civilization.

2

Defining Equality

*. . . The position of women in the
Bahá'í teachings . . . is not only legal
but also spiritual and educational.*
—Shoghi Effendi

*Only as women are welcomed into
full partnership in all fields of
human endeavor will the moral
and psychological climate be
created in which international
peace can emerge.*
—The Universal House of Justice

THE SIGNIFICANCE OF EQUALITY

Universal acknowledgment of the equality of men and women is fundamental to peace and the survival of humanity. Implementation of the principle of equality challenges traditional practices, necessitates a reexamination of the long-held assumptions underlying all human relationships from the family to society at large, and even demands a reconsideration of the concept of individual identity. Because it is so interwoven with all other facets of life, the practice of the equality of the sexes impinges on all human beings—women and men alike.

A major obstacle to acceptance of the equality of women and men is the lack of a clear definition of the meaning of equality and the lack of understanding of how it applies in daily life. The absence of a definition leads to the expression of conflicting and often hotly contested views, a retreat into sexual stereotypes, and the projection of one's worst fears onto the situation. Not only are people unclear about the meaning of equality, but, given the changes that have taken place in recent years in the structure of the family and in the degree of participation of women in society, the old certainties have been removed, and most individuals feel that they have no sure basis for evaluating the appropriateness of their behavior.

This chapter presents a brief survey of the manner in which women have been treated in ages past to provide a framework in which the significance of the Bahá'í teachings on the equality of men and women can best be appreciated. The basic features of these teachings are set out here, with certain aspects being discussed in greater detail in succeeding chapters.

A BRIEF HISTORICAL SURVEY

This brief survey is no more than an introduction to a complex and controversial subject about which much has been written and which will be seen in a clearer light as future scholars attach greater significance to it. A study of the treatment of women in ancient days is of value, not only as a useful subject of historical inquiry, but—even more important—because we believe that discriminatory attitudes toward women which were apparent at distant times find their echo in the modern day. Through the insights provided by the Bahá'í teachings it becomes apparent that a survey of the effect of religion on the status of women must also distinguish between the illumined attitudes toward women expressed by the Manifestations of God, Who were the Founders of the great religions of the world, and the unfortunate conduct and attitudes exhibited by many of the adherents of these religions in subsequent decades and centuries.

ATTITUDES TOWARD WOMEN IN ANTIQUITY

As the sciences of archaeology and anthropology continue to develop, greater insight will doubtless be obtained into the role of women in antiquity. While there is now impressive evidence that, in some areas, there were periods in which women occupied a position of power and even dominance in society, this was the exception rather than the rule.[1] The world was ruled by force, and pursuits dependent on physical strength—warfare, the hunting of animals, the construction of edifices— were recognized as being vital to the survival of a social group in a hostile world. In such a setting women were often at a disadvantage and at the mercy of their menfolk. They were socialized to adopt a passive and subservient role when confronted with the aggressive attitudes that were characteristic of men engaged in a daily struggle for survival. Thus 'Abdu'l-Bahá states,

The world in the past has been ruled by force, and man has dominated over woman by reason of his more forceful and aggressive qualities both of body and mind. But the balance is already shifting; force is losing its dominance, and mental alertness, intuition, and the spiritual qualities of love and service, in which woman is strong, are gaining ascendancy.[2]

In such times, with warfare prevalent, the demographic balance was altered by the killing of men in battle. This may have been one of the factors that gave rise to polygamy in the past.

Our knowledge of the past is too fragmentary to permit a comprehensive analysis of the attitudes toward women which existed in the diverse cultures of the world over a vast span of time; it is possible, however, to identify some of the principal attitudes that were apparent. Studies in the psychology of women have characterized these attitudes as having a mythic form, representing beliefs that served to explain that which was mysterious and unknown. As social scientist Juanita Williams has pointed out, "The tenacity and continuity of these beliefs in different eras and cultures must mean that they serve potent needs in the human experience."[3]

One attitude found in many cultures derived from the association of the female of the species with Mother Nature as a source of fertility and the appearance of new life. Since nature was manifestly unfathomable, capricious, and uncontrollable, these characteristics became associated with women. The worship of fertility found its expression in the mythological mother goddesses of creation. In some cultures the need to appease nature and prevent it from exercising its violent and destructive potential on the frail inhabitants of its domain led to the sacrifice of girls and women at critical times in the succession of seasons. Woman, subject to the periodicity of natural biological processes, was regarded at such times as being intrinsically unclean and in need of ritual purification and seclusion.[4] Even today there is a tendency to stigmatize women as irrational and unpredictable, to regard them as prisoners of uncontrollable hormonal influences, and to assess them as having minimal social value beyond the reproduction of the species and the performance of domestic duties. Societies under stress still tend to choose women as their scapegoats, blaming them for such complex problems as unemployment, the fragmentation of the family, and the rise of juvenile delinquency.

Another theme prevalent in certain areas was that of woman as an agent of evil, having access to powers that could divert men from the exalted purpose of their lives. Ambivalence about the mysterious powers of sexual attraction resulted in woman's being condemned as an enchantress, sexually promiscuous, and irresistible if approached too closely. Hence women were to be veiled and confined to a restricted area lest they shamelessly tempt a virtuous male to fall from grace. Misfortunes were ascribed to the actions of witches, whose manipulation of evil forces could only be terminated by their execution. Vestiges of these attitudes are to be found today, even in those societies that pride themselves in their enlightenment, in the occasional tendency to blame victims of rape and sexual harassment for the violence and degradation to which they have been subjected.

Woman was, in many parts of the world, considered to be inferior and thus not worthy of the rights assigned to men. She was weak and vulnerable, included in the property of the men, and required to carry out the most menial of tasks without any thought that she, too, might be a being of emotion, sensitivity, intelligence, and aspiration. As 'Abdu'l-Bahá says in commenting on the position of women in Asia in the past,

> Formerly in India, Persia and throughout the Orient, she was not considered a human being. Certain Arab tribes counted their women in with the live stock. In their language the noun for woman also meant donkey; that is, the

same name applied to both and a man's wealth was accounted by the number of these beasts of burden he possessed. The worst insult one could hurl at a man was to cry out, "Thou woman!"[5]

It is impossible to comprehend adequately the degree of suffering and degradation one-half of the human race has endured over countless centuries in a world where force prevailed and dominance belonged to the physically strong and aggressive.

TEACHINGS OF THE MANIFESTATIONS OF GOD

It is a cardinal element of Bahá'í belief that Manifestations of God have come to humanity at intervals throughout history, each one revealing divine teachings that include a reiteration of eternal spiritual principles and an application of these principles to the needs and opportunities of the social milieu in which the Manifestation appears.

All Manifestations have taught that there is no spiritual distinction between men and women. 'Abdu'l-Bahá explains that

. . . women are accounted the same as men, and God hath created all humankind in His own image, and after His own likeness. That is, men and women alike are the revealers of His names and attributes, and from the spiritual viewpoint there is no difference between them. Whosoever draweth nearer to God, that one is the most favored, whether man or woman.[6]

A consequence of the Bahá'í perspective on the revealed religions of the world is the belief that if it were possible to have access to the authentic record of the messages of the Manifestations who lived thousands of years ago, historical evidence in support of this viewpoint would be found. Such evidence is to be found in both the Bible and the Qur'án. In the Book of

Genesis we read that "God created man in his own image . . . ; male and female he created them" (Gen. 1:27*), thus affirming that men and women possess identical spiritual natures. The New Testament contains many examples of the spiritual equality that was expressed in the attitude of Jesus Christ toward women: The inclusion of women as well as of men in the parables, the healing of women and of men, and the crucial role assigned to Mary Magdalene are but a few examples of this perspective. Much insight might be obtained from John 4, which tells of the encounter between Jesus and the woman from Samaria; she is treated with a courtesy and respect that amazes the disciples, she is converted by Jesus to the new religion, and she becomes His emissary in proclaiming His coming to the Samaritans in the city of Sychar. The spiritual condition of women is described in the words of the New Testament, which says, "There is neither Jew nor Greek, there is neither slave nor free, there is neither male nor female; for you are all one in Christ Jesus" (Gal. 3:28).

In several places in the Qur'án, Muḥammad sets out the spiritual equality of men and women. The following passage provides an example:

> Surely the men who submit and the women who submit, and the believing men and the believing women, and the obeying men and the obeying women, and the truthful men and the truthful women, and the patient men and the patient women, and the humble men and the humble women, and the charitable men and the charitable women, and the fasting men and the fasting women, and the men who guard

---

* This and all subsequent references to the Bible refer to the Revised Standard Version.

their chastity and the women who guard, and the men who remember Allāh much and the women who remember— Allāh has prepared for them forgiveness and a mighty reward. (Qur'án 33:35*)

Here and in other passages of the Qur'án emphasis is placed on the lack of distinction between men and women in their quest for spiritual development and in their spiritual natures. A distinction must be made between the spiritual equality of men and women, which is reiterated by 'Abdu'l-Bahá in the statement that "God has created all mankind, and in the estimation of God there is no distinction as to male and female," and the expression of social equality in the rights and functions that were assigned to women in the life of the community. Because of the nature of the society in which each Manifestation appeared, the reaffirmation of spiritual equality was not matched by social equality in the authentic teachings of these religions. In the words of 'Abdu'l-Bahá, "From the beginning of existence until the Promised Day men retained superiority over women in every respect." Referring again to the uniqueness of the social equality ordained in the message of Bahá'u'lláh, 'Abdu'l-Bahá states, "He establishes the equality of man and woman. This is peculiar to the teachings of Bahá'u'lláh, for all other religions have placed man above woman."⁷

It is clear that the social position of women was advanced significantly by the account of the life of Jesus and by His teachings. Women were encouraged to participate fully in religious activities, and the record of the Acts of the Apostles indicates that women were engaged in regular study of the scriptures, in

---

* This and all subsequent references to the Qur'án refer to the Maulānā Muḥammad 'Ali translation (1963).

proclaiming the good news of the coming of the Son of God, and in forming part of a community in which their voice was heard and their opinions accorded respect. In matters of marriage and divorce, Jesus ordained that men and women be treated evenhandedly, thus giving women greater rights than they had previously been assigned. However, there was no prohibition on polygamy, and the selection of men as the twelve disciples formed the basis for the male hierarchy of the church, because there were no statements from Jesus setting out the rights of women to participate in the organization of the religious community.

The Qur'án did much to raise the status of women, forbidding female infanticide, providing a limitation on polygamy and extending to women the right to initiate divorce proceedings, giving to women rights of inheritance and of retention of their own earnings, specifying a dowry to be given to the wife by her husband at the time of marriage, and prescribing an equitable approach to the resolution of marital discord. Despite such improvements, social equality was not ordained in the Qur'án; in setting out conditions for formulation of a contract governing the lending of money, either one man or two women are to witness the document. In the administration of the household the husband is given rights superior to those of his wife. The Qur'án states, in reference to the rights of men and women in marriage, "And women have rights similar to those against them in a just manner, and men are a degree above them" (Qur'án 2:228).

A particularly important passage that is often quoted in discussions of the position of women is Qur'án 4:34, which states,

> Men are the maintainers of women, with what Alláh has
> made some of them to excel others and with what they spend

out of their wealth. So the good women are obedient, guarding the unseen as Allāh has guarded. And (as to) those on whose part you fear desertion, admonish them, and leave them alone in the beds and chastise them. So if they obey you, seek not a way against them. Surely Allāh is ever Exalted, Great.

As might be expected, this passage has been the subject of considerable disagreement and controversy among Muslim commentators. The Arabic term *nushúz*, translated here as "desertion," is described by eminent Arabic scholars as covering a wide range of meanings, including revolting against the husband; resisting, hating, and deserting him; leaving his place and taking up an abode which he does not like. Commentators agree that the three penalties set out are progressive, dependent on the degree of violation; for example, resistance to the husband's authority is to be remedied with a simple admonition; if hatred is combined with resistance to authority, marital separation is to occur; in extreme cases, when there is desertion, hatred, and a state of revolt against the husband's authority, chastisement, including corporal punishment, is permitted. It would be quite misleading to attempt to assess the appropriateness of such a set of penalties, which were designed for use in the social system of that period in history, according to present-day standards which assume an organized society and a developed legal system that has its own set of penalties for undermining the social order.

RELIGIOUS PRACTICE

The attitudes toward women set out in the Christian Gospels and in the Qur'án differ quite significantly from the approach to women that Christian and Muslim societies have exhibited in the statements of many of their religious leaders about women, in their laws regulating female conduct, and in their treatment of women. The hierarchies of both religions have consistently accorded women an inferior position that is not supported by the authoritative statements of their Founders and have, at times, even gone to the extreme length of denying the spiritual equality of men and women.

Before examining this development in detail, it is worthwhile to inquire how so significant a departure from the principles set out in the statements of Christ and Muḥammad could have occurred. In essence, the discriminatory attitudes that existed in ancient times were permitted to reemerge and to become dominant, casting women back into the inferior position from which the Founders of these religions had sought to rescue them.

The Bahá'í teachings provide insight into the reasons for the failure of a religious community to preserve its pristine purity. They are manifold but include the following: the lack of a universally accepted source of authoritative interpretation of the words of the Founder, with the result that some crucial terms were open to being understood in a variety of ways, thereby giving rise, in certain instances, to a highly discriminatory interpretation; the assignment of unwarranted authority to the views of charismatic religious leaders, who were often unwittingly influenced by the discriminatory culture from which they arose, and whose words were given an authority equal to that of the Founder; the admission to the sacred canon of oral traditions, many of which were of questionable validity and accuracy, and which came to possess an authority equivalent to that of the Sacred Text; the unjustified generalizations made from the specific action of the Founder in a particular situation of which all the details are not known; the compromises made to the presentation of the new teachings to accommodate prevailing cultural views about the inferiority of women, motivated by the desire to make the religion more palatable to the masses and thus to increase the number of converts; and the vested interests of an exclusively male ecclesiastical establishment in preserving its position, privileges, and prerogatives through the suppression of women. The end result has been the inferior position assigned to women in much of the Christian and Islamic worlds. This brief analysis shows why great importance is attached to the Covenant of Bahá'u'lláh as the guarantor that the Bahá'í Dispensation will not be subject to the loss of integrity and purity that has occurred in the past, and why the provisions of the Covenant are regarded as occupying a central position in the Bahá'í prescription for the emancipation of women.

The Christian attitude toward women was strongly influenced by the epistles to the early churches, many of which were either written by, or are attributed to, Paul. While the advice and admonitions set out in these epistles may have been intended for a particular time and circumstance, their inclusion in the New Testament led to their being accorded a much more general applicability. Among the statements to be found there are that "the head of a woman is her husband" (1 Cor. 11:3), that "any woman who prays or prophesies with her head unveiled dishonors her head" (1 Cor. 11:5), and that "the women should keep silence in the churches. For they are not permitted to speak, but should be subordinate, as even the law says. If there is anything they desire to know, let them ask their husbands at home. For it is shameful for a woman to speak in church" (1 Cor. 14:34–35). Statements such as these have no basis in the words of Jesus Christ and stand in striking contrast to His attitude toward women during His ministry.

A particularly significant element of Paul's view of women is set out in the following passage:

Let a woman learn in silence with all submissiveness. I permit no woman to teach or to have authority over men; she is to keep silent. For Adam was formed first, then Eve; and Adam was not deceived, but the woman was deceived and became a transgressor. (1 Tim. 2:11–14)

In this passage is to be found a revival of the pre-Christian view of woman as a source of evil and as a temptress, as well as the basis for what became the Christian view that woman, through Eve, was responsible for original sin. As stated in another epistle, "the serpent deceived Eve by his cunning" (2 Cor. 11:3). This literal interpretation of Genesis 3:1–7 was reinforced by Saint Augustine in the fifth century A.D. in his work *The City of God,* in which he follows Paul by asserting that the serpent, being commissioned by a fallen angel to bring about the fall of man from his pure condition, "tried his deceit upon the woman, making his assault upon the weaker part of that human alliance, that he might gradually gain the whole, and not supposing that the man would readily give ear to him, or be deceived, but that he might yield to the error of the woman."[8] The Christian doctrine of original sin is thus associated with a transgression induced by the weakness of Eve and by her temptation of Adam.

From a Bahá'í perspective this interpretation of Genesis is quite incorrect. In a talk, 'Abdu'l-Bahá summarizes the account of Adam and Eve in Genesis, stating,

If we take this story in its apparent meaning, according to the interpretation of the masses, it is indeed extraordinary. The intelligence cannot accept it, affirm it, or imagine it; for such arrangements, such details, such speeches and reproaches are far from being those of an intelligent man,* how much less of the Divinity.⁹

'Abdu'l-Bahá clarifies that "this story of Adam and Eve who ate from the tree, and their expulsion from Paradise, must be thought of simply as a symbol," and then offers a symbolic interpretation that is far removed from that enshrined in Christian theology. 'Abdu'l-Bahá rejects the doctrine of original sin as being "far from the justice of God" and asserts that "Such an idea is beyond every law and rule and cannot be accepted by any intelligent person."¹⁰

Although it is beyond the scope of this work to attempt to trace the attitude toward women which developed in Christian

---

* The writings of Bahá'u'lláh and 'Abdu'l-Bahá were written in the Persian and Arabic languages. In the translation of these writings into English, and in other authoritative Bahá'í texts written in English, masculine pronouns and words such as "man" and "men" are frequently used in a generic rather than a gender-specific sense. The English language is fortunate in having a common gender; generic terms are intended to encompass all humankind and not to apply only to males.

The question of gender in language can present difficulties for many people at this time when there is a determined effort to eliminate the unconscious bias and the discriminatory attitudes that are so often conveyed in the choice of terms used in speech or writing. The concerns arising from the use of gender-specific nouns and pronouns can be resolved by means other than changing the usage of such terms if the consciousness of sexual equality is permitted to modify the meaning of words as they are commonly used. In many instances, the use of these terms within the context of equality of the sexes restores to primacy the generic meaning which is attached to these words in their dictionary definition.

As the equality of the sexes is accepted throughout the world, and as this principle is expressed in practice universally, the meaning commonly attached to certain words will change accordingly, as will their usage. Language is a living entity and changes as the culture that it reflects evolves.

theological thought through the centuries, mention needs to be made of Saint Thomas Aquinas since his work was destined to become a central element in the formulation of dogma in the Roman Catholic Church. His *Summa Theologica,* written in the thirteenth century A.D., aimed to provide a systematic treatment of the theological doctrines arising from the Scriptures and to present a rational justification for these doctrines. Aquinas's view of women, derived in part from Aristotle, is that

> As regards the individual nature, woman is defective and misbegotten, for the active force in the male seed tends to the production of a perfect likeness in the masculine sex; while the production of woman comes from defect in the active force or from some material indisposition. . . .[11]

Aquinas goes on to state that, "as regards human nature in general, woman is not misbegotten, but is intended by nature, and ordered for the work of generation." Having categorized woman as being fit only for childbearing, he contrasts her function with that of man, stating that man's role is to participate in the sexual act, but that "man is yet further ordered to a still nobler vital action, and that is intellectual operation." A logical consequence of the intellectual inferiority he ascribes to woman is his assertion that "woman is naturally subject to man, because in man the discretion of reason predominates."[12] This grossly distorted line of thought, far removed from the attitude and statements of Jesus Christ, may be regarded as contributing to the degrading mistreatment of women during the centuries of orthodox Christian influence on society, as well as to the psychological and physical abuse of women, to the denial of education and legal rights to women, to the suppression of their participation in religious leadership or in the intellectual activity of their community, and, in the more shameful periods of human history, to the condemnation of women as witches and as embodiments of evil, and to the idealization of the celibate state.

Turning now to Islam, one can see that the Muslim attitude toward women differed generally from that set down in the Qur'án. This is due to a combination of factors of which the predominant may be the authority given by Muslims to hadith, oral statements attributed traditionally to Muḥammad. These traditions came, ultimately, to possess an authority equivalent to that of the Qur'án in prescribing law and conduct. The major collections were formulated some two centuries after the death of Muḥammad and included a vast amount of spurious material; Al-Bukhari, the compiler of *Al Sahih,* a well-known collection, reported that he had assembled 600,000 hadith, of which he regarded only some 7,200 as authentic! An analysis of the circumstances under which spurious hadith were circulated revealed that some were formulated by people anxious to enhance their own reputation, while others arose from those seeking ideological advantage through the manufacture of hadith which reinforced their own viewpoint; other individuals who were the source of hadith can best be characterized as honest but mistaken. Beyond that, many hadith were subject to inadvertent distortion in the process of transmission from one person to another in the two hundred years intervening between a statement by Muḥammad and its inclusion in a compilation. Further problems arise from the tendency to generalize statements made by Muḥammad in response to specific and unusual circumstances, the precise details of which may well have been lost with the passage of time. Despite these limitations it must be admitted that not all hadith suffered from such defects, and some provide interesting and useful insights into the application of the principles set out in the Qur'án or into Muslim history.

The result of the attribution of authority to oral statements was a tendency to the reemergence of the highly discriminatory pre-Islamic attitudes toward women under the guise of hadith ascribed to Muḥammad. Fatima Mernissi, a contemporary

Muslim author, has studied the origins of two such hadith, which had been accepted by Al-Bukhari after he had rejected 593,000 of his original collection of 600,000, and has shown them to be highly unlikely to be valid. These two hadith—"Those who entrust their affairs to a woman will never know prosperity" and "The dog, the ass, and woman interrupt prayer if they pass in front of the believer"—are indicative of the manner in which the rights conferred upon women in the Qur'án and the spiritual equality set out in that Book were undermined by some influential members of the male-dominated Muslim hierarchy through the use of hadith in the years following Muhammad's passing.[13]

Further diminution of the rights of women occurred as a consequence of a distortion of the intent of Qur'ánic verses prescribing modesty of dress and conduct, resulting in the creation of a spurious justification for the veiling of women and their seclusion from the society outside the confines of the home; this may well be regarded as the reassertion of the ancient view that woman is a temptress from whom virtuous men are to be protected and that she is mentally inferior and thus unqualified for education or participation in the intellectual life of the community. The seclusion of women created conditions that reinforced male prejudices about the inferiority of women: Unable to secure education or to participate in those activities that would be culturally enriching, intellectually stimulating, or financially remunerative, women were condemned to ignorance and total dependence on the male members of their family. The feminine ideal became the docile woman who was totally submissive to her male authority—initially her father and then her husband or her brothers—and vulnerable to punishment, abuse, or desertion if she dared to show signs of self-assertiveness or independence. Some hadith falsely claimed that Muhammad had remarked upon the high female population of hell, which was purportedly due to so many women's being ungrateful and unfaithful to their husbands. Such views introduced distortions into a religion that had been successful in eliminating the worship of idols, endorsing women's idolatrous worship of their husbands under penalty of consignment to the fires of hell.[14]

With the natural equilibrium arising from equality between the sexes disturbed, male arrogance and preoccupation with honor were inflated. An indolent wife became a sign of her husband's affluence, and her engagement in work outside the home reflected adversely on his honor. If she produced female children, his honor was again debased, since the prevailing folklore held that the sex of the embryo was determined by that of the dominant parent.

The tendency to debase women into sexual objects was reinforced by the generally accepted scholarly interpretations of Qur'ánic verses. An example is to be found in Qur'án 52:20, where the rewards of the afterlife for faithful believers are suggested by the statement, "We shall join them to pure; beautiful ones," who are designated by the Arabic term *húr*, the literal translation of which is generally taken to be "those who are pure." Interpreters built upon this a vivid description of a male paradise in which an inexhaustible supply of beautiful virgin females were readily available for the sexual gratification of the male appetite. This licentious image has persisted despite the careful analysis of contemporary Muslim commentators such as Maulānā Muḥammad 'Ali, who have shown, on the basis of the meaning and usage of the original Arabic words and of the Qur'ánic statements that both men and women will enjoy the rewards of the afterlife, that the term *húr* should properly be taken to refer to spiritual insights and previously unknown truths.[15]

In summary, there are significant elements in the practice of both Christianity and Islam that have departed greatly from the teachings on spiritual equality given by their Founders. Traditional attitudes succeeded in diminishing the status and freedom that were prescribed for women, and untold millions of faithful female adherents of these religions consequently suffered lives of misery, degradation, and ignorance. The present-day reaction in some quarters to this distressing record of oppression has been, most unfortunately, to engage in condemnation of the Founders for the actions of their misguided or malicious followers, and some critics have proceeded to the extreme of advocating the discarding of religion itself as a necessary prerequisite to the emancipation of women. Neither of these views is valid. The Bahá'í Faith aims to use the power of religion to accomplish this necessary emancipation and has, in the provisions of the Covenant that is a crucial element of its teachings, carefully designed safeguards to avoid the distortion and deviation that have been so highly destructive of the aims of the Manifestations of God in past Dispensations.

BAHÁ'Í TEACHINGS ON EQUALITY

The principle of the oneness of humankind is described in the Bahá'í writings as the pivot around which all the teachings of Bahá'u'lláh revolve. Stressing the significance of this principle, the Universal House of Justice, in a letter written on its behalf, states,

> It has widespread implications which affect and remold all dimensions of human activity. It calls for a fundamental change in the manner in which people relate to each other, and the eradication of those age-old practices which deny the intrinsic human right of every individual to be treated with consideration and respect.[16]

The equality of men and women is an important element in the achievement of the oneness of the human family. The Bahá'í Faith is the first revealed religion in the entire span of recorded history to have affirmed, as an integral element of its teachings, not only that the equality of women and men must be regarded as a spiritual reality, but that this equality must be expressed in both individual and social practice. This total commitment to the full expression of equality in all aspects of human life is a hallmark of the Bahá'í Faith. From the Bahá'í perspective, equality is not solely a matter of obtaining personal rights and opportunities. It is an essential prerequisite to the establishment of peace, and its attainment is indispensable for the full development of both men and women. The definition of equality expressed in the Bahá'í Faith is best discerned through consideration of the entire range of its teachings and cannot be summarized in a succinct phrase or statement.

The changes on a personal and social level necessary to make equality an established reality are far-reaching. The practice of equality requires not only basic changes in attitudes and behavior by both women and men but also a fundamental alteration to the structure of society to provide the necessary legal rights and to provide educational and employment opportunities for women. A distinguishing feature of the approach to change outlined in the Bahá'í writings is that it fosters the practice of equality by men and women in such a way as to preserve and indeed strengthen the fundamental unity of the family and society. The methods employed emphasize cooperation, mutual encouragement and support, and consultation.

A SPIRITUAL AND SOCIAL PRINCIPLE

Bahá'u'lláh unequivocally asserts the spiritual equality of women and men. He states that "All should know . . . Women and men have been and will always be equal in the sight of God," and He indicates that, "In this Day the Hand of divine grace hath removed all distinctions. The servants of God and His handmaidens are regarded on the same plane." Bahá'u'lláh affirms that "The most beloved of people before God are the most steadfast and those who have surpassed others in their love for God. . . ."[17]

'Abdu'l-Bahá confirms that men and women alike are the revealers of the names and attributes of God, clearly stating that "from the spiritual viewpoint there is no difference between them."[18] In one of His Tablets He provides the following comment about the nature of the soul:

> Know thou that the distinction between male and female is an exigency of the physical world and hath no connection with the spirit; for the spirit and the world of the spirit are sanctified above such exigencies, and wholly beyond the reach of such changes as befall the physical body in the contingent world.[19]

In the same Tablet, 'Abdu'l-Bahá provides insight into what is required now, in contrast to times past, in relation to the practical expression of this spiritual principle:

> In former ages, men enjoyed ascendancy over women because bodily might reigned supreme and the spirit was subject to its dominion. In this radiant age, however, since the power of the spirit hath transcended that of the body and assumed its ascendancy, authority and dominion over the human world, this physical distinction hath ceased to be of consequence; and, as the sway and influence of the spirit have become apparent, women have come to be the full equals of men. Today, therefore, there is no respect or circumstance in which a person's sex provideth grounds for the exercise of either discrimination or favor.[20]

As a spiritual principle, the equality of men and women has relevance to humankind as a whole. The equality of the sexes is, therefore, not an injunction that applies to only one-half of the human race. Its practice is a spiritual duty for all Bahá'ís, women and men alike. All Bahá'ís are required, as a matter of belief, to commit themselves to implementing it in their personal conduct, to encouraging its practice by others, and to fostering the means by which it is reflected in the operation of the institutions of society. In addition to emphasizing spiritual equality, the Bahá'í teachings clearly affirm that women's moral qualities and intellectual abilities are equal to those of men and that women are entitled to rights and opportunities equal to those of men.

In the Bahá'í writings are to be found specific practical provisions for promoting the equality of women and men, for fostering the development of full partnership, and for modifying the "harmful attitudes and habits" that stand in the way of the emancipation of women. From the Bahá'í perspective, there are a number of important prerequisites to the emancipation of women. These include the right of women to be respected as human beings, to be accorded civil and legal rights equal to those of men, and to have these rights protected by the society at large. In one of His Tablets Bahá'u'lláh explicitly states that women enjoy "a station and rank on the same plane" as men. 'Abdu'l-Bahá indicates that "Women have equal rights with men upon earth; in religion and society they are a very important element," and He calls attention to the fact that "Divine Justice demands that the rights of both sexes should be equally respected since neither is superior to the other in the eyes of Heaven."[21]

The Bahá'í writings spell out some of the implications of equal rights for women. Such rights include equality of opportunity in education and employment, the right to vote and to participate in government, and equality in all departments of life. It is important to recognize that these authoritative statements from the Bahá'í writings are regarded by Bahá'ís as expressions of the Divine Will; thus Bahá'ís regard it as a religious obligation to heed the call of these writings for changes in both attitudes and legal systems to accommodate this new reality. To deprive women arbitrarily of these rights and privileges is both immoral and unjust, a violation of God's law. It has a detrimental effect on the individual woman's sense of self and her peace of mind and undermines the "moral and psychological climate" of society.[22]

The emancipation of women and the achievement of "full equality" demands the recognition that women and men alike are endowed with talents and abilities. In the words of 'Abdu'l-Bahá, ". . . it is well established that mankind and womankind as parts of composite humanity are coequal and that no difference in estimate is allowable, for all are human."[23] The achievement of equality requires that women have the opportunity to demonstrate their abilities by obtaining education and participating in all fields of human endeavor.

THE EDUCATION OF GIRLS AND WOMEN

The Bahá'í writings affirm that many of the differences apparent between women and men, the differing functions assigned to them, and the inequities that persist, are due to the fact that women have been, and in many parts of the world continue to be, deprived of education and the opportunity to develop those skills that would enable them to participate fully in society. In one of His talks 'Abdu'l-Bahá makes the following observation:

The difference in capability between man and woman is due entirely to opportunity and education. Heretofore woman has been denied the right and privilege of equal development. If equal opportunity be granted her, there is no doubt she would be the peer of man.[24]

'Abdu'l-Bahá further stresses the role of education in establishing the equality of women:

... if woman be fully educated and granted her rights, she will attain the capacity for wonderful accomplishments and prove herself the equal of man. She is the coadjutor of man, his complement and helpmeet. Both are human; both are endowed with potentialities of intelligence and embody the virtues of humanity. In all human powers and functions they are partners and coequals. At present in spheres of human activity woman does not manifest her natal prerogatives, owing to lack of education and opportunity. Without doubt education will establish her equality with men.[25]

'Abdu'l-Bahá underlines the importance of according women opportunities equal to those open to men. He indicates that "The sex distinction which exists in the human world is due to the lack of education for woman, who has been denied equal opportunity for development and advancement," and He states that "Equality of the sexes will be established in proportion to the increased opportunities afforded woman in this age."[26]

In the Bahá'í teachings great emphasis is placed on the acquisition of knowledge in all of its forms, and education is highly valued. According to 'Abdu'l-Bahá, the education of each child is compulsory. He asserts that "Universal education is a universal law" and draws attention to the means, through the implementation of this instruction, for changing traditional and prejudiced attitudes, removing barriers between the sexes, and promoting recognition of the oneness of humanity.[27] Writing on this subject, 'Abdu'l-Bahá states,

. . . inasmuch as ignorance and lack of education are barriers of separation among mankind, all must receive training and instruction. Through this provision the lack of mutual understanding will be remedied and the unity of mankind furthered and advanced.[28]

Likewise, the Universal House of Justice notes in a statement on peace that "ignorance is indisputably the principal reason for the decline and fall of peoples and the perpetuation of prejudice." Consequently "No nation can achieve success unless education is accorded all its citizens."[29]

The importance accorded to the education of girls and women in the Bahá'í Faith is unique in religious history and quite revolutionary in its vision. Going beyond statements that access to education is vital for the development of women so that they can play an equal part in society, 'Abdu'l-Bahá also states that, under certain circumstances, preference is to be given to the education of girls. In His Tablets, calling attention to the responsibility of parents to educate all their children, 'Abdu'l-Bahá clearly specifies that the "training and culture of daughters is more necessary than that of sons," for girls will one day be mothers, and mothers are the first educators of each generation. If it is not possible, therefore, for a family to educate all the children, perhaps due to limitations on available resources, preference is to be given to daughters, thus opening the way to terminate the process by which ignorance is transmitted from one generation to the next through mothers deprived of education. The Universal House of Justice has reiterated the importance of 'Abdu'l-Bahá's instruction in calling upon "decision-making agencies" concerned with the "cause of universal education" "to consider giving first priority to the education of women and girls, since it is through educated mothers that the benefits of knowledge can be most effectively and rapidly diffused throughout society."[30]

One outcome of the Bahá'í emphasis on the education of daughters is that it draws attention to the value of the girl child. This emphasis is significant because, in many cultures, the girl child has a lower status and enjoys fewer rights and opportunities than her brothers. Many societies traditionally apply a different and discriminatory set of values and expectations to the girl child. All too often family decisions about the distribution of food, the allocation of household chores, the extent of health care and access to schooling, benefit boys to the detriment of the welfare of girls.[31]

The commitment to the education of girls and women, from the inception of the Bahá'í Faith, is demonstrated by 'Abdu'l-Bahá's encouragement of the Persian Bahá'ís to establish schools for girls at a time when there were no formal provisions for the education of girls in Persian society. Drawing attention to the importance of this activity, He states, "Devote ye particular attention to the school for girls, for the greatness of this wondrous Age will be manifested as a result of progress in the world of women."[32] The role of the Bahá'í family in the education of its female children is set out in chapter 3, and the present-day contribution of the worldwide Bahá'í community to the education of girls and women is described in chapter 6.

Another outstanding feature of the Bahá'í teachings on the equality of the sexes is that they call for the adoption of an identical program of education for men and women. 'Abdu'l-Bahá indicates that "Daughters and sons must follow the same curriculum of study," and He affirms that if woman were "given the same educational opportunities or course of study, she would develop the same capacity and abilities."[33] The introduction of a curriculum to be followed by both girls and boys would help to undercut the pervasive tendency to channel males and females into different fields of study irrespective of their capacities. Traditionally girls are encouraged to pursue such subjects as the humanities, social sciences, and domestic arts, while boys pursue the physical sciences, industrial arts, and the professions. As a result women and men tend to be segregated into different fields of work, having markedly different levels of remuneration. So pervasive is this tendency that it has reinforced the attitude that women have neither the ability nor the temperament to succeed in areas of work where men have traditionally predominated. The effects of adopting a curriculum that makes no distinction on the basis of sex will be profound and will give rise to far-reaching changes in society.

The Bahá'í teachings concerning the importance of educating girls and women are a vital means of bringing into existence the new definition of equality between the sexes. These teachings assert the value of women. They provide women with the opportunity to demonstrate their skills and abilities, to prepare themselves for active participation in all areas of human endeavor, and to perform more capably their function as mothers and educators of the next generation. They foster a reexamination of traditional attitudes toward girls and women, help to redress past discriminatory practices, and set the agenda for changing curricula and for removing existing sex-stereotyped barriers in the world of work.

THE PARTICIPATION OF WOMEN IN THE WORLD AT LARGE

The function of motherhood and being the first educator of the new generation is assigned a high position in the Bahá'í teachings. However, this does not mean that the Bahá'í Faith seeks to confine the role of women to the domestic setting. On the contrary, the Bahá'í concept of the equality of women and men calls for women to be involved in all fields of activity, as 'Abdu'l-Bahá affirms: "women must advance and fulfill their mission in all departments of life, becoming equal to men."[34] The standard of full partnership defined in the Bahá'í writings calls for women to be invited to participate in all fields of human endeavor. Indeed, the concept of "women's work" and "men's work" will become largely irrelevant. This is in dramatic contrast to religious practice in past ages—and in some parts of the world at the present time—where women were expected to be occupied solely with domestic pursuits, leaving to men the involvement in commerce and the professions. The movement of women into a wider field of endeavor in the twentieth century has been at the cost of their being accused of betraying their ordained female role and being blamed for the stress on family unity and for the adolescent behavioral problems that have occurred in the contemporary period.

In the statements of 'Abdu'l-Bahá, women are called upon, among other things, to "enter confidently and capably the great arena of laws and politics" and to devote their "energies and abilities toward the industrial and agricultural sciences."[35] That 'Abdu'l-Bahá mentions such pursuits should not be taken to imply that women should refrain from entering the multitude of other fields of professional activity He does not mention. It is interesting, however, to note that these particular fields have traditionally been restricted to males only and have been notorious for the degree of prejudice encountered by women seeking entry and acceptance therein.

The Bahá'í Faith calls for justice to be the controlling principle in the operation of social institutions to the extent that its governing institutions are designated to be Houses of Justice. The application of justice in such areas of employment as appointment, promotion, and remuneration will directly benefit women; furthermore, the Bahá'í moral code will protect women against workplace intimidation and harassment.

Women's full and equal participation in the life of society is a prerequisite to peace. The Universal House of Justice has clarified that

The emancipation of women, the achievement of full
equality between the sexes, is one of the most important,
though less acknowledged prerequisites of peace. The denial
of such equality perpetrates an injustice against one-half of
the world's population and promotes in men harmful attitudes and habits that are carried from the family to the workplace, to political life, and ultimately to international relations. There are no grounds, moral, practical, or biological,
upon which such denial can be justified. Only as women are
welcomed into full partnership in all fields of human endeavor will the moral and psychological climate be created
in which international peace can emerge.[36]

Education provides women with access to positions of authority in the world at large. Such prominent positions enable
women to influence thought, to bring to bear peace-inducing
attitudes in governmental and administrative settings, and to
be involved in making decisions that affect the future of society. 'Abdu'l-Bahá highlights the importance of women's contribution to peace, asserting that "when women participate fully
and equally in the affairs of the world . . . war will cease." He
also links the attainment of the equality of women and men
with lasting peace: "When . . . the equality of men and women
[shall] be realized, the foundations of war will be utterly destroyed. Without equality this will be impossible. . . ."[37] The
role of the Bahá'í family in the promotion of peace is described
in chapter 3.

COMPLEMENTARITY, NOT UNIFORMITY

One of the most interesting questions raised in recent years
as the quest for fuller understanding of the relationship be-

tween the sexes proceeds is that of the differences between men and women in other than the obvious physical characteristics. At one extreme are to be found those who insist that there are no other differences and that a rigid insistence on absolute equality of function and treatment should prevail. The other extreme accommodates those who regard men and women as fundamentally different in nature and characteristics. Such a perspective promotes stereotypical views of men as being distinguished by their rationality and women by their intuition, a characterization that can very easily be used as a basis for the discriminatory treatment of women and their exclusion from professions that are dependent on the power of rational thought. Attempts to resolve this question simply by observing present-day behavior are of limited value because such conduct occurs in a society that continues to reflect the traditional segregation of roles as well as the lack of equality and denial of opportunity accorded to women. Genetic and neurophysiological studies are at an early stage but will doubtless provide much useful information as they proceed in the future.

The vital contribution of the Bahá'í Faith to this interesting and complex issue is found in statements that refer to the complementarity of the functions of men and women. This implies that there would be some differences of function within the context of equality. Writing on this theme, the Universal House of Justice states,

> That men and women differ from one another in certain characteristics and functions is an inescapable fact of nature and makes possible their complementary roles in certain areas of the life of society; but it is significant that 'Abdu'l-Bahá has stated that in this Dispensation *"Equality of men and women, except in some negligible instances, has been fully and categorically announced."*[38]

The Bahá'í writings employ a number of graphic images to illustrate the similarities and differences that exist between women and men and the character of the relationship between them. For example, 'Abdu'l-Bahá states,

> The world of humanity has two wings—one is women and the other men. Not until both wings are equally developed can the bird fly. Should one wing remain weak, flight is impossible. Not until the world of women becomes equal to the world of men in the acquisition of virtues and perfections, can success and prosperity be attained as they ought to be.[39]

The wings of a bird are structurally equivalent and perform similar functions. They are simply attached to opposite sides of the bird's body, and one is not inherently to be preferred over the other. Both must work in cooperation for the bird to fly. Likewise, though differences exist between men and women, these differences are not so great as to prevent them from performing essentially similar functions. The qualities of the one reinforce those of the other. Each is indispensable to the other, and one wing cannot function adequately in isolation from the other.

'Abdu'l-Bahá provides another simple but profound example of the equal and complementary relationship that should exist between women and men, stating that in the "world of humanity"

> There is a right hand and a left hand, . . . functionally equal in service and administration. If either proves defective, the defect will naturally extend to the other by involving the completeness of the whole; for accomplishment is not normal unless both are perfect. If we say one hand is deficient,

we prove the inability and incapacity of the other; for single-handed there is no full accomplishment.[40]

Just as it is well-nigh impossible to complete even the most simple task—such as tying a knot—with only one hand, so the contribution of women is indispensable in the functioning of society. Women's qualities and skills cannot be discounted as "optional extras" in the work of the world.

Such analogies are very powerful in illustrating the significance of this relationship. The Bahá'í concept of complementarity stresses the equality and mutual interdependence between men and women and recognizes that, in certain instances, women's contributions may differ from men's. It affirms the value of both and recognizes that one cannot be legitimately undervalued simply because it derives from the female part of the world of humanity. It underscores the importance of the full partnership of women and men in all areas of human endeavor.

THE BAHÁ'Í APPROACH TO IMPLEMENTATION

The Bahá'í approach to implementing the principle of the equality of men and women is multifaceted. It involves individuals, women and men, Bahá'í institutions, and all members of the community. Some of the major features of the Bahá'í approach are set out below, while the application of this approach is described in chapters 5, 6, and 7.

CREATING THE PSYCHOLOGICAL CLIMATE FOR CHANGE

As described earlier, the Bahá'í Faith is intrinsically a religion of change, and its approach to the attainment of the sweeping change in human society associated with the universal recognition of the equality of men and women involves promoting in the Bahá'í community a positive attitude toward change as well as the patience and confidence necessary as the community proceeds toward that goal.

This climate of change is fostered when men and women examine their assumptions about women in light of the new reality set out in the Bahá'í writings. It calls for accepting the new definition of women's station and role in society, recognizing the concerted effort required of individual women and men and the community as a whole to modify negative and outdated attitudes and habits, and encouraging women's development and full participation in all areas of life.

Willingness to change is facilitated by a non-adversarial attitude in the Bahá'í community, with the believers being patient and understanding toward each other. Bahá'ís are encouraged to be tolerant of the diverse attitudes that may be manifested in the process of change, but such tolerance is not to be confused with complacency about conduct that does not correspond to that which is prescribed in the Bahá'í teachings. Collaboration between women and men, mutual encouragement, consultation and shared decision-making, and the commitment and support of the community for change are the hallmarks of the Bahá'í approach to implementing the principle of equality.

Another important element in creating the psychological climate that will facilitate change is the unified understanding of the believers about what is required of them in expressing the equality of men and women. Such a unified understanding is attainable through use of methods that are integral to Bahá'í community functioning, including consultation and reference to the Bahá'í institutions, and ultimately to the Universal House of Justice if necessary, of any matters that are obscure or are the source of differences. As a result, believers can approach the process of change confident that they are proceeding in the right direction, irrespective of the difficulties they may encounter along the way.

DESIGNING THE FUTURE

The implementation of the principle of the equality of women and men within the Bahá'í community is not left to chance. It results from promulgation of a clear vision of the ideal Bahá'í community life, which forms a basis for planful activity that is designed to create the future. The activities are of several kinds. They aim to instill and sharpen individual and community understanding of the principle of equality, to encourage the adoption of the value of equality and its practice, and to gain community support for implementing the principle in individual and social life.

Commitment to the ideal of equality gives rise to a determination to create a model community, one in which equality is truly practiced. The vision of the ideal community acts as a magnet to inspire and motivate individual and community alike to take steps to introduce changes so as to bring personal and social behavior into accord with the ideal. Commitment to the ideal also gives inspiration and courage to pursue the steps required for change.

One implication of having the ideal clearly in front of the community, on the horizon, is the realization that as we move toward the horizon, the horizon moves ahead, and the landscape changes. As time goes by in the journey toward the future, the understanding of the principle of equality, and consequently the way in which it is practiced, will most likely change. Increased understanding allows the Bahá'ís to reach enhanced levels of personal transformation and to plan new activities that enable all members of the community to implement the principle of equality more fully on a societal level. Both chapters 5 and 6 illustrate the progressive enlargement of the scope of Bahá'í activities in the promotion of equality.

Educational programs are designed both to enhance individual understanding of the principle and to provide opportunities for women and men to put the principle into action. Such programs aim to create a community that manifests the shared vision and which represents the gradual attainment of equality. Examples of these educational programs are set out in chapter 7.

METHODOLOGY

Involving, as it does, fundamental changes in ingrained individual values and discriminatory social systems, the implementation of the principle of equality will not come about immediately, nor simply because well-meaning people support the ideal and consider such support sufficient to change the social reality. Rather, the Bahá'í approach to achieving equality aims to establish the practice of equality of women and men on a firm foundation. It is characterized by the implementation of the spiritual principle in an evolutionary manner over a long period of time, sustained by a commitment to fundamental change and nurtured by educational programs designed to assist individuals and communities to gradually bring attitudes and actions into conformity with the spiritual principle. The approach is, therefore, non-utopian; it is realistic and evolutionary, proceeding in a phased manner, yet never losing sight of the long-term goal. While the approach may not satisfy the impatient, it has the advantage of leading to enduring change. The record of accomplishment described in chapters 5 and 6 supports this assertion.

Planning for change, which consists of concrete steps for a more conscious and thorough application of the spiritual principles of equality, is fostered by the Spiritual Assembly's acting in consultation with the members of the community. The Assembly not only supports the efforts of individual Bahá'ís to implement the principle of equality in daily life, but it arranges activities that both stress the importance of the principle and engage community members in actions that lead to a consolidation of behaviors that reflect equality. The planned activities enable individuals and the Bahá'í community to take the next step in their personal and collective development. A fuller description of the role of the Spiritual Assembly in facilitating changes in values and actions is given in chapter 7.

THE PRESENT DAY

The history of the nineteenth and twentieth centuries can well be regarded as a chronicle of human endeavor for emancipation, equality, and freedom. The efforts of women in the nineteenth century, and especially those in the Western world, to win such rights as access to education and participation in intellectual and commercial activities outside the home were followed by the quest for suffrage and for active involvement in the process of governance.

Many powerful forces are now at work to promote the fuller expression of the equality of the sexes. Technological advances, including computerization, automation, and a comprehensive system of worldwide communication, have provided the means for women to lead fuller lives. Jobs in industry, agriculture, and construction, which previously required physical strength, have been transformed such that their principal requirement is now technical skill in the use of complex instruments. Distance learning and telecommuting have enabled both men and women to receive education and to participate in professional endeavors from their homes or from remote locations. Equal-opportunity legislation and the provision of legal redress for those exposed to sexual harassment in the workplace have combined to facilitate the entrance of women into a wider sphere of remunerative activity. Television and radio programs have awakened hope and aspiration in women living in countries where they are deprived of their human rights, as they have become informed of the more enlightened circumstances in which women reside elsewhere in the world.

A realistic assessment of the present-day condition must not ignore or underestimate the strength and potential of those repressive forces that, in many parts of the world, seek to reverse the advances of recent decades and to return women to the narrow and confining world from which they have sought emancipation. As a society in transition experiences turmoil and upheaval, there is a growing tendency to make women the scapegoats for a variety of social problems, ignoring the root causes of these social maladies in the loss of values now afflicting humanity. People, insecure and uncertain about the future, hanker for an idealized past age of calm and stability with which was associated a sharp demarcation of sex roles and a lesser involvement of women in the affairs of the world. Increasing violence toward women and increasing aggression against the physically weaker members of the community offer further evidence of the profoundly disordered state of society, as does the general breakdown of law and order everywhere. The ominous rise in religious fanaticism and extremism among so many of the major faiths of humankind takes as one of its primary aims the repression of women.

Within this setting of simultaneously operating forces of emancipation and repression, the Bahá'í community is working, seeking to effect that fundamental transformation of values which will lead to an enduring change in human behavior. Although the achievement of its objectives is aided immeasurably by the forces of positive change, the Bahá'í Faith must inevitably be confronted by the entrenched forces of repression. It does not underestimate the magnitude of the challenge before it, but approaches its task with supreme confidence in the power of the spiritual forces associated with the Bahá'í Revelation to reinforce the endeavors of the Bahá'ís in all parts of the planet.

3

Family Dynamics and Peace

The denial of . . . equality perpetrates an injustice against one-half of the world's population and promotes in men harmful attitudes and habits that are carried from the family to the workplace, to political life, and ultimately to international relations.

—The Universal House of Justice

THE FAMILY AS MATRIX

Chapter 2 mentioned one of the most widespread concerns about implementing the principle of the equality of men and women: that it will lead to the disruption of family structure, bringing about marital breakdown, a rise in family disorder, and a general disturbance of the stability of human society. Supporters of this view have no difficulty in finding examples where radical feminism, expressed in an aggressive and adversarial attitude toward men, has created such conditions; this, in turn, provides ready ammunition for those who would mistakenly assert that the quest for equality is contrary to the natural order and that its abandonment is necessary for the preservation of marriage and a stable home in which children can be raised. If their aim is to preserve the time-honored patriarchal family structure, then it cannot be denied that the practice of the equality of the sexes will severely disrupt that form.

The purpose of this chapter is to explore the Bahá'í perspective on the impact of equality on the family and social relations. The Bahá'í teachings call for a new form of family dynamics, based on equality, that provides a family structure appropriate to the present age and intrinsically far stronger than that of ages past, a family structure that offers to all of its members—husband, wife, and children—a level of fulfillment and satisfaction otherwise inaccessible.

Beyond that, the Bahá'í Faith asserts that there is an intimate connection between this new approach to family functioning and the attainment and preservation of world peace.

The Bahá'í writings disclose a positive and inspiring vision of the future. They stress the inevitability of world peace—a peace based on the practice of moral and spiritual values and on the recognition of the oneness of the human family; a peace that embodies the emancipation and full partnership of women and men, that signals the unity and maturity of the human race; a peace that can be hastened by means of active and conscious choices by individuals to support its emergence. Not only do the Bahá'í writings underline the relationship between equality and peace, but they also stress the important role of the family as the environment in which attitudes are acquired—attitudes that can be either harmful or conducive to peace.

'Abdu'l-Bahá sees the family as a microcosm of the family of nations. He calls attention, in the following statement, to the impact of the psychological climate of the family and the effects of the behavior of individual members on the peace and security of the whole:

> Compare the nations of the world to the members of a family. A family is a nation in miniature. Simply enlarge the circle of the household, and you have the nation. Enlarge the circle of nations, and you have all humanity. The conditions surrounding the family surround the nation. The happenings in the family are the happenings in the life of the nation. Would it add to the progress and advancement of a family if dissensions should arise among its members, all fighting, pillaging each other, jealous and revengeful of injury, seeking selfish advantage? Nay, this would be the cause of the effacement of progress and advancement. So it is in the great family of nations, for nations are but an aggregate of families.[1]

Highlighting the challenge confronting each individual and each family in choosing attitudes and actions that promote unity and peace, 'Abdu'l-Bahá offers the following exhortation:

> Consider the harmful effect of discord and dissension in a family; then reflect upon the favors and blessings which descend upon that family when unity exists among its vari-

ous members. What incalculable benefits and blessings would descend upon the great human family if unity and brotherhood were established!²

In this chapter we explore ways in which the family serves as the matrix for the acquisition of values. We examine the source of some of the "harmful attitudes and habits" that originate in the family and the means by which they are transmitted to the workplace, to the world of politics, and to international relations.³ This approach demonstrates how the Bahá'í concept of the family, based on the explicit teachings of the Faith, serves to transform the moral and psychological climate and to promote positive attitudes and behavior in its individual members, contributing thereby to the creation of peace.

TRADITIONAL FAMILY VALUES AND WARFARE

We show here that the traditional family gives rise to harmful attitudes which are inevitably expressed also in the wider society, leading to aggression and conflict. The creation of enduring peace and unity in the world thus depends on the transformation of this form of family structure.

The Patriarchal Family

Throughout recorded history women have been denied full social equality with men. A natural consequence of this situation was the primary role assigned to the husband in marriage and in the family, which gave rise to patriarchy as the ideological form into which such relationships have been cast. In its broadest sense, patriarchy consists of a set of beliefs and values about the nature of men and women and about their relative worth and their roles in society. It is supported by social institutions and backed by implicit or explicit threats of violence.⁴

The significance of the family is that, as indicated in the passages from 'Abdu'l-Bahá quoted above, it constitutes the setting in which attitudes and values are not only formed and expressed but transmitted to the next generation. That which is learned in the family setting is then expressed far more widely in the larger society and, ultimately, in the behavior of decision-makers on a national level in their relationships with people of other nations and races.

The patriarchal family, which is characterized by the "institutionalization of male dominance over women and children," has been, until recent decades, the structure found universally. Even in the present day it still represents the family structure most commonly found in most of the world. In such a family, with divorce being highly discouraged or impossible, husband and wife are bound together in a relationship of inequality; this disparity of rights becomes the kernel, embedded in the matrix of the family relationship, from which grow the attitudes apparent today. In some instances the love between the couple, their spiritual qualities, or the pressing need to meet external challenges from famine, warfare, or natural disasters give rise to cooperative relationships and to attitudes distinguished by mutual respect and consideration. All too often, however, the sense of inequality between male and female facilitates the development of a differentiation of treatment that has been amplified over a vast number of generations. This sense of inequality and differentiation of treatment, in the words of the Universal House of Justice, promote "in men harmful attitudes and habits that are carried from the family to the workplace" and beyond to all levels of society.[5]

While it is beyond the scope of this chapter to review the evolution of patriarchy, it is possible to identify three harmful effects deriving from that system and from its lack of equality in the treatment of women within the family. The first of these effects is the categorization of women as a group subordinate to the dominant male group, with the women and girls being assigned a place in the family structure subordinate to their fathers, brothers, husbands, and, in extreme but not uncommon instances, to their sons.

The implications of this attitude are profound. As Jean Baker Miller, a contemporary psychologist, has written,

> Once a group is defined as inferior, the superiors tend to label it as defective or substandard in various ways. . . .
>
> Dominant groups usually define one or more acceptable roles for the subordinate. Acceptable roles typically involve providing services that no dominant group wants to perform for itself. . . . Functions that a dominant group prefers to perform, on the other hand, are carefully guarded and closed to subordinates. Out of the total range of human possibilities, the activities most highly valued in any particular culture will tend to be enclosed within the domain of the dominant group; less valued functions are relegated to the subordinates.
>
> Subordinates are usually said to be unable to perform the preferred roles. Their incapacities are ascribed to innate defects or deficiencies of mind or body, therefore immutable and impossible of change or development. It becomes difficult for dominants even to imagine that subordinates are capable of performing the preferred activities. More importantly, subordinates themselves can come to find it difficult to believe in their own ability.[6]

The operation of the dynamic described by Miller has direct application in the family in which women are regarded as subordinate to men. It gives rise to a condition defined by Gerda Lerner, a contemporary writer on patriarchy, as "paternalistic dominance," which

> describes the relationship of a dominant group, considered superior, to a subordinate group, considered inferior, in which the dominance is mitigated by mutual obligations and reciprocal rights. The dominated exchange submission for protection, unpaid labor for maintenance. In the patriarchal family, responsibilities and obligations are not equally distributed among those to be protected: the male children's subordination to the father's dominance is temporary; it lasts until they themselves become heads of households. The subordination of female children and of wives is lifelong. Daughters can escape it only if they place themselves as wives under the dominance/protection of another man. The basis of paternalism is an unwritten contract for exchange: economic support and protection given by the male for subordination in all matters, sexual service, and unpaid domestic service given by the female.[7]

The patriarchal family underlines the traditional view, which held sway for many centuries, that women were intellectually inferior and hence incapable of intellectual development or education, that their views should be disregarded, and that, in times of scarcity, the female family members should have lesser access to the food than should the men. From such a position it is but a small additional step to decide that the inferior individual should be compelled to be obedient to her husband or father, even if this requires use of force or violence. Another consequence of the relegation of women to an inferior role in the family has been, in some instances, sexual abuse in the form of marital rape or incest, in attempted justification for which is offered the spurious argument that the woman concerned is, in essence, the property of the male.

Closely related to the first harmful effect of patriarchy, the subordination of women, is the second harmful effect, which is the inculcation of attitudes that are restrictive or even crippling in both women and men. Women are expected to be submissive and non-assertive and to refrain from showing initiative or being venturesome. By contrast men in such a family setting are socialized into being aggressive and competitive even to the point of violence and are discouraged from manifesting such attributes as sensitivity, generosity, and a sense of caring, lest they be stigmatized as effeminate and lacking in masculinity.

Psychologists call attention to the fact that healthy personality development involves equal and complementary emphasis on individuality and relatedness for both women and men. They note that the underdevelopment of interpersonal relatedness in men and of a sense of self in women results in both sexes' being deprived of their full potential as human beings. In Western cultures men as a group generally tend to give more attention to self-development and to underemphasize interpersonal relatedness. On the other hand, women are usually more developed in the interpersonal realm. Relational development represents both a culturally undervalued strength and a vulnerability because women risk losing themselves in their relationships.[8]

Such an analysis illuminates the significance of statements by 'Abdu'l-Bahá that restriction on the expression of equality for women has the effect of damaging the development of men. He states,

> The world of humanity consists of two parts: male and female. Each is the complement of the other. Therefore, if one is defective, the other will necessarily be incomplete, and perfection cannot be attained. There is a right hand and

a left hand in the human body, functionally equal in service
and administration. If either proves defective, the defect will
naturally extend to the other by involving the completeness
of the whole; for accomplishment is not normal unless both
are perfect.[9]

He further states, "As long as women are prevented from attaining their highest possibilities, so long will men be unable to
achieve the greatness which might be theirs."[10] One could quite
properly construct on this foundation a self-interest argument
for men to exert themselves to work for the equality of the sexes
on the basis that such a condition would liberate men to develop aspects of their personality that have been stunted by the
society of inequality and would thus lead them to a greater
sense of fulfillment and contentment.

The third harmful effect of patriarchy, which is closely related to the two effects already described, is the creation of a
rigid sense of role definition between the sexes that goes far
beyond a simple division of labor and is characterized by certain functions' being reserved for each sex. Some justification
could perhaps have been provided in the past for such discrimination, because of variation in physical strength. However, in
practice the distinction was more commonly based on the notion that female household members belonged to the dominant male. The confinement of women to domestic pursuits
was thus a means of preserving his property from loss. The
resulting rigid role distinction was reinforced by the discriminatory view that women lacked the powers of rational thought
that men enjoyed. The stereotype of the irrational, emotional
female was reinforced by denial of facilities for her education
and for her access to information about the world from other
sources.

Traditional sex-role expectations have created separate worlds for the sexes and have interfered with the mutual communication and respect needed for the development of equal and non-exploitive relationships between men and women. These rigid role expectations have also been found to contribute to the likelihood of depression, family violence, and sexual abuse of female children.[11]

A patriarchal family structure of the form described will necessarily be vulnerable to strain or disruption as its female members claim their right to be treated as equals, and in this sense there is some validity to the criticism that implementing the Bahá'í teachings on this subject would indeed weaken that particular form of family; however, the response to such criticism is not to retreat into inequality but rather to create a new, stronger, and more fulfilling family structure. Despite the likelihood of some initial disruption, Bahá'ís are confident that a stronger, more balanced family structure than was possible under the old patriarchal system can be built on the firmer foundation of two equal partners in marriage. While the strictly patriarchal family is gradually being modified in many parts of the world, there is also a tendency to return to its inflexibility and hierarchy in societies where there is insecurity and disorder. The advance of education for women and the movements for human rights and emancipation are beginning to create a climate in which increasing numbers of men are more likely to admit the legitimacy of equal rights for women, even on those occasions when their conduct is deficient, paternalistic, or hypocritical.

Great emphasis is placed on the need for wisdom and unity and on the evolutionary nature of change in implementing the Bahá'í teachings. Such an approach minimizes the disruption experienced by a family that is practicing the principle of sexual

equality, and all who are involved have the opportunity to ad-
just progressively to the new conditions, to lovingly help and
encourage each other, and to become aware of the resulting
benefits to the entire family. It should be recognized, however,
that appeals for such a progressive approach to implementation
can also be used, under some circumstances, as an excuse for
procrastination or avoidance of constructive action—a short-
sighted and ethically improper strategy that will often yield dis-
location and disunity in the longer term.

THE TRANSMISSION OF ATTITUDES TO THE WIDER SOCIETY

As the Universal House of Justice states, the "harmful attitudes and habits" that result from the denial of equality to
women "are carried from the family to the workplace, to political life, and ultimately to international relations."[12] The relationship between the manifest needs on a world scale—such as
world peace and harmonious relationships between peoples and
nations—is only now becoming clear to those who are deeply
concerned about the betterment of society.

The family is where individuals first learn, by example and
by how they are treated, how people relate to each other and
how they ought to relate to each other. Parents tend to shape a
child's attitudes and behaviors by a variety of means: articulat-
ing expectations about how boys and girls should act, reinforcing desired behaviors, punishing those forms of conduct that
are considered unacceptable, and providing models for the child
to emulate. At an early age children are able to state clearly the
stereotypical expectations regarding appropriate and inappropriate behaviors for women and men.[13]

Emphasizing the role of the family as a matrix for the transmission of values and attitudes, a report by the Center for Partnership Studies calls attention to the importance to the wider

society of the expression of human rights, including women's rights within the family, stating that

> as long as violations of human rights are condoned in people's most intimate relations—the relations between women and men and parents and children—not only will these continue in family relations from generation to generation, but so also will human rights violations outside the family. For it is in our intimate relations that we first learn, and continually apply, equitable or inequitable standards for human relations. And it is also here that we learn to accept, or reject, authoritarian rule and violence as a means of conflict resolution. . . .[14]

Susan Moller Okin, a political scientist concerned with social justice, has underlined the need for justice within the family unit. She makes the point that women will not be able to gain equality in politics, at work, or in any other sphere until there is justice within the family. She asserts that a just family is an essential foundation to a just society, stating,

> unless the first and most formative example of adult interaction usually experienced by children is one of justice and reciprocity, rather than one of domination and manipulation or of unequal altruism and one-sided self-sacrifice, and unless they themselves are treated with concern and respect, they are likely to be considerably hindered in becoming people who are guided by principles of justice.[15]

If the structure of the family is that of dominance and subordination, the attitudes learned within the home are ultimately amplified and projected on the world scene. Those who are accustomed to dominate will regard others who appear to be different—be they of another gender, race, class, ethnic group, or nation—as being appropriate for subjugation, even if this has to be accomplished by force. The concept of human rights will become perverted, with the subordinates being denied equal treatment, and thus regarded as partaking of a lesser degree of humanity. This becomes apparent in the epithets and caricatures used to characterize opponents during warfare, in the denial that such antagonists also have human sensitivities and emotions, and in the pitiful attempts to justify genocide or torture on the basis of sweeping generalizations about the segment of humankind that is being oppressed.

The fostering of male aggression within the family setting provides the predisposition to achieve the dominance described above through warfare, violence, and conquest. Military prowess is taken to be an expression of masculinity, and conquerors are exalted to the rank of the heroes of a victorious nation. Fathers are encouraged not only to expose their sons to experiences that will bring out latent tendencies toward aggression and domination through violent sports and recreational pursuits, but also to prevent mothers from exerting a restraining influence. This aggression is expressed not only in the military sphere but also in the realm of business and economic activity; some popular books on management advocate the development of a "killer instinct" from the earliest age as the best preparation for success in business.

Rigid sex-role definition extends beyond the family environment into the manner in which society is organized and into restrictions on the participation of women in professional activities and in public affairs. Riane Eisler, a cultural historian with a special interest in the rights of women, describes the effect of inequality between the sexes on the totality of society. She draws attention to the "fundamental correlation between sexual inequality and a generally unjust, unequal and violent form of social organization."[16]

Women are, in such a setting, largely confined to service positions in employment, where they are expected to be subservient. Those who aspire to advancement and promotion by moving out of the subservient role are likely to be criticized for being "unfeminine." Little importance is attached to their education, and the ignorance they exhibit as a result of the deprivation of opportunities for learning is taken as fulfilling the prejudiced assessment of their lack of capacity and confirming their intellectual inferiority to men.

This restriction of women from involvement in the wider society has a direct effect on the prolongation of warfare. As 'Abdu'l-Bahá points out,

> Woman by nature is opposed to war; she is an advocate of peace. Children are reared and brought up by the mothers who give them the first principles of education and labor assiduously in their behalf. Consider, for instance, a mother who has tenderly reared a son for twenty years to the age of maturity. Surely she will not consent to having that son torn asunder and killed in the field of battle. Therefore, as woman advances toward the degree of man in power and privilege, with the right of vote and control in human government, most assuredly war will cease; for woman is naturally the most devoted and staunch advocate of international peace.[17]

The creation of a society in which there is equality between the sexes will doubtless liberate men to participate more fully in processes such as child rearing that conduce to the development of greater sensitivity and tenderheartedness. Beyond that, at a time when the world stands so urgently in need of peace, the greater involvement of women in decision-making and governance is of vital importance so that their experience in nurturance and the preservation of harmony may exert a beneficial influence on humanity's quest for peace.

BAHÁ'Í FAMILY VALUES AND PEACE

An entirely new model for the family is provided by the Bahá'í teachings. This form of family structure expresses equality and provides a means by which all family members can develop attitudes and patterns of behavior that are conducive to a peaceful and harmonious society.

THE BAHÁ'Í FAMILY

The distinctiveness of the Bahá'í family, as prescribed in the Bahá'í teachings, is that it rests on the foundational principles of the equality of the sexes and respect for the rights of all members of this social unit.

The attitude and relationship between husband and wife in a Bahá'í marriage play a determining role in the manner in which the family functions and in the values the couple inculcates in the new generation. In the selection of a marriage partner, both man and woman are to be left free from interference from others and are called upon to strive to become well informed of each other's character. An example of the application of the principle of equality is found in the fact that either one is free to propose marriage, as stated by Shoghi Effendi in a letter written on his behalf: "'. . . there is absolute equality between the two, and . . . no distinction or preference is permitted.'"[18]

This spirit of equality carries through to the actual marriage ceremony, which contains no statement of subservience of one partner to the other, but rather directs them to a mutual endeavor to conform their lives to the Will of God. As is discussed in chapter 4, the sense of equality is reinforced by the provision of a dowry to be given by the husband to the wife, an implication of which is his endorsement of her right to the ownership of property and the disposition of resources.

The nature of the Bahá'í family should be considered within the context of a marriage in which equality between husband and wife is affirmed and practiced as a matter of course.

Within the family setting the rights of all members must be respected. This contrasts with the traditional patriarchal family, in which the father and the other male members enjoy privileges at the expense of the females. It also contrasts with the authoritarian family, in which the rights of the children are denied and the parents are subject to no restraint in the treatment of their children in such matters as education, discipline, and duties. In the Bahá'í context, where a sound foundation is to be set for the unity of the family, no one member has the right to usurp or infringe on the rights of the others. 'Abdu'l-Bahá states,

> The integrity of the family bond must be constantly considered, and the rights of the individual members must not be transgressed. The rights of the son, the father, the mother—none of them must be transgressed, none of them must be arbitrary. Just as the son has certain obligations to his father, the father, likewise, has certain obligations to his son. The mother, the sister and other members of the household have their certain prerogatives. All these rights and prerogatives must be conserved. . . .[19]

The preservation of the rights and prerogatives of the individual family members ensures that respect is accorded to all, irrespective of sex or age. It encourages an appreciation for the unique contribution that each can make to the family and fosters individual development, collaboration, mutual support, and a more equitable sharing of tasks and resources. The practice of equality within the context of family unity creates a nurturing and positive climate that helps to lay the foundation for full partnership between the members and thereby further strengthens the family unit.

THE ROLE OF PARENTS

The Bahá'í writings define, in broad terms, the primary responsibilities of the mother and father along lines that may well appear to be, at first sight, conventional. The distinctive feature of the Bahá'í approach is that the roles of mother and father are not rigidly exclusive and are best seen within the context of mutual support and cooperation. There is considerable flexibility in the functions assigned to each, and changes and adjustments can be made to suit particular family situations, including the interests and capacities of each party to the marriage. Within this degree of role flexibility, the Bahá'í teachings set out a complex of duties and responsibilities that the members of the family have toward each other and toward the family as a whole. Shoghi Effendi, in a letter written on his behalf, states that

> The task of bringing up a Bahá'í child . . . is the chief responsibility of the mother, whose unique privilege is indeed to create in her home such conditions as would be most conducive to both his material and spiritual welfare and advancement. The training which a child first receives through his mother constitutes the strongest foundation for his future development. . . .[20]

This statement should not be taken to imply that the father has no part in influencing the conditions within the home, or that he is not to consider himself responsible for playing a role in the early training of the child as circumstances permit.

According to the Universal House of Justice, "a corollary of this responsibility of the mother is her right to be supported by her husband—a husband has no explicit right to be supported by his wife."[21] This imposes a spiritual obligation on the husband to make every effort to secure employment in order to support his family. The husband's responsibility to support the wife has revolutionary implications in those cultures in which the women currently do a disproportionate share of the work, including growing the food, collecting water and fuel, and generally taking care of the survival needs of the family.

While the man has primary responsibility for the financial support of the family, it must also be noted that this function is not inflexibly fixed and can be adjusted to suit particular family situations. There is nothing in the Bahá'í teachings to preclude a wife from assuming the role of major breadwinner or a husband from taking principal responsibility for care of the children and of the home, if the couple chooses to do so.

The role of mothers is rehabilitated within the Bahá'í context and given importance beyond the immediate family setting. Motherhood is not only concerned with the rearing of children, it is also allied with no less exalted an aim than the attainment of peace. While mothers have the chief and primary responsibility to be the first educators of the next generation, they are not excluded from the world at large, as they would be in a rigidly patriarchal social structure, nor are men excluded from participation in homemaking activities. Bahá'ís envisage and indeed support the involvement of women and men in both the private and public spheres of activity.

Fathers not only have the major responsibility to provide for the financial support of the wife and family and to pay for the education of the children, but they also have a significant part to play in the education of the children. In the Kitáb-i-Aqdas (literally, "the Most Holy Book"), the chief repository of Bahá'u'lláh's laws, He reveals, "Unto every father hath been enjoined the instruction of his son and daughter in the art of reading and writing and in all that hath been laid down in the Holy Tablet." The Universal House of Justice affirms that the father's responsibility to educate his children is "so weighty that Bahá'u'lláh has stated that a father who fails to exercise it forfeits his rights of fatherhood."[22] Commenting further on the important role of the father in this regard, the House of Justice states in a letter written on its behalf,

> The great importance attached to the mother's role derives from the fact that she is the *first* educator of the child. . . . This does not mean that the father does not also love, pray for, and care for his baby, but as he has the primary responsibility of providing for the family, his time to be with his child is usually limited, while the mother is usually closely associated with the baby during this intensely formative time when it is growing and developing faster than it ever will again during the whole of its life. As the child grows older and more independent, the relative nature of its relationship with its mother and father modifies and the father can play a greater role.[23]

It should be noted that, rather than prescribing that fathers should spend less time with the children than the mothers, the House of Justice appears to be describing the situation that now exists in many countries in the world.

Hence the roles of the mother and father are neither narrowly defined nor mutually exclusive. Each has a part to play in nurturing and educating the children, and both can be breadwinners. It is clear from the statement of Bahá'u'lláh cited above and from the following extract from the writings of 'Abdu'l-Bahá that the educational responsibilities of the parents apply to daughters as well as to sons:

> ... it is enjoined upon the father and mother, as a duty, to strive with all effort to train the daughter and the son, to nurse them from the breast of knowledge and to rear them in the bosom of sciences and arts. Should they neglect this matter, they shall be held responsible and worthy of reproach in the presence of the stern Lord.[24]

COLLABORATION, COOPERATION, AND ENCOURAGEMENT

Though cooperation is basic to society, in many existing family settings men very early in life tend to learn to expect females to serve them. For men to cooperate and to share, therefore, may well be interpreted by them as a personal loss or, at best, an act of altruism. The Bahá'í model of the family demonstrates a new approach both to the relationship between the sexes and to the marital relationship. It is a model in which selfishness, aggression, and the use of force are to be eliminated and replaced by cooperation and consultation.

In one of His Tablets 'Abdu'l-Bahá stresses the importance of cooperation and reciprocity to the progress of human society. He states,

> Were one to observe with an eye that discovereth the realities of all things, it would become clear that the greatest relationship that bindeth the world of being together lieth in the range of created things themselves, and that co-operation, mutual aid and reciprocity are essential characteristics in the unified body of the world of being, inasmuch as all created things are closely related together and each is influ-

enced by the other or deriveth benefit therefrom, either directly or indirectly. . . .

And thus when contemplating the human world thou beholdest this wondrous phenomenon shining resplendent from all sides with the utmost perfection, inasmuch as in this station acts of co-operation, mutual assistance and reciprocity are not confined to the body and to things that pertain to the material world, but for all conditions, whether physical or spiritual, such as those related to minds, thoughts, opinions, manners, customs, attitudes, understandings, feelings or other human susceptibilities. In all these thou shouldst find these binding relationships securely established. The more this interrelationship is strengthened and expanded, the more will human society advance in progress and prosperity. Indeed without these vital ties it would be wholly impossible for the world of humanity to attain true felicity and success.[25]

Central to cooperation and sharing is a recognition of the equality and interdependence of the family members. Appreciation of mutuality encourages women and girls to endeavor to develop themselves and to enrich their own lives, and it increases the likelihood that their efforts will not be misinterpreted as an attempt to diminish or imitate men. Such appreciation also enhances the likelihood that men will actively encourage and support women's efforts for self-development, since they understand the relationship between the development of women and the greater development of the family unit and of the society at large. The development of girls and women is not at the expense of the male members of the family, and it accrues to the good of the family unit.

Understanding the link between the development of women and girls and the fuller development of the family has implications not only for the personal enrichment and self-esteem of the female members, but it also discourages rigid role definition and influences the willingness of men and women to share family tasks and resources. Such understanding will progressively create an environment in which girls and women are no longer deprived of an adequate share of the food and access to educational opportunities and health care, and in which females cease to be forced to undertake an inequitable share of the work that must be done within the family. Likewise, the greater malleability of roles enables women to seek employment and to participate fully in the public sphere and frees up men to share a number of functions that have been traditionally regarded as "women's work."

It is interesting to note the benefits of this greater flexibility and sharing. A number of social scientists have observed that the fullest development of both boys and girls is more likely if both parents are actively engaged in parenting so that an infant can become deeply attached to both. Greater involvement by fathers in childrearing could result in a cultural shift away from exaggerated individualism. Psychologists writing on the changing roles of men have found a positive relationship between improved mental health in men and their contributing in a significant way to household and family tasks; they have also drawn attention to the value of sharing the nurturing role—it tends to increase personal sensitivity and foster empathy, qualities that are linked to the development of a sense of justice.[26]

DECISION-MAKING

The Bahá'í approach to group decision-making and interaction is based on a distinctive process of consultation. This process is used in the functioning of Bahá'í administrative institutions such as Spiritual Assemblies. But consultation is not restricted to decision-making groups; it applies also to the interaction between the participants in Bahá'í meetings such as National and Unit Conventions and Nineteen Day Feasts, whose purpose is to ensure that issues are properly ventilated, that a unity of vision is established, and that suggestions and recommendations are made to the decision-making body.

Within the Bahá'í family are found the application of the principles of Bahá'í consultation in these two forms: as a means of decision-making and as a process for the thorough exploration of issues and the attainment of unity of vision. It is clear that the ultimate decision-making role is assigned to the parents and that the children are expected to obey their parents. As the Universal House of Justice explains in a letter written on its behalf,

> The members of a family all have duties and responsibilities towards one another and to the family as a whole, and these duties and responsibilities vary from member to member because of their natural relationships. The parents have the inescapable duty to educate their children—but not vice versa; the children have the duty to obey their parents—the parents do not obey the children. . . .[27]

This duty does not, however, empower the parents to act in an authoritarian manner, for the Universal House of Justice, in a letter written on its behalf, refers to "the principle that the rights of each and all in the family unit must be upheld, and the advice that loving consultation should be the keynote, that all matters should be settled in harmony and love. . . ."[28]

Bahá'í consultation is distinguished by the spirit of inquiry into what is best for all concerned, rather than by a desire to prove oneself right or an aim to pressure the group to accept one's view. Thus the participants are urged not to be possessive about their own ideas, but rather to offer these views with an attitude of detachment, regarding them as a contribution to the group as it strives to reach its conclusions.

Essential to the successful functioning of the consultative process is its atmosphere and the freedom that each participant has to express his or her views without fear of being belittled, humiliated, insulted, or ignored. Such an atmosphere can only be established on the secure bases of acceptance of the oneness of humankind and the equality of the sexes, and recognition of the importance of courtesy and respect in all manner of human relations.

The Bahá'í teachings provide the foundation for the believers' conduct in their individual and collective activities. Thus the consultation of the parents and the entire family is, in its essence, an inquiry into the application of the values and precepts of the Bahá'í Faith to the issue at hand. It is, in a very real sense, an expression of devotion to God and the commitment of the family members to walk in His path and to do that which will be pleasing to Him.

When applied within the family setting, consultation represents another significant element of the Bahá'í model of family life. In this context, consultation is described by the Universal House of Justice as the "panacea" for family problems, provided, of course, it is conducted in the right spirit and in the appropriate manner. The Universal House of Justice states in a letter written on its behalf,

> Bahá'u'lláh . . . stressed the importance of consultation. We should not think this worthwhile method of seeking solutions is confined to the administrative institutions of the Cause. Family consultation employing full and frank discussion, and animated by awareness of the need for moderation and balance, can be the panacea for domestic conflict.[29]

The consultative decision-making of husband and wife must necessarily be carried out in a spirit of equality, far removed from the adversarial approach and patriarchal tone that is found so often in the wider society. Although it follows the form used in Bahá'í community consultation, it differs from such gatherings in the manner in which it handles situations in which unanimity cannot be reached—at which time the larger group relies on a majority vote, with the obligation of all group members to give their full support to the majority decision. The Universal House of Justice provides the following guidance for applying Bahá'í consultation to parental decision-making:

> In any group, however loving the consultation, there are nevertheless points on which, from time to time, agreement cannot be reached. In a Spiritual Assembly this dilemma is resolved by a majority vote. There can, however, be no majority where only two parties are involved, as in the case of a husband and wife. There are, therefore, times when a wife should defer to her husband, and times when a husband should defer to his wife, but neither should ever unjustly dominate the other. In short, the relationship between husband and wife should be as held forth in the prayer revealed by 'Abdu'l-Bahá which is often read at Bahá'í weddings: "Verily, they are married in obedience to Thy command. Cause them to become the signs of harmony and unity until the end of time."[30]

Elaborating on this deference, a letter written on behalf of the House of Justice states, ". . . there are times when the husband and the wife should defer to the wishes of the other. Exactly under what circumstances such deference should take place, is a matter for each couple to determine."[31] It is evident that the procedure of deference in the case of disagreement is open to abuse through insistence and denigration and could, under adverse circumstances, degenerate into a reversion to the patriarchal decision-making that is antithetical to the Bahá'í teachings on the equality of the sexes. The Bahá'í approach to the relationship between husband and wife cannot be reduced to the mechanical application of a set of procedural rules; it requires instead the fostering of love, respect, and mutual consideration so that matters such as decision-making can be handled properly.

Family consultation plays a vital role in building and maintaining family unity and in training the children to develop good judgment and the capability to examine complex issues fully and dispassionately. It may well be expected that, as the children grow up, the range of issues that are considered in family consultation will be extended, and the parents' reliance in their decision-making on the conclusions arrived at during family consultation will increase.

A novel feature of Bahá'í community life is that some individuals are assigned certain functions without being given powers of decision-making greater than those of other members of a group; these functions may, in the case of a Spiritual Assembly, include those of acting as a point of reference, of convening meetings, or of executive action in carrying out the consultative decisions. A similar flexibility applies within the Bahá'í family, together with a corresponding absence of superiority in decision-making. Although the Universal House of Justice states, in a letter written on its behalf, that "it can be inferred from a number of the responsibilities placed upon him, that the father can be regarded as the 'head' of the family," it also points out, in response to a request for further elucidation of this matter, that by inference from a number of responsibilities placed upon him, the father can be regarded as the "head" of the family. However, this term does not have the same meaning as that used generally. Rather, a new meaning should be sought in the light of the principle of the equality between men and women, and of statements of the Universal House of Justice that neither husband nor wife should ever unjustly dominate the other. The House of Justice has stated previously, in response to a question from a believer, that use of the term "head" "does not confer superiority upon the husband, nor does it give him special rights to undermine the rights of the other members of the family." It has also stated that if agreement cannot be reached following loving consultation, "there are times . . . when a wife should defer to her husband, and times when a husband should defer to his wife, but neither should ever unjustly dominate the other"; this is in marked contrast to the conventional usage of the term "head" with which is associated, frequently, the unfettered right of making decisions when agreement cannot be reached between husband and wife.[32]

The emphasis on consultation should not be taken to imply that the individual family members are unduly restricted in the exercise of initiative or the expression of diversity. The purpose of the Bahá'í teachings is to foster the fullest expression of the talents, capabilities, and interests of all, and this can only be accomplished if an appropriate degree of freedom is accorded to each family member. Certain issues are reserved for individual decision-making, and none is more important than that of the right of religious belief. Shoghi Effendi states, in a letter written on his behalf,

> It is one of the essential teachings of the Faith that unity should be maintained in the home. Of course this does not

mean that any member of the family has a right to influence the faith of any other member; and if this is realized by all the members, then it seems certain that unity would be feasible.[33]

In the matter of selecting a prospective marriage partner, family consultation can well serve as a means of clarifying issues and obtaining valuable advice. Nevertheless, 'Abdu'l-Bahá writes,

> As for the question regarding marriage under the Law of God: first thou must choose one who is pleasing to thee, and then the matter is subject to the consent of father and mother. Before thou makest thy choice, they have no right to interfere.[34]

Although the couple wishing to marry are free to reach their decision without interference from the parents, it would be quite natural for them to turn to their parents for advice and counsel in the process of exercising their choice, and such a warm and loving interaction is far removed from that which might be characterized as interference. The parents have, as stated above, the freedom to give or refuse that consent which is a prerequisite for Bahá'í marriage to take place.

THE BAHÁ'Í FAMILY'S CONTRIBUTION TO CREATING PEACE

The redefinition of family contained in the writings of the Bahá'í Faith fosters a transformation in the moral and psychological climate of the family. It addresses, thereby, a number of the problems associated with patriarchy, problems that are linked to the perpetuation of attitudes of inequality and dominance, the assignment of women to sex-stereotyped roles, their virtual confinement to the private sphere of activity, and their exclusion from positions of public decision-making. Such attitudes and discriminatory behaviors not only limit the development of the individual, both male and female, but they also prevent the expression of peace-inducing attitudes and actions and, as a result, deprive women of the opportunity to enjoy full partnership with men in the family and in society at large.

In the Bahá'í view, enduring peace can only exist when unity is achieved. Bahá'u'lláh attests that "The well-being of mankind, its peace and security, are unattainable unless and until its unity is firmly established."[35] The attainment of the equality of men and women is a vital prerequisite to achieving the oneness of humanity, since the continued existence of discriminatory attitudes and practices is a lingering source of discord and conflict.

The Bahá'í family serves as a model for the transmission of attitudes and skills that are calculated to undermine the very foundations of war. It addresses the essential prerequisites of peace by aiming to achieve unity in human relationships and the acceptance of the equality of women and men. Its approaches include changing fundamental attitudes and values, teaching behaviors and skills that foster peace, and facilitating the involvement of women in the public sphere, where they can bring to bear their unique capabilities in the service of peace and international arbitration.

CHANGING ATTITUDES

Parents are concerned with teaching and modeling the values and behaviors that they hold dear and that they want their children to acquire. The commitment of husband and wife to equality, service, and loving solicitude, and their efforts to practice these attitudes and values in daily life have a far greater impact on children's behavior than mere oral instruction and training.

Within a Bahá'í family husband and wife are coequal. They are encouraged to act as a team, to appreciate the contribution made by the other, and to offer each other mutual support and encouragement. They are committed to demonstrating respect for all family members and a real appreciation for the girl as well as the boy child, helping, thereby, to counteract the preference for males and the all-too-pervasive superiority and self-importance of boys that exists in many different cultures of the world—attitudes that give rise to aggressive conduct and warfare. Parents also protect the rights of all family members. They endeavor to ensure the fair and equitable distribution of resources and family tasks and, by sharing roles, help to break down artificial barriers between "men's work" and "women's work."

Because the practice of the equality of women and men is enjoined in the Bahá'í religion, its implementation is a spiritual responsibility for all members of the Bahá'í community. Consequently the attitudes and behaviors associated with equality must be taught to both male and female family members. Equality cannot be achieved merely by training the daughters. Real and fundamental social change will come about only as both men and women, together, act on this spiritual principle. Furthermore, community support of the individual's effort to align his or her behavior with the spiritual standard is important to cement the desired attitudes and actions.

TEACHING THE SKILL OF CONSULTATION

One of the major contributions of the family to peace is that it provides its members with the opportunity to learn the important skill of consultation for use in the wider society in which the family members participate through their professional and social endeavors. In addition to serving as an effective means for decision-making and peaceful conflict resolution, consultation is a vehicle for putting into practice the attitudes and values associated with peace and justice. Decisions are made in the light of spiritual principles. They reflect the group's understanding of the truth of the matter under discussion and its effort to arrive at a solution that is equitable and just. Such decisions are willingly supported by the community.

Children who are taught the skill of consultation recognize that one may be different but equal. They learn to be more concerned with the good of all and less motivated by self-interest, to solve problems and make decisions without recourse to violence or threat, and they understand the importance and wisdom of obedience to, and support of, a decision once it is made. These insights are very relevant to their future participation in decision-making in government and in the realm of international relations, where even after decisions are finally made, all too often, these conclusions tend not to be supported either by those who participated in the decision-making or by those on whose lives the decisions impinge.

FOSTERING WOMEN'S DEVELOPMENT AND PARTICIPATION

Bahá'í families place great importance on the moral and intellectual education of all children. However, because girls grow up to be mothers, and mothers are the first educators of the next generation, special emphasis is accorded to the education of daughters. 'Abdu'l-Bahá states that

> . . . it is incumbent upon the girls of this glorious era to be fully versed in the various branches of knowledge, in sciences and the arts and all the wonders of this preeminent time, that they may then educate their children and train them from their earliest days in the ways of perfection.[36]

He further encourages the Bahá'ís to

> ... teach the young girls and the children, so that the mothers may educate their little ones from their earliest days, thoroughly train them, rear them to have a goodly character and good morals, guide them to all the virtues of humankind, prevent the development of any behavior that would be worthy of blame, and foster them in the embrace of Bahá'í education.[37]

'Abdu'l-Bahá spells out the implications of inculcating such qualities into the next generation:

> Thus shall these tender infants be nurtured at the breast of the knowledge of God and His love. Thus shall they grow and flourish, and be taught righteousness and the dignity of humankind, resolution and the will to strive and to endure. Thus shall they learn perseverance in all things, the will to advance, high-mindedness and high resolve, chastity and purity of life. Thus shall they be enabled to carry to a successful conclusion whatsoever they undertake.[38]

It is interesting to observe that the qualities 'Abdu'l-Bahá calls for are those required to achieve worthy and challenging ends. It is also of note that 'Abdu'l-Bahá calls for the development of such qualities in both girls and boys.

Access to education is a vital means of compensating for the past lack of opportunities for women to acquire training and to develop their skills and capacities and thereby demonstrate that their abilities have merely been latent. Education is a prerequisite to women's equal participation in the workforce so that they can be welcomed into full partnership by their male colleagues and can bring to bear the values of cooperation, negotiation, and service. When this occurs, their voices will be heard and listened to with respect in the councils of the world. Then will women have the moral and temporal authority to refuse to send their sons to war, to become a vital force for peace-building. The family that is committed to the equality of women and men can hasten the advent of peace by helping to lower the barriers to women's participation in education and, indeed, in the world at large. This can be achieved first by providing the means—both time and money—to allow the female members to obtain an education, then by encouraging them to study, to acquire the qualities called for by 'Abdu'l-Bahá, to persevere in their efforts and to have the courage to excel in all fields of human endeavor and, finally, by taking pride in their accomplishments.

The unique significance of the family's potential contribution to the development of society and the attainment of peace becomes clear in the light of the following statement from 'Abdu'l-Bahá:

> When all mankind shall receive the same opportunity of education and the equality of men and women be realized, the foundations of war will be utterly destroyed. Without equality this will be impossible because all differences and distinction are conducive to discord and strife. Equality between men and women is conducive to the abolition of warfare for the reason that women will never be willing to sanction it.[39]

4

Women and Bahá'í Law

We make mention of the handmaidens of God at this time and announce unto them the glad-tidings of the tokens of the mercy and compassion of God and His consideration for them. . . .

—Bahá'u'lláh

EQUALITY AND LAW

The Bahá'í Faith affirms the equality of the sexes, and its teachings express this equality in all aspects of practical life on both an individual and social level. The purpose of chapter 4 is to explore those aspects of the Bahá'í teachings that are especially pertinent to the role and functions of women in their activities as members of the Bahá'í Faith.

As will be evident from the discussion set out here, the pertinent issues are far from simple, due to the necessity to accommodate differences in function while maintaining equality. Some reference to this matter has been made in chapter 2 and is further emphasized in the following extract from a letter written by the Universal House of Justice:

> Concerning your questions about the equality of men and women, this, as 'Abdu'l-Bahá has often explained, is a fundamental principle of Bahá'u'lláh; therefore the Laws of the Aqdas should be studied in the light of it. Equality between men and women does not, indeed physiologically it cannot, mean identity of functions. In some things women excel men, for others men are better fitted than women, while in very many things the difference of sex is of no effect at all.[1]

To explore this question adequately, it is necessary to consider first the unique features of Bahá'í law. It differs markedly from the law found in other religions in ways that affect profoundly the manner in which Bahá'í law is applied to women. Such a consideration forms a framework in which to examine in some detail certain Bahá'í laws found in the Kitáb-i-Aqdas (the Book of Laws) and in other passages of Bahá'u'lláh's writings.

THE NATURE OF BAHÁ'Í LAW

Bahá'í law differs fundamentally from those systems of law that are designed principally to regulate and harmonize the interaction of all elements of society and to bring about equity and justice in human relations. By contrast, Bahá'í law has as its ultimate aim, in the words of the Universal House of Justice, "the relationship of the individual soul to God and the fulfillment of its spiritual destiny."[2] To attain this spiritual purpose requires a system of law that expresses justice and promotes harmony. However, it must never be forgotten that the ultimate purpose is a spiritual one, and hence the full justification for some components of this law may not readily be apparent to individuals who fail to take into consideration the spiritual dimension of creation. There is a vital element of faith in the acceptance of Bahá'í law, but this should not be confused with blind faith. Adherence to Bahá'í law comes as a consequence of using the human faculties, including the power of reason, to independently investigate Bahá'u'lláh's claim to be a Manifestation of God before committing oneself to acceptance of this claim and the consequences that derive from it.

Closely associated with such a perspective is the fact that some of the laws of the Kitáb-i-Aqdas have been described, in a letter written on behalf of the Guardian, as "formulated in anticipation of a state of society destined to emerge from the chaotic conditions that prevail today."[3] The form of that future society is not yet evident, although one can be certain that it must necessarily include full equality between the sexes. The social functions of some of the provisions of the Kitáb-i-Aqdas will not be fully apparent until that future society has emerged and the need for regulation of certain aspects of conduct becomes clear.

Bahá'í law is applied progressively to the followers of the Faith at the discretion of the Head of the Faith as the community matures in its practice of the laws already in force and in its understanding of its distinctive identity. Such a practice of progressive application is not unique to the Bahá'í Dispensation. For example, in Islam in the days of Muḥammad, the interdiction on the consumption of alcohol was introduced gradually through initial discouragement, followed by the admonition not to recite prayers while intoxicated, leading ultimately to prohibition of the drinking of alcohol. An example of progressive application in a Bahá'í setting will be found in the discussion of Bahá'í marriage law.

An inevitable consequence of progressive application is that a religion renders itself vulnerable to criticism or derision from those who ignore the time sequence and take satisfaction in pointing out obvious contradictions between the various statements made authoritatively in prescribing religious law. Ignoring the fact that there is no contradiction if the various statements are looked at as elements in the evolutionary process of application, critics take the distinction between statements made at various times as manifest evidence that either the Founder of the religion did not know His own mind or that He yielded to expediency or compromise under differing circumstances. Despite such criticism, progressive application is a vital element in the process of transformation necessary to bring together disparate elements to form a new and dynamic community.

Bahá'í law has a flexibility greater than that found in other religions because of the existence of the Universal House of Justice, to which Bahá'u'lláh has assigned the right to formulate authoritative legislation on matters not covered explicitly in the laws He has revealed, and the right to alter its own legislative decisions at a future time when conditions have changed. No change can be made to the laws specified by Bahá'u'lláh, which are to remain in effect until the coming of the new Manifestation of God, after a thousand or more years. Because Bahá'u'lláh has refrained from legislating on certain matters, including some of secondary detail, the Universal House of Justice is free to operate in that arena, changing its own decisions as society progresses along the path of "an ever-advancing civilization" and a new social condition emerges.[4] Thus the Bahá'í Faith avoids becoming an agent of restraint upon progress, innovation, and social development. 'Abdu'l-Bahá writes,

> Those matters of major importance which constitute the foundation of the Law of God are explicitly recorded in the Text, but subsidiary laws are left to the House of Justice. The wisdom of this is that the times never remain the same, for change is a necessary quality and an essential attribute of this world, and of time and place. Therefore the House of Justice will take action accordingly. . . .[5]

The efficacy of such a provision is dependent on the authority of the Universal House of Justice being clearly apparent and accepted by all Bahá'ís as an article of faith, and on the existence of ironclad guarantees that the Universal House of Justice, in its legislative functions, will not deviate from the spirit and intent of the Bahá'í teachings. The Covenant of Bahá'u'lláh provides the necessary assurance that these conditions are met. If it were not so, the Bahá'í Faith would be doomed to suffer a corruption of its purity similar to that which has damaged the unity and integrity of other religions, through the grafting of individuals' ideas onto the body of the law.

Knowing that such provisions are in place, one can appreciate why statements of law in the Bahá'í teachings are intentionally far from complete and can be misleading if considered without the elucidations of the Universal House of Justice. Commenting on these laws, the Universal House of Justice writes,

> A salient characteristic is their brevity. They constitute the kernel of a vast range of law that will arise in centuries to come. This elaboration of the law will be enacted by the Universal House of Justice under the authority conferred upon it by Bahá'u'lláh Himself.[6]

In considering the application of Bahá'í law to women, it must always be borne in mind that many of the laws of the Kitáb-i-Aqdas are expressed only from the perspective that the male segment of the population is being addressed, due apparently to the social conditions at the time this Book was revealed, a time when women were denied their fundamental rights and the call of the Bahá'í Faith for equality of the sexes was in the very earliest stages of its implementation. Such an orientation of the revealed law should cause no difficulties for women, because the Universal House of Justice states,

> In general, the laws of the Kitáb-i-Aqdas are stated succinctly. An example of this conciseness can be seen in the fact that many are expressed only as they apply to a man, but it is apparent from the Guardian's writings that, where Bahá'u'lláh has given a law as between a man and a woman, it applies *mutatis mutandis* between a woman and a man unless the context makes this impossible. For example, the text of the Kitáb-i-Aqdas forbids a man to marry his father's wife (i.e. his stepmother), and the Guardian has indicated that likewise a woman is forbidden to marry her stepfather. This understanding of the implications of the Law has far-reaching effects in light of the fundamental Bahá'í principle of the equality of the sexes, and should be borne in mind when the sacred Text is studied.[7]

At the same time, such a formulation of Bahá'í law renders it open to unfounded criticism from those who would assess the application of Bahá'í law to women yet ignore, for whatever reason, the profound importance of the pronouncements of the Universal House of Justice. Examples of clarifications provided by the Universal House of Justice are to be found in the succeeding sections of this chapter.

WOMEN AND THE LAWS OF PERSONAL CONDUCT

This section does not attempt to provide a comprehensive survey of the laws of the Faith concerning personal conduct; instead it confines itself to those aspects of such laws in which there has historically been a distinction between the treatment of men and women. It will be apparent that some distinction persists in Bahá'í law, but it is within the context of equality of the sexes and does not imply any assessment of women as being inferior to men.

DEVOTIONAL PRACTICES

The devotional practices enjoined in the Bahá'í teachings are central to the spiritual life of the believer and are the principal means for developing and maintaining the relationship between the individual and the Creator.

As discussed earlier, the Bahá'í teachings assert unequivocally that, from a spiritual viewpoint, there is no distinction between men and women. Hence it may come as a surprise to students of Bahá'í law to find, in the Kitáb-i-Aqdas, that a distinction is made between the devotional practices prescribed for men and those set out for women, including an exemption from certain devotional activities during menstruation. Such a distinction could well raise a concern as to whether the Bahá'í teachings endorse the concept of ritual impurity. This concern can be removed completely by a closer study of the statements set out in the Kitáb-i-Aqdas.

The concept of ritual impurity is strongly established in the practices of many religions. It holds that an individual can be in a state of impurity under certain defined conditions that render it improper for the person to perform some specific devotional actions that require purification through the performance of prescribed rituals such as ablutions. As mentioned in chapter 2, women have historically been regarded as agents of evil in certain cultures, due to their association with sexuality, and so women have been held to be impure and thus to be excluded from areas or practices that are sacred and liable to defilement by their presence or participation. Even when such a stigma is not attached to women, there has been a widespread belief that menstruation gives rise to ritual impurity, with women being physically isolated during that time or debarred from participation in religious activities such as prayer and fasting.

The Bahá'í teachings are unambiguous on this subject. Bahá'u'lláh states, in the Kitáb-i-Aqdas, that "God hath, likewise, as a bounty from His presence, abolished the concept of 'uncleanness,' whereby divers things and peoples have been held to be impure." The explanatory notes to the Kitáb-i-Aqdas point out that this passage repudiates the concept of ritual impurity, although the Bahá'í teachings encourage all believers, male and female alike, to be "the very essence of cleanliness" and to cling "unto the cord of refinement."[8]

The Kitáb-i-Aqdas includes exemptions from the laws of obligatory prayer and fasting for women who are menstruating, but those who utilize these exemptions are required to carry out other devotional practices of a physiologically less demanding nature. Bahá'í law also provides an exemption to women from the performance of pilgrimage, in contrast to men, whose exemption is only applicable when circumstances render them unable to carry it out. Central to the understanding of these provisions is the clarification given by the Universal House of Justice that these formulations are exemptions rather than prohibitions. Much misunderstanding arises from confusion between the differing concepts of exemption and prohibition. Any woman is free to avail herself of these exemptions if she so wishes, but she is under no obligation to do so. That the matter is left to her discretion, and that she is entirely free not to invoke these exemptions, serve to illustrate the fundamental difference between these exemptions and that discrimination to which women have been subjected for countless centuries in the name of the invalid concept of ritual impurity.

One might well inquire as to the reason for these exemptions for women. It is significant to note that the pilgrimage exemption is described in the Kitáb-i-Aqdas as "a mercy on His part," and that this Book of Laws also includes exemptions from prayer and fasting applicable to men and women alike for such reasons as illness or the infirmities of old age. It is thus reasonable to conclude that the exemptions are granted simply for physiological reasons quite unrelated to the spiritual condition of the believer. The decision whether or not to avail oneself of an exemption would consequently be taken by the believer concerned, having regard to the individual's physiological condition at the time. As the Universal House of Justice points out, "That men and women differ from one another in certain characteristics and functions is an inescapable fact of nature."[9]

No discussion of this subject would be complete without mentioning the ablutions prescribed in Bahá'í law, since this practice has so often been associated with remedial actions prescribed for ritual impurity. It is apparent from religious literature and from studies in cultural anthropology that, historically, ablutions have served several purposes other than that of achieving physical cleanliness: as a symbolic act performed in marking the transition from mundane daily activities to an act of devotion; as a rite of passage to a new stage in one's life, such as that of Christian baptism of a new believer; or as a purificatory act to compensate for pollution through contact with an entity that is in a state of ritual impurity. With this background one might well inquire what is the purpose of ablutions in Bahá'í devotional practice.

It is clear from the prescriptions for ablutions in the Kitáb-i-Aqdas that they are intended to have a purely spiritual significance; note, for example, that they must precede the offering of obligatory prayer by either men or women and that they are to be performed even if the individual has just finished bathing. Consequently it should not be surprising that, when an exemption is provided from obligatory prayer and fasting for a menstruating woman, she is nevertheless required to perform ablutions before reciting the particular verse specified as part of the exemption. Further evidence of the symbolic nature of ablutions is obtained from the fact that, when water is not available or when the application of water to the face or hands would be harmful to an individual, men and women alike are free to recite a specified verse in place of the ablution.

SEXUAL CONDUCT

As is the case in other religions, the Bahá'í Faith includes in its teachings laws regulating sexual conduct. However, there are two fundamental differences between the Bahá'í teachings and those conventionally associated with religion.

The first of these fundamental differences concerns the nature of sexuality, which has so often been regarded by religious authorities as antithetical to spiritual development. Sexual activity was thus to be avoided by adherents seeking spirituality, and those exercising a priestly function were called upon to adopt celibacy. Underlying this view was the concept of the material world as being the province of the Devil in eternal contest with the Divinity, with the sexual impulse regarded as designed by the Devil for the purpose of diverting humankind from spiritual endeavors.

In contrast, the Bahá'í view of sexuality is expressed in the following statement written on behalf of the Guardian:

> The Bahá'í Faith recognizes the value of the sex impulse, but condemns its illegitimate and improper expression such as free love, companionate marriage and others, all of which it considers positively harmful to man and to the society in which he lives. The proper use of the sex instinct is the natural right of every individual, and it is precisely for this very purpose that the institution of marriage has been established. The Bahá'ís do not believe in the suppression of the sex impulse but in its regulation and control.[10]

This balanced approach to sexuality, recognizing "the value of the sex impulse" and prescribing that its expression occur only within marriage, sets the Bahá'í Faith apart from much of conventional religious philosophy and has far-reaching implications that are gradually being explored by Bahá'í scholars and authors, including psychologists and psychiatrists who use their professional expertise to provide insights into this aspect of the Bahá'í teachings.

The second fundamental difference in the Bahá'í teachings on sexual conduct lies in the Bahá'í perception of women, who have so often in the past been stigmatized as agents of evil through their association with sexual attraction. This misguided perception has led to the imposition of rules designed to diminish women's influence in this regard, through specification of certain types of female clothing, proscription of adornment with jewelry, censure of the use of cosmetics, and, in even more extreme cases, the requirement that a woman cover her hair, veil her face, or remain secluded within the confines of the home. 'Abdu'l-Bahá refers to the status of women in earlier times, pointing out that "If she pursued educational courses, it was deemed contrary to chastity; hence women were made prisoners of the household."[11]

Such erroneous concepts have no place in the Bahá'í teachings, which set forth an identical standard for both men and women. The Guardian's secretary has written on his behalf,

> Briefly stated the Bahá'í conception of sex is based on the belief that chastity should be strictly practiced by both sexes, not only because it is in itself highly commendable ethically, but also due to its being the only way to a happy and successful marital life.[12]

The Bahá'í teachings call for both men and women to be modest and decent in their dress, but provide a wide latitude in the form of apparel; the Kitáb-i-Aqdas states that "The Lord hath relieved you, as a bounty on His part, of the restrictions that formerly applied to clothing," but warns the believers to "make not yourselves the playthings of the ignorant."[13]

A false and dangerous theory that has been used in some cultures to justify the mistreatment of women, either reducing them to objects for male sexual gratification or forcing them to be veiled, is that the male sexual impulse is uncontrollable and that consequently men cannot be held responsible for the sexual abuse of women. This view has its modern counterpart in the blame sometimes attached to rape victims, who are accused of having brought the abuse on themselves by their dress or behavior. In striking contrast are the following words written on behalf of the Universal House of Justice:

> The lack of spiritual values in society leads to a debasement of the attitudes which should govern the relationship between the sexes, with women being treated as no more than objects for sexual gratification and being denied the respect and courtesy to which all human beings are entitled. Bahá'u'lláh has warned: *"They that follow their lusts and corrupt inclinations, have erred and dissipated their efforts. They, indeed, are of the lost."* Believers might well ponder the exalted standard of conduct to which they are encouraged to aspire in the statement of Bahá'u'lláh concerning His *"true follower,"* that: *"And if he meet the fairest and most comely of women, he would not feel his heart seduced by the least shadow of desire for her beauty. Such an one, indeed, is the creation of spotless chastity. Thus instructeth you the Pen of the Ancient of Days, as bidden by your Lord, the Almighty, the All-Bountiful."*[14]

This standard of conduct has direct bearing on the elimination of sexual harassment of females in the workplace. Its application would create an environment in which women could confidently anticipate employment in a setting where they would not be subjected to sexual advances and would be free to carry out their duties without humiliation or fear.

A statement of the Kitáb-i-Aqdas that bears upon the subject of the freedom of women to follow employment opportunities, and that might easily be misunderstood if there were no additional clarification, is "And he who would take into his service a maid may do so with propriety." In response to a question, Bahá'u'lláh later explained that this provision of Bahá'í law removes the restriction, specified in earlier religions, that an unmarried woman should not be employed by a man, as that employment tended to carry with it the implication of a sexual relationship between the man and his female employee, or even of prostitution on her part. Women were thus severely restricted in their professional or industrial life under the penalty of social condemnation and irreparable damage to their reputations. By contrast, the Bahá'í Faith aims, as 'Abdu'l-Bahá states, for women to "'advance and fulfill their mission in all departments of life.'"[15] To achieve this aim requires that women be free to advance without fear of sexual harassment and that moral and legal force be used, if necessary, to restrain men who wish to use the workplace setting for predatory sexual activities. The Bahá'í teachings are thus a safeguard and a liberating influence for women as they strive to fulfill the vastly expanded role to which these teachings summon them.

In some parts of the world the degrading practice of female genital mutilation is prevalent and is the source of incalculable distress to its victims. This practice is contrary to the spirit of the Bahá'í teachings, and Bahá'í agencies have been forthright in its condemnation at international conferences in which they have participated.[16]

As indicated above, the Bahá'í teachings state that "Sex relationships of any form, outside marriage, are not permissible."[17] Apart from its implications for heterosexual premarital and extramarital conduct, this standard of chastity also finds expression in the prohibition of homosexual relationships. Certain laws of the Kitáb-i-Aqdas have been formulated in anticipation of a future condition when the continued spread of the Bahá'í Faith and the size of its community will have led progressively to nations' choosing to incorporate Bahá'í laws in their national legislative codes; the Kitáb-i-Aqdas envisages, at such a time, the imposition of penalties for sexual offenses, including unlawful heterosexual intercourse and also such violations of the moral code as sodomy. 'Abdu'l-Bahá indicates that the aim of these provisions of the Kitáb-i-Aqdas is to penalize offenders through public exposure of their misdeeds such that they are shamed in the eyes of society.

One of the most deplorable features of present-day society is the prevalence of rape, which Bahá'u'lláh condemns in the Kitáb-i-Aqdas, assigning to the Universal House of Justice the duty to determine the penalty for this and other sexual offenses when, in the future, the Bahá'í laws become the basis for the legislative system of a society. At the present time the Universal House of Justice, in a letter written on its behalf, discusses the consequences of rape in the following terms:

> One of the most heinous of sexual offences is the crime of rape. When a believer is a victim, she is entitled to the loving aid and support of the members of her community, and she is free to initiate action against the perpetrator under the law of the land should she wish to do so. If she becomes pregnant as a consequence of this assault, no pressure should be brought upon her by the Bahá'í institutions to marry. As to whether she should continue or terminate the pregnancy, it is left to her to decide on the course of action she should follow, taking into consideration medical and other relevant factors, and in the light of the Bahá'í Teachings. If she gives birth to a child as a result of the rape, it is left to her discretion whether to seek financial support for the maintenance of the child from the father; however, his claim to any parental rights would, under Bahá'í law, be called into question, in view of the circumstances.[18]

The discussion here is necessarily brief and may well be regarded as no more than an introduction to the Bahá'í perspective on sexual conduct and the uniqueness of its approach. Other Bahá'í authors have explored this subject more fully.[19]

MARRIAGE AND DIVORCE

The Bahá'í teachings on marriage are quite distinctive not only for their unequivocal prescription of monogamy but also for the manner in which they incorporate the principle of equality of the sexes in the structure, form, and purpose assigned to the marital relationship.

'Abdu'l-Bahá refers to Bahá'í marriage in the following terms: "The true marriage of Bahá'ís is this, that husband and wife should be united both physically and spiritually, that they may ever improve the spiritual life of each other, and may enjoy everlasting unity throughout all the worlds of God."[20] The mutuality of effort required and the spiritual purpose assigned to marriage imply clearly that the practice of equality is an essential prerequisite to attaining this exalted aim.

Shoghi Effendi, as authorized interpreter of the Faith, writes that the Kitáb-i-Aqdas "prescribes monogamy."[21] However, the manner in which it is prescribed illuminates a number of vital principles about the application of Bahá'í law. It is apparent that polygamy, or more specifically polygyny, is a very ancient practice among most of the people of the world, of all cultures and religious traditions. It was permitted under Mosaic law, although there was a general tendency toward monogamy with the passage of the centuries. Jesus did not prohibit polygamy, and the historical record provides evidence of polygamy in early Christian communities. Muḥammad restricted the number of wives to a maximum of four but made plurality of wives contingent on justice.

At the time of the revelation of the Kitáb-i-Aqdas, the Bahá'ís were drawn entirely from the Muslim society and were thus accustomed to polygamy. In fact, Bahá'u'lláh contracted marriages before the revelation of the Bahá'í laws and so had three wives. The Bahá'í teachings introduced monogamy gradually, beginning with the following statement in the Kitáb-i-Aqdas which outwardly conveys the impression that taking two wives is permitted: "Beware that ye take not unto yourselves more wives than two. Whoso contenteth himself with a single partner from among the maidservants of God, both he and she shall live in tranquillity." This may be taken as an illustration of the progressive application of Bahá'í law, since account must necessarily be taken of the fact that Bahá'u'lláh specified 'Abdu'l-Bahá to be the infallible Interpreter of His writings, and the believers were enjoined in the Kitáb-i-Aqdas to "refer . . . whatsoever ye understand not in the Book to Him."[22]

'Abdu'l-Bahá followed the progressive approach in that initially He did not forbid marriage to a second wife, but discouraged it with statements to the effect that marriage with a second wife is dependent upon justice, and the implementation of justice is extremely difficult, and it is more conducive to one's well-being and happiness to practice monogamy.[23] He later clarified the matter precisely in the following statement: "In accordance with the text of the Kitáb-i-Aqdas, the law on marriage is, in reality, based on monogamy, because bigamy has been made dependent on an impossible condition."[24] This clarification was further elaborated in the following passage from 'Abdu'l-Bahá:

> Know thou that polygamy is not permitted under the law of God, for contentment with one wife hath been clearly stipulated. Taking a second wife is made dependent upon equity and justice being upheld between the two wives, under all conditions. However, observance of justice and equity towards two wives is utterly impossible. The fact that bigamy has been made dependent upon an impossible condition is clear proof of its absolute prohibition. Therefore it is not permissible for a man to have more than one wife.[25]

For this reason Shoghi Effendi states, as 'Abdu'l-Bahá does, that the Kitáb-i-Aqdas prescribes monogamy; the practice of polygamy, which had the sanction of religious teaching for thousands of years, has been abrogated in the Bahá'í Dispensation after a transitional period of no more that a few decades immediately following the revelation of the Kitáb-i-Aqdas.

An interesting insight into the practice of equality in relation to monogamy is obtained from a Tablet of 'Abdu'l-Bahá to an early believer during the transitional period concerning the need to practice monogamy. In this Tablet 'Abdu'l-Bahá calls attention to the fact that both physically and spiritually the feelings of women are like those of men. If a woman were repeatedly to seek a new husband she would be considered unchaste. He further stresses that the same standard applies to men also.[26]

The need to express equality and to protect the rights of women informs other aspects of the Bahá'í teachings concerning marriage such as the right of either the man or the woman to propose marriage.

Betrothal, or engagement, cannot occur before the age of at least fifteen and requires the consent of both parties, thus outlawing practices of the past in which girls were betrothed as children, often against their will or with no respect for their preferences. Bahá'í law, which is now being applied progressively under the direction of the Universal House of Justice, specifies that the betrothal period may not exceed ninety-five days. The effect of this law is to put an end to the unjust practice of contracting an engagement and then leaving an individual to languish for years, uncertain whether the marriage will ultimately occur and not free to seek another prospective marriage partner.

The concept of dowry is associated historically, in many instances, with the humiliation of women or their reduction to no more than a commodity to be bought or sold. In some cultures the dowry is a payment made by the bridegroom to the parents of the bride and is described as the bride-price or bride-wealth; at best, it is the monetary expression of his pledge to her parents that he will treat her well, but it has so often degenerated to being no more than her purchase price. Another form of dowry is the payment of a sum to the bridegroom by the bride's family, in which case it can be regarded, at best, as a generous contribution to the expenses of setting up the new household; the reality is that it has frequently been reduced to being a payment made to him by her parents, who are thereby relieved of the expenditure of maintaining an economically unproductive female in their household. In light of the historical record it may come as a surprise to find that the concept of a dowry is to be found in the Bahá'í teachings, where it can be an important element in raising the status of women and reinforcing their equality with men.

The Bahá'í dowry is a specified sum of money, or its equivalent, to be given by the bridegroom to the wife, and not to her parents; she is entirely free to dispose of it as she wishes. The giving of the dowry may be regarded as a symbolic act, since the sum involved may be only around U.S. $800, depending on the price of gold, for those living in an urban setting with its cash economy. However, the significance of the act is great, since it represents a tangible expression of the wife's inalienable right to hold property in her own name and to maintain a degree of economic independence from her husband if she so desires. The practice, in Western societies, of the groom's giving the intended bride a diamond engagement ring is, to some extent, reminiscent of the Bahá'í dowry. It is also interesting to note that in Islam the Qur'án calls for the bridegroom to provide a dowry to the bride but does not specify the amount, with the result that the practice became open to possible abuse. So important is the dowry in the Bahá'í teachings that if the bridegroom is unable to pay the specified sum in full, the alternative is to give the bride a promissory note for the amount owed, with the express understanding that he will honor this note when he is financially in a position to do so.[27]

The Bahá'í teachings also provide for the possibility that the parties to a marriage may, if so inclined, follow the practice of some cultures in drawing up a formal marriage contract with defined conditions and provisions that are binding on both parties. The Kitáb-i-Aqdas provides that if such a contract has been drawn up with one of its provisions being that the marriage is conditioned on the woman's virginity, and if it is later found that she is not a virgin, the dissolution of the marriage can be demanded. In such a case, however, Bahá'u'lláh advises that it would be highly meritorious in the sight of God if the husband were to conceal the matter and not make an issue of it. The bride is likewise free to put a similar condition on the bridegroom's virginity in the marriage contract, if she wishes, and to demand dissolution of the marriage if she later receives reliable evidence that he is not a virgin.[28]

The Bahá'í teachings place great emphasis on the preservation of the marriage bond, and application of the Bahá'í family values described in chapter 3 has the direct effect of strengthening that bond. The institutions of the Faith are available to provide guidance and advice to couples experiencing marital difficulties, and the Universal House of Justice states in a message written on its behalf that a couple in need of assistance should not hesitate to consult "professional marriage counsellors, individually and together if possible, and also to take advantage of the supportive counselling which can come from wise and mature friends. Non-Bahá'í counselling can be useful but it is usually necessary to temper it with Bahá'í insight."[29]

While the causes of marital breakdown can be many, one common cause is domination of the wife by the husband. Such behavior, as indicated in chapter 3, is contrary to explicit statements set out in the authoritative Bahá'í texts. An extreme form of such domination is domestic violence, when a wife is physically abused by her husband. Such behavior is condemned in the Bahá'í Faith. Bahá'u'lláh Himself states that

> The friends of God must be adorned with the ornament of justice, equity, kindness and love. As they do not allow themselves to be the object of cruelty and transgression, in like manner they should not allow such tyranny to visit the handmaidens of God. He, verily, speaketh the truth and commandeth that which benefitteth His servants and handmaidens. He is the Protector of all in this world and the next.[30]

The Universal House of Justice states in a letter written on its behalf, "For a man to use force to impose his will on a woman is a serious transgression of the Bahá'í Teachings." It also warns that "No husband should ever beat his wife, or subject her to any form of cruel treatment; to do so would be an unacceptable abuse of the marriage relationship and contrary to the Teachings of Bahá'u'lláh."[31]

Another form of violence in marriage occurs when the husband subjects his wife to sexual abuse, often seeking to justify his conduct with the excuse that the marital relationship confers upon him the right to do as he wishes, irrespective of his wife's feelings. The Universal House of Justice clarifies that this is an erroneous line of thinking. Referring to sexual conduct within marriage, it explains in a letter written on its behalf,

> In this aspect of the marital relationship, as in all others, mutual consideration and respect should apply. If a Bahá'í woman suffers abuse or is subjected to rape by her husband, she has the right to turn to the Spiritual Assembly for assis-

tance and counsel, or to seek legal protection. Such abuse would gravely jeopardize the continuation of the marriage, and could well lead to a condition of irreconcilable antipathy.[32]

Divorce is permissible in the Bahá'í teachings, although it is strongly discouraged, and believers are enjoined to make a sustained and wholehearted effort to repair the breakdown in their relationship. Shoghi Effendi affirms that both husband and wife "have equal right to ask for divorce" whenever either partner "feels it absolutely essential to do so." Divorce is permissible after the lapse of one full year if, in the words of the Kitáb-i-Aqdas, "resentment or antipathy arise between husband and wife."[33] During the year of waiting (commonly referred to as a year of patience), the couple is urged, under the guidance of their Spiritual Assembly, to strive to reconcile their differences if possible; if this effort is unsuccessful, a divorce is effected. The husband is obliged nonetheless to provide both for the financial support of his wife and children during this period, and for the continuing support of his children, in accord with his responsibility for the financial support of the family, as discussed in chapter 3.

An interesting example of a law expressed as between a man and a woman, but applied also between a woman and a man, is found in the case of adultery. 'Abdu'l-Bahá states that the year of waiting preceding divorce is waived in the case of adultery on the part of the wife. The Universal House of Justice explains that the time to apply this law has not yet come; when that time arrives, this aspect of the law of divorce will require elucidation and supplementary legislation by the Universal House of Justice, which states that the exemption will apply equally to the case of adultery on the part of the husband.[34]

FINANCIAL RIGHTS

No discussion of Bahá'í law as it pertains to women and the implementation of the equality of the sexes would be complete without reference to the financial rights of women in marriage, since, as professor of law Ian F. G. Baxter points out in his article on family law in the *Encyclopædia Britannica*, "The history of marriage is bound up with the legal and economic dependence of women upon men and the legal incapacities of women in owning and dealing with property."[35]

Several aspects of this matter have already been discussed in earlier chapters. It is clear that in the Bahá'í teachings the way is open for women to be actively involved in the "social and economic equation" and to participate in such professions as law, public administration, and industrial and agricultural sciences, to name but a few.[36] The wife's right to have her own possessions is affirmed in the Bahá'í concept of dowry, while other passages of the Bahá'í writings envision a wife owning property of her own, quite distinct from that of her husband, and accumulated through her profession, craft or trade, her dowry and her inheritance, or even through the provisions of a marriage contract.

Regarding inheritance, every believer, man or woman, is instructed as a matter of religious obligation to make a will. Bahá'u'lláh states in the Kitáb-i-Aqdas, "Unto everyone hath been enjoined the writing of a will." The importance of this instruction should not be underestimated. 'Abdu'l-Bahá refers to it as "one of the binding laws of this mighty Dispensation" and indicates that any Bahá'í who neglects to do this "disobeyeth the divine command."[37]

Bahá'u'lláh affirms that, in formulating one's will, "a person hath full jurisdiction over his property," since "God, verily, hath permitted him to deal with that which He hath bestowed upon him in whatever manner he may desire." In preparing a will, a Bahá'í would heed the admonition of 'Abdu'l-Bahá that "Everyone must in his lifetime draw up a will, and dispose of his property in whatsoever manner he deemeth fit, while having due regard for the need to observe justice and equity." It would be natural for a Bahá'í to make provisions in the will for any financial dependents such as a spouse or children who have no other source of income. 'Abdu'l-Bahá clarifies that the testator is, in the will, "free to bequeath the residence to whomsoever he wisheth" while observing the aforementioned justice and equity.[38] There is no restriction on leaving one's property to individuals who are not Bahá'ís; thus a believer whose spouse is not a Bahá'í might well feel that "justice and equity" require that a substantial portion of the assets be bequeathed to the spouse, including the residence in which the couple has been living.

Another consideration relevant to the formulation of a will is the following statement, which appears in a letter written on behalf of Shoghi Effendi:

> . . . even though a Bahá'í is permitted in his will to dispose of his wealth in the way he wishes, yet he is morally and conscientiously bound to always bear in mind, while writing his will, the necessity of his upholding the principle of Bahá'u'lláh regarding the social function of wealth, and the consequent necessity of avoiding its overaccumulation and concentration in a few individuals or groups of individuals.[39]

An unusual situation occurs when a Bahá'í neglects to follow the command to draw up a will. In the event that intestacy arises from such a failure to observe this aspect of Bahá'í law, or in the case where the will cannot be found, the Kitáb-i-Aqdas provides detailed inheritance laws, two features of which are directly relevant to the principle of the equality of the sexes. The first is that a distinction is made between male and female heirs in certain categories, with the father of the deceased receiving a somewhat greater portion than the mother, and brothers receiving more than sisters. This disparity can best be understood in relation to the principle of the equality of the sexes by noting that, as stated in chapter 3, the husband has the primary responsibility for the financial support of the family, irrespective of the wife's income and financial position.

The second feature is that the intestacy provisions include allocation of the residence of the deceased father, or his principal residence if he has more than one, to the eldest son. It means that this residence does not have to be sold at the time of the father's death in order that distribution can be made to a number of heirs. It also affords a significant measure of protection to his widow, if she has been living there and the house was entirely in the husband's name, since the Bahá'í teachings clearly assign to the eldest son the responsibility to care for his mother and to consider the needs of the other heirs. However, the full implications of this provision may not become apparent until there is further clarification of the role and responsibilities of the eldest son in the future, through guidance from the Universal House of Justice.

SERVICE ON BAHÁ'Í INSTITUTIONS

No survey of the role of women in religion can fail to take account of the extent to which women in the past have been systematically debarred from access to positions of administrative authority or decision-making in the organization of the religious community.

It is possible to make a few broad generalizations about the role assigned to women in the functioning of a religion in the past. During its earliest period, that associated with the Founder of a religion, women could be found playing a significant and highly admirable role in its defense, propagation, and emancipation. In Christianity, Mary Magdalene played an important role around the time of the crucifixion, and the Gospel of John records the spectacular success of the woman of Samaria in attracting a large number of adherents to the new faith. In Islam, Khadijah was among the first to believe in Muḥammad and remained of staunch faith in the face of persecutions, while His daughter Fatimih courageously served in the defense and preservation of the community; following His passing, Ayesha influenced significantly the development of the early religious community through her actions, including her military leadership in the armed conflict between factions competing for power.[40]

As the body of adherents crystallized into a religious community and an ecclesiastical structure came into being, women were increasingly excluded from positions of authority and relegated to a minor or supportive role. Since, in the past, the Founder of each of the religions did not prescribe, in any degree of detail, how the community was to be organized, the social inequality between the sexes became a determining factor in the development of a male organizational hierarchy. In the religions arising in Western Asia, rabbis, priests, and mullahs were all male. Although in some instances female religious orders were established to perform an educational or healing function, their female leaders were assigned authority only over other women.

In the contemporary scene, the movement for equality has found limited expression in some modification of this segregation. Within certain liberal denominations of Judaism and Christianity women are to be found exercising ecclesiastical functions over congregations that include men and women, and in Islam some female scholars have emerged recently. Yet it must be admitted that they remain very much the exception rather than the rule, and religious organization continues to be an overwhelmingly male preserve.

The Bahá'í Faith stands in direct contrast to the historical precedent. Its Administrative Order, based directly on explicit statements of Bahá'u'lláh Himself, has as one of its most striking and distinctive features the involvement of women in positions of responsibility at local, national, and international levels. Women serve as Hands of the Cause of God and as Counselor members of the International Teaching Center, discharging vital responsibilities worldwide in stimulating the expansion of the Bahá'í community, preserving its integrity, and fostering its spiritual life. Each of the five Continental Boards of Counselors includes women as well as men among its members, and women are elected as members of National and Local Spiritual Assemblies throughout the world and participate at the grassroots level of Bahá'í community life, consulting at the Nineteen Day Feast and at conventions and conferences. Chapters 5 and 6 set out in some detail the initiatives that the institutions of the Faith at its World Center have taken to promote the involvement of women, and such measures are actively being pursued now in many countries where the traditional culture has inhibited women's participation in all aspects of community life.

In light of the distinguished record of the Bahá'í Faith in this regard, it may well surprise those inquiring into the Bahá'í teachings about the role of women to find that the Bahá'í writings specify clearly that membership on its supreme administrative body, the Universal House of Justice, is confined to men. Many will not be unduly concerned by this aspect of the Bahá'í teachings, directing their attention to the multitude of women whose lives have been transformed by the promulgation of the

Bahá'í principle of equality of the sexes. However, it is quite understandable that some will be disturbed by it and that this exclusion of women from the highest administrative body of the Bahá'í Faith will raise a number of questions for them. For this reason it is necessary to examine this matter in considerable detail and to explore at length some of the questions that might naturally come to mind.

Such an exploration must begin with an examination of the passages of the authoritative Bahá'í writings in which the membership of the Universal House of Justice is specified. Here we find again the processes of progressive clarification and progressive application of Bahá'í law. Bahá'u'lláh ordained both the Universal House of Justice and Local Houses of Justice in His writings, leaving to 'Abdu'l-Bahá the ordination of the Secondary House of Justice, now known as the National Spiritual Assembly. In several passages in the Kitáb-i-Aqdas Bahá'u'lláh refers to the "House of Justice," leaving open for later clarification the level or levels of the entire institution to which His statements were to be applied; among these passages of the Kitáb-i-Aqdas is one that refers to members of the House of Justice as "Men of Justice."[41]

During the ministry of 'Abdu'l-Bahá the intent of these passages of the Kitáb-i-Aqdas was clarified when He wrote to the Bahá'ís in America, who were at that time forming Spiritual Assemblies and embarking on the construction of a Bahá'í Temple:

> According to the ordinances of the Faith of God, women are the equals of men in all rights save only that of membership on the Universal House of Justice, for as hath been stated in the text of the Book, both the head and the members of the House of Justice are men. However, in all other bodies, such as the Temple Construction Committee, the Teaching

Committee, the Spiritual Assembly, and in charitable and scientific associations, women share equally in all rights with men.[42]

This clarification was restated and given further authoritative elaboration when Shoghi Effendi specified, in a letter written on his behalf to an individual believer,

> As regards your question concerning the membership of the Universal House of Justice: there is a Tablet from 'Abdu'l-Bahá in which He definitely states that the membership of the Universal House is confined to men, and that the wisdom of it will be fully revealed and appreciated in the future. In the local as well as the National Houses of Justice, however, women have the full right of membership. It is, therefore, only to the International House that they cannot be elected. . . .[43]

While the Bahá'í teachings specify the manner in which the Universal House of Justice is to be elected by members of the Secondary Houses of Justice, which are now called National Spiritual Assemblies, many details about election procedures, the number of members, and the term of office have not been set out in the writings of Bahá'u'lláh, or in the interpretations of 'Abdu'l-Bahá and Shoghi Effendi, and are thus left to the Universal House of Justice itself to determine. In accordance with the provisions of the Covenant, the Universal House of Justice is free to change its decisions whenever it judges conditions to have changed. This has raised in the minds of some the question of whether it might be possible for the Universal House of Justice to change the present stipulation that its membership is to be confined only to men. The Universal House of Justice addresses this subject, stating,

Further, in response to a number of questions about eligibility for membership and procedures for election of the Universal House of Justice, the Guardian's secretary writing on his behalf distinguished between those questions which could be answered by reference to the "explicitly revealed" Text and those which could not. Membership of the Universal House of Justice fits into the former category. The letter stated:

> The membership of the Universal House of Justice is confined to men. Fixing the number of members, the procedures for election and the term of membership will be known later, as these are not explicitly revealed in the Holy Text.
> (27 May 1940)

Hence, 'Abdu'l-Bahá and the Guardian progressively have revealed, in accordance with divine inspiration, the meaning and implications of Bahá'u'lláh's seminal teachings. Their interpretations are fundamental statements of truth which cannot be varied through legislation by the Universal House of Justice.[44]

Associated with this progressive clarification has been a progressive implementation of the provisions of the Bahá'í writings. Initially, when matters were not clear, the membership of the embryonic Local Houses of Justice established in the Western world through the initiative of the Bahá'ís living in these areas was confined to men. Later, when 'Abdu'l-Bahá clarified that the exclusion of women from membership applied only to the Universal House of Justice, women became eligible for service at both the local and national levels. The progressiveness of application in the Eastern world is discussed in greater detail in chapter 6, where the steps Shoghi Effendi took to bring about the full participation of women in the administrative activities of the Faith at both a local and national level are considered. As can readily be imagined, the Bahá'í approach to progressive clarification, with associated gradual implementation, has provided abundant ammunition to antagonists of the Bahá'í Faith seeking to direct at it accusations that can be disproved only through patient and careful examination of the facts. 'Abdu'l-Bahá has been falsely accused of yielding to the pressure to make the Bahá'í Faith more palatable to Western tastes and of changing the law of Bahá'u'lláh to allow women to serve on local and national bodies. At the other extreme are those who have argued unsuccessfully that the statements of Bahá'u'lláh were not intended to exclude women from the Universal House of Justice, but that 'Abdu'l-Bahá and Shoghi Effendi yielded to male pressure in imposing a restriction at the international level. No doubt other more ingenious accusations will be leveled against the Bahá'í institutions as the Bahá'í community grows in size and prestige and as those who are opposed to its values seek means of retarding its spread and influence.

A fundamental Bahá'í principle is illustrated when one considers the reason for excluding women from membership of the Universal House of Justice. 'Abdu'l-Bahá writes, "The House of Justice, . . . according to the explicit text of the Law of God, is confined to men; this for a wisdom of the Lord God's, which will erelong be made manifest as clearly as the sun at high noon." Similar statements are made by the Guardian in a letter written on his behalf in response to a query: "Regarding your question, the Master said the wisdom of having no women on the International House of Justice would become manifest in the future. We have no other indication than this." The Universal House of Justice, in a letter written on its behalf, states, "Bahá'ís believe that to gain a fuller understanding of the reason women are excused from membership of the Universal House of Justice, we must await the evolution of society, and, we are confident that the wisdom of women's exclusion will become manifest as society develops and becomes more united."[45]

Clearly, these responses from the central Bahá'í institutions do not indicate what the reason for exclusion is, and the believers are enjoined to have faith in the wisdom of this law and to trust that, in the course of time, the reason will become evident to the people of that future period.

This situation provides a useful example of the role of faith in the structure and operation of Bahá'í belief. A basic principle of the Bahá'í Faith is that of independent investigation of truth, by which a seeker after truth is encouraged to exercise independent judgment in determining whether or not to accept Bahá'u'lláh's claim to be a Manifestation of God and thus the source of religious truth for humanity in this Dispensation. A decision of such far-reaching consequences for the spiritual life of the individual should be reached without an unquestioning dependence on the views and conclusions of others. When a person accepts Bahá'u'lláh's claim and becomes a believer, he or she is accepting that whatever is revealed by Bahá'u'lláh is divine truth, irrespective of the extent to which the reasons for any given provision are clear. To hold to a contrary view is inconsistent with belief in Bahá'u'lláh as a Manifestation of God, and such a logical contradiction is best resolved by reexamining the evidence that led the individual to identify with the claims of the Bahá'í Faith. It is the spiritual obligation of every believer to endeavor, in applying the principle of independent investigation of truth, to obtain a deeper understanding of the Bahá'í teachings. In the course of that endeavor the believer will gain insight into the reasons for many of the provisions in Bahá'í law that a Bahá'í accepts on the basis of faith in Bahá'u'lláh. However, such a position should not be confused with blind faith, in which the views of a supposed source of truth are accepted without adequately investigating the validity of the alleged source.

It is not unusual, in the physical and biological sciences, to make use of an equation, concept, or chemical compound when the evidence about its validity or utility is compelling, even if the reasons are not clear. Medical compounds are used in healing because those who prescribe them are convinced of their efficacy, even if the mechanism by which the remedial action takes place is unknown. There are many examples in the physical sciences of equations that have been employed successfully, sometimes for many decades, before a theoretical justification was established.

The Bahá'í teachings contain many aspects that must, at present, be accepted on faith by the believer, including statements about life after death, predictions of the future condition of human society, and references to cosmology and to sciences of the future. It is in such a context that Bahá'ís might well view the call to them, as followers of Bahá'u'lláh, to accept with complete faith the statements in the Bahá'í teachings that the reason for the exclusion of women from membership of the Universal House of Justice will become evident in the future. The Universal House of Justice addresses this subject:

> Though at the present time it may be difficult for the believers to appreciate the reason for the circumscription of membership on the Universal House of Justice to men, we call upon the friends to remain assured by the Master's promise that clarity of understanding will be achieved in due course. The friends, both women and men, must accept this with faith that the Covenant of Bahá'u'lláh will aid them and the institutions of His World Order to see the realization of every principle ordained by His unerring Pen, in-

cluding the equality of men and women, as expounded in the Writings of the Cause.[46]

As might well be anticipated, there has been considerable speculation in the Bahá'í community about the reason for this explicit provision in the Faith. The views of individuals on this matter should not, of course, be regarded as authoritative statements of the Bahá'í Faith. In some instances the theories put forth may be regarded as logically inconsistent with the teachings of the Faith; other speculative views may well appear to reflect unconscious bias or unwarranted inferences drawn from the experiences of the male-dominated cultures that have prevailed throughout recorded history. In response to a question from a believer about a view propounded to the effect that women cannot make objective decisions because of their compassion and hence are excluded from the Universal House of Justice, a letter written on behalf of the House of Justice states,

> While individuals are free to speculate on the reason for the membership of the Universal House of Justice being confined to men, there is no authoritative text to support the assertion that it is due to women being so compassionate as to be unable to make objective decisions. Indeed, it might well be argued that if this were the reason, the teachings would have provided also for the exclusion of women from Local and National Spiritual Assemblies, whereas a letter written on behalf of Shoghi Effendi to an individual believer contains this statement: "In the local, as well as the national Houses of Justice, however, women have the full right of membership."[47]

This example illustrates the scrupulous care that should be taken not to give unjustified authority to the views of individual Bahá'ís on a subject that awaits the passage of time before it will become clear. In the meanwhile the Bahá'í community in all parts of the planet is summoned to persevere in the endeavor, which must extend over many generations, to create a world society that has translated the Bahá'í commitment to equality into established and unprejudiced social practice.

Those who are not Bahá'ís naturally find the Bahá'í teachings on membership of the Universal House of Justice puzzling and are not persuaded by the reasons given for Bahá'í adherence to this provision, since their perception of Bahá'u'lláh's station and the authority of His statements differs from that of Bahá'ís. Bahá'ís should be sympathetic and understanding of the concern others might feel about this aspect of the Faith, while maintaining their own resolute commitment to unqualified adherence to whatever Bahá'u'lláh has ordained.

Inquirers into the Bahá'í Faith often raise some probing questions in their exploration of the implications of this provision. The questions most frequently posed are set out below with our responses to them.

Question: How does the provision that women are excluded from membership of the Universal House of Justice accord with the Bahá'í principle of the equality of the sexes; does it not introduce an inconsistency in the application of this principle?

Response: The Bahá'í principle of the equality of the sexes does not imply identity of function, but it denies any implication of superiority associated with this functional differentiation. This is clarified by the Universal House of Justice, which writes,

> With regard to the status of women, the important point for Bahá'ís to remember is that in face of the categorical pronouncements in Bahá'í Scripture establishing the equality of men and women, the ineligibility of women for membership of the Universal House of Justice does not constitute evidence of the superiority of men over women. It must

also be borne in mind that women are not excluded from any other international institution of the Faith. They are found among the ranks of the Hands of the Cause. They serve as members of the International Teaching Centre and as Continental Counsellors. And, there is nothing in the Text to preclude the participation of women in such future international bodies as the Supreme Tribunal.*[48]

While there are differences of rank between the constituent elements of the institutions of the Bahá'í Administrative Order, and while the Universal House of Justice indicates that "Courtesy, reverence, dignity, respect for the rank and achievements of others are virtues which contribute to the harmony and well-being of every community," it also emphasizes the vital principle that "The true spiritual station of any soul is known only to God. It is quite a different thing from the ranks and stations that men and women occupy in the various sectors of society."[49] The importance of this distinction between rank in the Administrative Order and spiritual station lies not only in its resolution of the putative inconsistency referred to above. Clearly comprehending that administrative rank does not carry with it the implication of a higher spiritual station precludes the possibility of sullying the Bahá'í electoral process with the poison of ambition and preserves the prescribed attitude of humble willingness to serve in whatever function is assigned by the electors.

Question: Does not the exclusion of women from membership of the Universal House of Justice deny them access to the highest rank in the Faith?

---

* The Supreme Tribunal, a body that is to be elected and established by the peoples and governments of the world, will arbitrate disputes of an international character and will be a guardian of international peace. For further information, see *Messages from the Universal House of Justice, 1963–1986*, no. 422.

Response: Throughout the duration of the Bahá'í Dispensation, the highest rank to which a believer can be assigned is that of Hand of the Cause of God, and the Hands of the Cause outrank the members of the Universal House of Justice. Not only have several women been appointed as Hands of the Cause, but the Hand of the Cause whom Shoghi Effendi designated "the foremost Hand raised by Bahá'u'lláh since 'Abdu'l-Bahá's passing" was a woman, Miss Martha Root.[50]

Question: Does not the fact that the membership of the Universal House of Justice is all male imply that this body will concern itself principally with the welfare of men, or even with the preservation of male privilege, rather than being equally concerned with the welfare of women?

Response: In responding to a question of this nature the Universal House of Justice called attention to the fact that, in its decision-making, the House of Justice is the recipient and beneficiary of a unique assurance enshrined in the Covenant quite independent of the composition of its membership. The letter written on its behalf states,

> A vital distinction between the opinions and perceptions of the individual members of this body and the decision of the Universal House of Justice, is emphasised by 'Abdu'l-Bahá in the statement:
>
>> Let it not be imagined that the House of Justice will take any decision according to its own concepts and opinions. God forbid! The Supreme House of Justice will take decisions and establish laws through the inspiration and confirmation of the Holy Spirit, because it is in the safekeeping and under the shelter and protection of the Ancient Beauty . . .
>
> (From *Wellspring of Guidance: Messages 1963–1968*, The Universal House of Justice, pp. 84–85)

In describing the functions of the Universal House of Justice, Bahá'u'lláh has written that:

> We exhort the men of the House of Justice and command them to ensure the protection and safeguarding of men, women and children. . . .
>
> (From *Tablets of Bahá'u'lláh Revealed after the Kitáb-i-Aqdas* pp. 69–70)[51]

Some examples of actions taken by the Universal House of Justice to promote the equality of the sexes are given in chapter 6.

Question: History shows that the actions of men in past Dispensations have severely curtailed the freedom and rights granted to women by the Founder of each religion. What is there to prevent a similar erosion from occurring in the Bahá'í Dispensation?

Response: Were it left only to the followers of the Faith, no guarantee could be provided that such a restriction would not occur. The historical record indicates that in other religions such deviation from the purpose and intent of the Founders occurred partially through the misguided actions of those who were unconsciously influenced by the culture from which they came, and partially through the conscious efforts of those who feared a loss of power and privilege and who felt that changed circumstances justified their departure from the statements of the Founder. In the Bahá'í Faith the unassailable guarantee is provided by the institution of a Covenant entirely unique in religious history, with no parallel in the Dispensations of the past. Its provisions guarantee that the integrity of the teachings will be preserved and that their purity will remain free from corruption by manmade ideas or schemes. Without the Covenant, the high ideals of the Faith are doomed to ultimate failure, irrespective of the good intentions of its faithful adherents. Equipped with the Covenant of Bahá'u'lláh, the Faith is destined to bring about, to an extent now inconceivable, all the provisions of the Kitáb-i-Aqdas, a consequence of which will be the realization of the equality of the sexes and the liberation of women from the millennia of social inferiority that they have endured.

THE APPLICATION OF BAHÁ'Í LAW

The laws of every religion must necessarily take account of the consequences of the physiological differences between the sexes. Unfortunately, in times past these differences have often been used as a basis for the imposition on women of laws that acted as an unwarranted restriction on their freedom and that were in many instances humiliating.

Bahá'í law recognizes certain functional differences between men and women. However, this law is formulated in such a manner that the equality of the sexes is safeguarded and the freedom of women to develop their potential is not circumscribed. While its essential features are apparent now, its full implications will only become evident in the course of time as it is applied on a wider scale.

Through adherence to this law on the part of the Bahá'í community, the conduct of its members is modified. These changes in behavior serve to reinforce the attitudes that are enjoined in the Bahá'í teachings and are thus a potent means of implanting firmly in the consciousness of the Bahá'ís an ever-growing conviction of the equality of men and women.

5

Implementing Equality: The Ministries of Bahá'u'lláh and 'Abdu'l-Bahá

. . . *In every land the world of women is on the march, and this is due to the impact of the Most Great Manifestation, and the power of the teachings of God.*

—'Abdu'l-Bahá

BELIEF AND PRACTICE

Chapters 5, 6, and 7 discuss a number of aspects of implementing the principle of the equality of women and men. Chapter 5 highlights strategies and actions taken by Bahá'u'lláh and 'Abdu'l-Bahá during Their ministries. Chapter 6 focuses on the role of Shoghi Effendi and the Universal House of Justice to facilitate the understanding and practice of this principle. Chapter 7 examines the Bahá'í approach to implementation, drawing attention to its distinctive features and its multifaceted approach.

A religion such as the Bahá'í Faith must necessarily expect to be criticized by some as being no more than a utopian expression of high ideals and exalted principles, doomed to failure in its attempt to translate its teachings into practical reality. One aspect of the refutation of such an inaccurate assessment of the Faith is to draw attention to the actions taken by the central authority in the Faith since its inception to foster the progressive implementation of equality, in all its many aspects, and to demonstrate consistent and unyielding adherence to the principle of equality of the sexes.

The Bahá'í Faith lays unusually strong emphasis on the application of its laws and principles. Bahá'u'lláh states that "True belief in God and recognition of Him cannot be complete save by acceptance of that which He hath revealed and by observance of whatsoever hath been decreed by Him and set down in the Book by the Pen of Glory."[1] This passage illustrates the essential element of the Bahá'í commitment to implementation of religious requirements such as that of the equality of the sexes. The acceptance by a believer of such clearly stated principles and the practice of them are related directly and unambiguously to the central aim in the spiritual life of the individual, that of belief in God and unreserved acceptance of His teachings. This can give rise to a motivation far stronger than that of idealists, social reformers, and other fair-minded people who see clearly the need to practice the equality of the sexes and who strive to contribute to its implementation.

Such a perspective derives from a recognition that religion, in its pure form, uncorrupted by the pollution and distortion of dogmatic additions from erroneous sources, is the most powerful means of effecting constructive change in the world. As 'Abdu'l-Bahá states in *The Secret of Divine Civilization,*

> Religion is the light of the world, and the progress, achievement, and happiness of man result from obedience to the laws set down in the holy Books. Briefly, it is demonstrable that in this life, both outwardly and inwardly the mightiest of structures, the most solidly established, the most enduring, standing guard over the world, assuring both the spiritual and the material perfections of mankind, and protecting the happiness and the civilization of society—is religion.[2]

THE ACTIONS OF BAHÁ'U'LLÁH

The historical record of the actions taken by Bahá'u'lláh as Founder of the Bahá'í Faith to promote the implementation of this cardinal principle of His religion is far from complete. Much material remains untranslated and other significant information unrecorded because of the conditions in the Muslim societies of the nineteenth century. Nevertheless, even at this early stage, enough examples have been accumulated to allow some illuminating insights to be derived.

HIS TEACHINGS

Chapters 1 through 4 demonstrate in some detail that Bahá'u'lláh's unequivocal pronouncements on the equality of

men and women are an integral component of His vision of
the world of justice, unity, and liberation that His teachings are
designed to bring into being. He affirms that "such means as
lead to the elevation, the advancement, the education, the protection and the regeneration of the peoples of the earth have
been clearly set forth by Us and are revealed in the Holy Books
and Tablets by the Pen of Glory." Bahá'u'lláh also states that
His "counsels . . . constitute the supreme animating power for
the advancement of the world and the exaltation of its peoples."[3]

Within this context should be viewed the definitive statements of Bahá'u'lláh such as

> Praised be God, the Pen of the Most High hath lifted dis-
> tinctions from between His servants and handmaidens, and,
> through His consummate favours and all-encompassing
> mercy, hath conferred upon all a station and rank of the
> same plane. He hath broken the back of vain imaginings
> with the sword of utterance and hath obliterated the perils
> of idle fancies through the pervasive power of His might.[4]

The simplicity of the following passage should not be allowed to obscure its categorical nature and its far-reaching consequences: "Women and men have been and will always be equal
in the sight of God. The Dawning-Place of the Light of God
sheddeth its radiance upon all with the same effulgence."[5]

It is a familiar theme that the prescription of Bahá'u'lláh for
the rights of women stood in sharp contrast to the oppressive
conditions under which women were forced to exist in the nineteenth century within Iran and neighboring regions of the Ottoman Empire. What is less clearly understood is that His laws
and principles called for women to have rights far beyond those
enjoyed at that time by women in the Western world, where
there had already been a significant improvement in their state
and circumstances.

This point is illustrated by an analysis of the Declaration of Sentiments and the resolutions of the historic Seneca Falls Women's Rights Convention held in the United States in 1848. These statements called for women to be accorded human rights, including those of participation in the electoral process and in the legislative process, and the right to hold property within marriage. They deplored the lack of equity accorded to women in marriage and in the provisions for divorce, and sought removal of the formidable barriers to the education of women and to their participation in employment at other than the most menial and nonprofessional levels. In addition, they condemned the distinction in moral standards applied to men and women, the exclusion of women from public participation in religious affairs, and the destruction of the self-respect and self-confidence of women as a consequence of the manner in which they were being treated.[6] This eloquent call for the emancipation of women issued in Seneca Falls was far surpassed by the provisions enunciated by Bahá'u'lláh a few years later, in a distant land, for the liberation of women and their full participation in the affairs of humanity.

His Guidance and Encouragement to Women

Bahá'u'lláh did not confine Himself to the expression of the statements that form the foundation of the Bahá'í teachings. He modeled to His followers practical applications of the principle of equality, continually supporting and encouraging the female members of the Bahá'í community in their aspirations to develop themselves and be of service to others.

It is impossible to overestimate the reassurance, comfort, and encouragement that Bahá'í women continue to receive from the tenderness and consideration Bahá'u'lláh conveys in these words:

We make mention of the handmaidens of God at this time
and announce unto them the glad-tidings of the tokens of
the mercy and compassion of God and His consideration
for them, glorified be He, and We supplicate Him for all His
assistance to perform such deeds as are the cause of the exaltation of His Word.[7]

In the early days of the Bahá'í Faith it required great courage
for a woman to defy the pressure of her spouse and extended
family in expressing her adherence to this new religion. The
weight of a time-honored patriarchal social structure bore down
upon her, and her manifest assertion of the right to independence of thought rendered her subject to ridicule, condemnation, and derision. Bahá'u'lláh, in a Tablet, addressed one such
woman in these terms:

> Blessed art thou, doubly blessed art thou! Thou art reck-
> oned amongst those handmaidens whose love for their kin
> hath not prevented them from attaining the shores of the
> Sea of Grace and Mercy. God willing, thou shalt rest eter-
> nally neath the shade of the favours of the All-Merciful and
> shalt be assured of His bounties. Engage in the praise of the
> True One and rejoice in His loving-kindness.[8]

The handmaiden's courageous stand is praised, the spiritual
impact of her action is described, and she is promised a future
tranquillity and happiness. She is advised not to bemoan her
plight, but rather to rejoice in the opportunity that circumstances have given her to stand firm in the face of opposition
and to thus demonstrate the strength of her belief.

Bahá'u'lláh encouraged and recognized the participation of
women in the work of the Bahá'í Cause, thereby further affirming a role for women in religion. In this regard, it is very signifi-

cant that Bahá'u'lláh revealed Tablets in honor of some of His female followers and, in one such Tablet, admonished His "handmaiden" to "do that which will serve to promote the interests of the Cause of God amongst men and women." Not only does Bahá'u'lláh define a role for women in religion, but He specifies that women are to be on an equal footing with men in service to the Cause of God and that all must recognize and appreciate the important contribution that women have to make in this realm of activity. Women are not simply confined to teaching and ministering to the spiritual needs of women, but are called upon to operate "amongst men and women."[9]

From His Tablets it is evident that Bahá'u'lláh was most appreciative of the services of the female believers. He bestows the title of "handmaiden" upon those women who have had the blessing of recognizing and serving the Manifestation of God.[10] He indicates that

> The title "O My handmaiden" far excelleth aught else that can be seen in the world. Ere long the eyes of mankind shall be illumined and cheered by recognizing that which Our Pen of Glory hath revealed.[11]

In another Tablet addressed to one of the female believers, He asserts,

> Wert thou to perceive the sweetness of the title "O My handmaiden" thou wouldst find thyself detached from all mankind, devoutly engaged day and night in communion with Him Who is the sole Desire of the world.[12]

Bahá'u'lláh praises the services of the female believers and calls attention to their "station." In one of His Tablets He states,

> In words of incomparable beauty We have made fitting mention of such leaves and handmaidens as have quaffed

from the living waters of heavenly grace and have kept their
eyes directed towards God. Happy and blessed are they indeed. Ere long shall God reveal their station whose loftiness
no word can befittingly express nor any description adequately describe.[13]

And in another Tablet He affirms,

> By My Life! the names of handmaidens who are devoted
> to God are written and set down by the Pen of the Most
> High in the Crimson Book. They excel over men in the sight
> of God. How numerous are the heroes and knights in the
> field who are bereft of the True One and have no share in
> His recognition, but thou hast attained and received thy fill.[14]

EXAMPLES FROM HIS PERSONAL RELATIONSHIPS

In studying the life of any individual, including no less exalted a figure than a Manifestation of God, useful insights are
obtained by observing informal contact and association.
Religious history has been enriched by the Gospel accounts of
the interactions of Jesus with those of both high and low
estate, and many useful lessons have properly been drawn from
the record of the quotidian association of Muḥammad with
the people of Mecca and Medina.

There are pitifully few fragments in the Bahá'í literature accessible in the English language that illuminate the attitudes
and statements of Bahá'u'lláh toward the women with whom
He came in contact amid the restrictions of a life spent mostly
as a prisoner of implacable ecclesiastical and secular antagonists. Nonetheless, the brief accounts that are available are profoundly instructive to His followers, for they exemplify the acute
sensitivity, courtesy, respect, and consideration that distinguish
this contact.

Ásíyih Khánum. We begin with the most personal and intimate of relationships, that of Bahá'u'lláh and His faithful and devoted wife Ásíyih Khánum, on whom He conferred the title of honor *Navváb* (meaning "highness"), by which she is known. The information available about her is lamentably sparse, and the most detailed biography of her life is no more than a lengthy essay, despite the diligent endeavors of the author to glean material from sources in Arabic and Persian as well as English. Nevertheless, enough remains to provide useful glimpses, one of which concerns the hardships endured by the family of Bahá'u'lláh during its exile, at which time, in the words of her daughter Bahíyyih Khánum,

> Ásíyih Khánum, my dear mother, was in delicate health, her strength was diminished by the hardships she had undergone, but she always worked beyond her force.
>
> Sometimes my father himself helped in the cooking, as that hard work was too much for the dainty, refined, gentle lady. The hardships she had endured saddened the heart of her divine husband, who was also her beloved Lord. He gave this help both before his sojourn in the wilderness of Sulaymáníyyih, and after his return.[15]

Bahá'u'lláh's assisting Navváb with domestic duties and grieving over her ill health, other accounts of His consolation to her when their son Mírzá Mihdí fell to his death in an accident while the family was confined to the prison in 'Akká, and His solicitude to her in the last hours of her earthly life—all provide fragmentary but compelling evidence of a relationship of love and consideration.

In a Tablet of Visitation revealed after her passing, Bahá'u'lláh praises her exalted spiritual qualities and affirms that the sorrow caused by her death changed the light of the day to the darkness of night, transformed joy to sadness, and transmuted calmness into agitation.[16] He addresses her in these terms:

> O Navváb! O Leaf that hath sprung from My Tree, and been My companion! My glory be upon thee, and My loving-kindness, and My mercy that hath surpassed all beings. We announce unto thee that which will gladden thine eye, and assure thy soul, and rejoice thine heart. Verily, thy Lord is the Compassionate, the All-Bountiful. God hath been and will be pleased with thee, and hath singled thee out for His own Self, and chosen thee from among His handmaidens to serve Him, and hath made thee the companion of His Person in the daytime and in the night season.
>
> Hear thou Me once again, God is well-pleased with thee. . . .[17]

Bahá'u'lláh calls upon those who visit Navváb's resting-place to recite these words:

> Salutation and blessing and glory upon thee, O Holy Leaf that hath sprung from the Divine Lote-Tree! I bear witness that thou hast believed in God and in His signs, and answered His Call, and turned unto Him, and held fast unto His cord, and clung to the hem of His grace, and fled thy home in His path, and chosen to live as a stranger, out of love for His presence and in thy longing to serve Him. May God have mercy upon him that draweth nigh unto thee, and remembereth thee through the things which My Pen hath voiced in this, the most great station. We pray God that He may forgive us, and forgive them that have turned unto thee, and grant their desires, and bestow upon them, through His wondrous grace, whatever be their wish. He, verily, is the Bountiful, the Generous. Praise be to God, He Who is the Desire of all worlds, and the Beloved of all who recognize Him.[18]

Bahíyyih Khánum. Our attention turns next to Bahíyyih Khánum, the daughter of Bahá'u'lláh who is referred to as the Greatest Holy Leaf, a title of honor. The warmth of His relationship with her is evident in the following passage addressed to her:

> How sweet thy presence before Me; how sweet to gaze upon thy face, to bestow upon thee My loving-kindness, to favour thee with My tender care, to make mention of thee in this, My Tablet—a Tablet which I have ordained as a token of My hidden and manifest grace unto thee.[19]

Bahíyyih Khánum played a vital role in the work of the Faith during the ministry of Bahá'u'lláh. Perhaps the most striking example of how He availed Himself of the services of female believers is the way in which He called upon her to undertake important and challenging tasks on behalf of the Faith. Shoghi Effendi, in a letter dated 17 July 1932, attests that

> . . . this revered and precious member of the Holy Family, then in her teens, came to be entrusted by the guiding hand of her Father with missions that no girl of her age could, or would be willing to, perform, with what spontaneous joy she seized her opportunity and acquitted herself of the task with which she had been entrusted! The delicacy and extreme gravity of such functions as she, from time to time, was called upon to fulfill, when the city of Baghdád was swept by the hurricane which the heedlessness and perversity of Mírzá Yaḥyá had unchained, as well as the tender solicitude which, at so early an age, she evinced during the period of Bahá'u'lláh's enforced retirement to the mountains of Sulaymáníyyih, marked her as one who was both capable of sharing the burden, and willing to make the sacrifice, which her high birth demanded.[20]

She was, in this way, the archetype for those Bahá'í women
who have, in subsequent decades, played a courageous and crucial role in protecting the Faith from adversaries who sought to
extirpate it or to foment dissension within its ranks, and in
establishing the institutions of its Administrative Order. The
services she rendered through the guidance and encouragement
of Bahá'u'lláh were of such preeminent distinction as fitted one
described by Him as having "a station such as none other woman
hath surpassed."[21]

Other Bahá'í Women. Yet another example of Bahá'u'lláh's
confidence in the capacity of women to render important services to the Faith, and of His determination to provide them
with opportunities to do so, is found in His decision concerning the custodianship of the House of the Báb. After the passing of Khadíjih Bagum, the wife of the Báb, in 1882, Bahá'u'lláh
assigned this function to Zahrá Bagum, a sister-in-law of the
Báb, and to her descendants. Given the importance of the House
of the Báb in Shíráz as a center of formal pilgrimage and the
holiest place in Persia, the appointment of a woman to shoul-
der this important responsibility is indicative, not only of Bahá'u'lláh's trust in Zahrá Bagum's stewardship, but also of His
willingness to break with tradition. Such an appointment stands
in sharp contrast to the prevailing Islamic practice in which
women were generally excluded from religious office, for the
custodianship of holy places was the exclusive province of men.[22]

A further indication of Bahá'u'lláh's appreciation of the services of Bahá'í women is His extension of assistance and hospitality to a number of devoted female believers who had suffered
in the path of service to the Cause, including the widows and
children of distinguished Bahá'í martyrs. In *Memorials of the
Faithful,* 'Abdu'l-Bahá describes how Bahá'u'lláh directed
Fáṭimih Begum, the widow of the King of Martyrs, and members of her family to "come to the Most Great Prison so that,

sheltered in these precincts of abounding grace, they might be compensated for all that had passed."[23]

Bahá'u'lláh's communications with His cousin Maryam might well be taken as an example of His trust in, and respect for, women.[24] In one of the several Tablets addressed to her, revealed soon after His return from Sulaymáníyyih, Bahá'u'lláh pours out His heart to her, recounting the rigors of His exiles and His retirement to the mountains of Kurdistan, and the afflictions He endured at the hands of unfaithful relatives and friends:

> The wrongs which I suffer have blotted out the wrongs suffered by My First Name [the Báb] from the Tablet of creation. . . . After countless afflictions, We reached 'Iráq at the bidding of the Tyrant of Persia, where, after the fetters of Our foes, We were afflicted with the perfidy of Our friends. God knoweth what befell Me thereafter! At length I gave up My home and all therein, and renounced life and all that appertaineth unto it, and alone and friendless, chose to go into retirement. I roamed the wilderness of resignation, travelling in such wise that in My exile every eye wept sore over Me, and all created things shed tears of blood because of My anguish. The birds of the air were My companions and the beasts of the field My associates. . . . By the righteousness of God! I have borne what neither the oceans, nor the waves, nor the fruits, nor any created thing, whether of the past or of the future, hath borne or will be capable of bearing.[25]

During the course of His ministry Bahá'u'lláh recalled on many occasions the loyalty and devotion of Maryam and honored her with the appellation "Crimson Leaf."[26] Upon her passing He revealed a special Tablet of Visitation in her memory.

The following description of an event that transpired in
Baghdad, taken from a compilation of anecdotal accounts of
Baháʼuʼlláhʼs life, illustrates vividly the kindness and respect that
were so characteristic of Baháʼuʼlláhʼs attitude toward the women
with whom He was in contact:

> The Blessed Beauty was a source of great bounty and mercy
> for all, but particularly for the poor to whom He gave special
> attention. Always He bestowed gifts upon the disabled, the
> orphans and the needy whom He met during His walks in
> the city.
>
> One of these was a woman of eighty who lived in a de-
> prived area through which Baháʼuʼlláh often passed. Each
> day, as He walked from His house towards the coffee-house
> of Sar-i-Jisr, she would wait for him in the roadway.
> Baháʼuʼlláh was exceedingly kind to her and always asked
> after her health. Although He would not let her kiss His
> hands, whenever she wanted to kiss His cheeks, because she
> was bent with age and short of stature, He would bend down
> so that she could realize her wish. Often He remarked, "Be-
> cause I love this old woman so much, she also loves Me."
> Throughout His time in Baghdád, He showered her with
> kindness, and before leaving for Constantinople, He arranged
> an allowance for her to the end of her days.[27]

Such anecdotes are far from inconsequential or trivial. They
cast light on the unprecedented level of honor, respect, and
consideration toward women that is enjoined in the Baháʼí teachings, and on the need for a constant striving, even in the most
circumscribed conditions, for means by which women can be
encouraged and aided to take their rightful place as equal members of society.

THE ROLE OF 'ABDU'L-BAHÁ

The cause of women was also championed by 'Abdu'l-Bahá, the son of Bahá'u'lláh. He not only elaborated and promoted the principle of equality in His writings and talks, but His life serves as an example, a model of how to apply this principle and the other aspects of the Bahá'í teachings.

'Abdu'l-Bahá occupies a unique position in the Bahá'í Faith. He served not only as the designated successor to Bahá'u'lláh and as "the unerring Interpreter of His Word," but He is also the "perfect Exemplar" of Bahá'u'lláh's teachings, the "embodiment of every Bahá'í ideal," and "the incarnation of every Bahá'í virtue."[28] His every action is, therefore, of significance as a full expression of the Faith applied in the world; Bahá'ís are encouraged to study His approach and to follow His example as a means of attaining a more concrete understanding of the Bahá'í way of life.

The example of 'Abdu'l-Bahá translates abstract spiritual principles into visible reality and demonstrates their application, thereby making it possible for the individual to strive to emulate His action. He is a recent historical figure Who lived and traveled in the East and the West. His life is well documented and available for scrutiny. Examination of His writings, the events in His life, and the nature of His relationships with people from diverse backgrounds and cultures evinces the relevance of His attitudes and behavior to contemporary life. His interactions readily demonstrate that His behavior was not culture bound; His example transcends traditional limitations and stereotypes. He defines and models a way of life that is appropriate in both the East and the West.

An examination of the statements and the life of 'Abdu'l-Bahá will illustrate the ways in which He clearly, authoritatively, and strategically, not only defines, but also exemplifies and encourages the application of the principle of the equality of women and men by the followers of Bahá'u'lláh throughout the world.

THE EXEMPLAR OF THE BAHÁ'Í FAITH

Examining the historical record for accounts of the attitudes and statements of 'Abdu'l-Bahá serves, through practical example, to illustrate the conduct that all Bahá'ís should strive to follow. Such inquiry is limited by the present lack of comprehensive documentation about the activities of women in the Middle East, but a sufficient number of episodes have been reported to serve our purpose.

We begin by examining the characteristics of 'Abdu'l-Bahá's relationship to the women with whom He was most closely associated in His daily activities—His illustrious sister Bahíyyih Khánum, known as the Greatest Holy Leaf, and His wife, Munírih Khánum. During the ministry of 'Abdu'l-Bahá Bahíyyih Khánum, to whom some references have already been made, continued to play a most important and highly responsible role in the work of the Faith. She shared His imprisonment, reinforced His efforts, and was His ever-loyal supporter entrusted by Him with the affairs of the Cause during His absences from the Holy Land. Shoghi Effendi describes the services she performed in these words:

Forgetful of her own self, disdaining rest and comfort, and undeterred by the obstacles that still stood in her path, she, acting as the honoured hostess to a steadily increasing number of pilgrims who thronged 'Abdu'l-Bahá's residence from both the East and the West, continued to display those same attributes that had won her, in the preceding phases of her career, so great a measure of admiration and love.

And when, in pursuance of God's inscrutable Wisdom, the ban of 'Abdu'l-Bahá's confinement was lifted and the Plan which He, in the darkest hours of His confinement, had conceived materialized, He with unhesitating confidence, invested His trusted and honoured sister with the responsibility of attending to the multitudinous details arising out of His protracted absence from the Holy Land.[29]

A brief compilation of letters from 'Abdu'l-Bahá to Bahíyyih Khánum conveys the warmth of His affection for her, His concern for her well-being, and His appreciation of her abilities and services. Distressed about the sufferings she had endured, He wrote to her on one occasion, "Not for one moment do I cease to remember thee. My sorrow and regret concern not myself; they centre around thee. Whenever I recall thine afflictions, tears that I cannot repress rain down from mine eyes. . . ."[30] At one time when she was ill and was absent from Him, 'Abdu'l-Bahá wrote,

It is to be hoped that out of the grace of the Blessed Beauty thy illness will be completely cured and thou wilt return in the best of health, so that once again I may gaze upon that wondrous face of thine.

Write thou a full account of thy condition by every post, for I am most anxious for news of thee. Let me know if thou shouldst desire anyone from here to come to thee, that I may send the person along—even Munírih—so that thou wilt not be homesick.[31]

'Abdu'l-Bahá instructed His daughter Ḍíyá to care for Bahíyyih Khánum in these terms:

O Ḍíyá! It is incumbent upon thee, throughout the journey, to be a close, a constant and cheerful companion to my

honoured and distinguished sister. Unceasingly, with the
utmost vigour and devotion, exert thyself, by day and night,
to gladden her blessed heart; for all her days she was denied
a moment of tranquillity. She was astir and restless every
hour of her life. Moth-like she circled in adoration round
the undying flame of the Divine Candle, her spirit ablaze
and her heart consumed by the fire of His love. . . .[32]

In these and other passages we see glimpses of the quality of
the relationship that should distinguish the male members of a
family in regard to the female members. It is beyond the scope
of this work to describe in detail the life of Bahíyyih Khánum,
but it is relevant to note how strongly she encouraged Bahá'í
women to strive to develop their intellectual and spiritual capabilities through letters such as the following passage written by
her to another Bahá'í woman in 1897:

> It is my earnest hope that you, His distinguished leaf,
> together with the other maidservants of the All-Merciful in
> that land, may be so enkindled by the flame set ablaze by the
> hand of God as to illumine the whole world through the
> quickening energy of the love of God, and that through the
> eloquence of your speech, the fluency of your tongue, and
> the confirmations of the Holy Spirit you will be empowered
> to expound divine wisdom in such manner that men of elo-
> quence, and the scholars and sages of the world, will be lost
> in bewilderment. This indeed would not be hard for Him.[33]

When 'Abdu'l-Bahá passed away it was the Greatest Holy
Leaf who steadied the Cause until the newly appointed Guardian felt able to take up his duties. Shoghi Effendi's touching
announcement of his decision to assign such a responsibility to
the Greatest Holy Leaf reads as follows:

This servant, after that grievous event and great calamity, the ascension of His Holiness 'Abdu'l-Bahá to the Abhá Kingdom, has been so stricken with grief and pain and so entangled in the troubles (created) by the enemies of the Cause of God, that I consider that my presence here, at such a time and in such an atmosphere, is not in accordance with the fulfilment of my important and sacred duties.

For this reason, unable to do otherwise, I have left for a time the affairs of the Cause both at home and abroad, under the supervision of the Holy Family and the headship of the Greatest Holy Leaf until, by the grace of God, having gained health, strength, self-confidence and spiritual energy, and having taken into my hands, in accordance with my aim and desire, entirely and regularly the work of service I shall attain to my utmost spiritual hope and aspiration.[34]

In addition to assuming the "headship" of the Cause during this critical period, Bahíyyih Khánum served as the Guardian's main source of encouragement and support until her passing in 1932.

Our attention now turns to Munírih Khánum, the second of the two women with whom 'Abdu'l-Bahá enjoyed close association in His daily life. We consider the exemplary features of the marriage of 'Abdu'l-Bahá and Munírih Khánum. The latter spoke of it to Lady Blomfield, an early Bahá'í from Britain who visited her in the Holy Land on two occasions. Lady Blomfield records her remarks as follows:

It is impossible to put into words the delight of being with the Master; I seemed to be in a glorious realm of sacred happiness whilst in His company.

You have known Him in His later years, but then, in the youth of His beauty and manly vigour, with His unfailing

love, His kindness, His cheerfulness, His sense of humour,
His untiring consideration for everybody, He was marvel-
lous, without equal, surely in all the earth![35]

Lady Blomfield also records Munírih Khánum's summary of her
life with 'Abdu'l-Bahá:

> For fifty years my Beloved and I were together. Never were
> we separated, save during His visits to Egypt, Europe, and
> America.
> O my Beloved husband and my Lord! How shall I speak
> of Him?
> You, who have known Him, can imagine what my fifty
> years have been—how they fled by in an atmosphere of love
> and joy and the perfection of that Peace which passeth all
> understanding, in the radiant light of which I await the day
> when I shall be called to join Him, in the celestial garden of
> transfiguration.[36]

Some ten years after Bahá'u'lláh's passing, Madame de Canavarro, an American Buddhist who was a student of religion,
visited the Holy Land. There she was able to meet with Bahíyyih
Khánum, who gave the following description of the married
life of her brother 'Abdu'l-Bahá and Munírih Khánum:

> My brother's marriage has proved exceedingly happy and
> harmonious. Several months ago my sister[-in-law] took two
> of her daughters to Beirut on account of their health, and
> this has been her first separation from her husband for any
> length of time. Since a short time after her departure a ques-
> tion repeated by my brother the first thing every morning to
> his daughter, who is his constant attendant, is, "Ruha, when
> do you think your mother will come back?"[37]

In the light of such a relationship one can well understand why 'Abdu'l-Bahá states, in encouraging Bahá'ís to strive to create a harmonious and loving atmosphere in their homes, "My home is the home of peace. My home is the home of joy and delight. My home is the home of laughter and exultation. Whoever enters through the portals of this home must go out with gladsome heart."[38]

From within such a household Munírih Khánum wrote letters to Bahá'í women concerning the need to educate girls and involve Bahá'í women in all aspects of the work of the Faith. The following extract from one of her letters provides an indication of the strength of her commitment to the advancement of women:

> By the grace and favor of God, 'Abdu'l-Bahá has elevated the station of women in this radiant age. He has altered the quranic verse: "Men are the custodians of women." He has taught that men and women are like the two wings of a bird, and neither is superior to the other. Girls should be educated in the same way as boys, perhaps even given preference.
>
> Bahá'u'lláh has said that in this age, leaves [i.e., women] will appear who will become the glory of the men of the world.
>
> Without a doubt the promises of God will come about and will be manifested soon. We have heard that nowadays in Tehran, fifty women have offered their enthusiastic services in any capacity. This news has made these servants very, very happy. I have asked for the names of each of those dear sisters, so that I can write to each one and let her know that the mention of her service has been made and is known in the Holy Land.
>
> And so, my dear and respected sisters, thanks be to God that the field of service in the Cause of God is extensive and

souls with capacity are ready. Seekers and thirsty ones are waiting, and those leaves are prepared and willing to sacrifice.[39]

Munírih Khánum's devotion to the work of the Faith during 'Abdu'l-Bahá's ministry and her relationship to Him were such that, at the time of her passing, Shoghi Effendi wrote in a cable, "WITH SADDENED HEARTS BAHÁ'ÍS EAST AND WEST CALL TO MIND INVALUABLE SERVICES WHICH HER HIGH STATION EMPOWERED HER RENDER DURING STORMIEST DAYS 'ABDU'L-BAHÁ'S LIFE." A letter written on Shoghi Effendi's behalf at that time states, "she is now re-united with her Lord, and is enjoying the blissfulness and peace which the great World Beyond alone can confer."[40]

The historical accounts now available provide no more than a few brief episodes that illustrate the relationship of 'Abdu'l-Bahá to the women of the household, since the prevailing customs of the time did not permit chroniclers access to that aspect of the domestic scene. However, the fragments that are available are highly illuminating in that they record relatively minor occurrences that convey volumes about His attitude. Consider, for example, the statement of Bahíyyih Khánum recorded by Madame de Canavarro concerning Bahá'u'lláh's arrival in 'Akká in 1868 with the members of His family and His associates:

> At that time there was no landing for the city: it was necessary to wade ashore from the boats. The governor ordered that the women be carried on the backs of the men. My brother ['Abdu'l-Bahá] was not willing that this should be done, and protested against it. He was one of the first to land, and procured a chair, in which, with the help of one of the believers, he carried the women ashore.[41]

Consider also the following comment about the women of 'Abdu'l-Bahá's household: "The women would often join the

Master for His talks with the pilgrims, assisting with translation and adding their own insights to the proceedings."[42] No doubt other anecdotes will emerge in the future as the process of translation and classification of the testimonies of those who visited 'Abdu'l-Bahá develops. They will further reinforce the perception of 'Abdu'l-Bahá as providing an ideal example of the relationship of courtesy, respect, consideration, and encouragement that should distinguish Bahá'í men and women.

'Abdu'l-Bahá consistently displayed a caring attitude toward women, respecting their sensitivity, upholding their dignity, and attending to their welfare, in a society that displayed very little consideration for their rights or for their well-being. This attitude is exemplified by two events, one relatively minor but highly illustrative, and the second of far-reaching consequence.

The first example is from an account of Ṭúbá Khánum, a daughter of 'Abdu'l-Bahá, regarding the care that He gave to the poor and ill people in 'Akká, who had no means of getting assistance from the state to relieve their distress. She states,

> . . . a poor, crippled woman named Na'úm used to come every week for alms; one day a man came running:
>
> "Oh! Master, that poor Na'úm has measles. She is lying by the hot room of the Hammám;* everybody is keeping away from her. What can be done about her?"
>
> The Master immediately engaged a woman to care for her; took a room, put comfortable bedding (His own) into it, called the doctor, sent food and everything she needed. He went to see that she had every attention, and when she died in peace and comfort, He it was Who arranged her simple funeral, paying all charges.[43]

---

* *Hammám* is an Arabic word referring to a Turkish bath.

The second example is the action 'Abdu'l-Bahá took to assist
the Bahá'í women in Iran who had no access to competent
medical care, especially regarding gynecological concerns, in a
society in which the medical profession was male.

When a number of Persian Bahá'í physicians appealed for
an American female doctor to reside in Tehran for the purpose
of caring for the women of Iran, 'Abdu'l-Bahá chose Dr. Susan
Moody, a gynecologist and specialist in women's diseases. She
was the first American Bahá'í woman to settle in Iran.

En route to Iran Dr. Moody visited 'Abdu'l-Bahá in the Holy
Land and received from Him the necessary instructions and
encouragement for the work. He gave her the designation
Amatu'l-A'lá, "the handmaid of the Most High," counseled her
to have patience, and assured her that He would always be with
her. Dr. Moody arrived in Tehran in November 1909, in the
fifty-ninth year of her life.

Her medical services were greatly appreciated by the population at large. She served high and low alike, providing primary
health care and holding classes for mothers. She also actively
promoted the education of girls and worked for the establishment of the Tarbíyat school for girls, which is discussed below.
She remained at her post for fifteen years before returning to the
United States. In 1928, at Shoghi Effendi's request, she proceeded again to Iran to continue her highly meritorious service.
She completely consecrated herself to her work and passed away
in that land in 1934. Other health professionals, including Dr.
Sarah Clock and Miss Elizabeth Stewart, assisted Dr. Moody
and carried on her tradition of providing selfless service to the
Bahá'ís and the general public.[44]

AUTHORITATIVE INTERPRETER

As is abundantly evident from the preceding chapters of this book, 'Abdu'l-Bahá, in carrying out His ordained function of providing authoritative interpretation of the Bahá'í teachings, clarified the ramifications and implications of the principle of the equality of the sexes and guided the Bahá'ís in the practical application of this principle in daily life.

This section examines 'Abdu'l-Bahá's approach to presenting this issue, because it provides a most useful example of ways to promulgate the principle of equality in present-day society. An analysis of His approach identifies three principal elements, which are discussed below in some detail: His stress on timeliness, His setting of the principle of equality in an enlarged context, and His methods for challenging stereotypic thinking about the status and abilities of women.

TIMELINESS

'Abdu'l-Bahá stressed the timeliness and importance of the "rights of woman and her equality with man" when He described this issue as one of the "questions of the utmost importance" that are "facing humanity" in "this radiant century."[45] He further underscored the inevitability of achieving equality, stating,

> The realities of things have been revealed in this radiant century, and that which is true must come to the surface. Among these realities is the principle of the equality of man and woman—equal rights and prerogatives in all things appertaining to humanity.[46]

One of the direct results of 'Abdu'l-Bahá's emphasis on timeliness is that it provides motivation for regarding the attainment of equality of the sexes as a matter that must be addressed now, not as something that can be deferred for some time in the future. Those who accept His statement that the attainment of equality is inevitable will naturally feel impelled to align themselves with a historical process that is moving inexorably toward a prescribed conclusion.

ENLARGING THE CONTEXT

'Abdu'l-Bahá's approach enlarges the context within which the equality of men and women should be considered, standing in sharp contrast to those movements for equality that focus only on eradicating discrimination against women while ignoring underlying issues.

Characteristic of His approach is a redefinition of the issue and an appeal to those basic, more encompassing principles that are both fundamental to the aims of the Bahá'í Faith and are, perhaps, potentially more acceptable to individuals threatened by the idea of equality. For example, 'Abdu'l-Bahá sets the issue of equality within the context of justice when He states, "Divine Justice demands that the rights of both sexes should be equally respected since neither is superior to the other in the eyes of Heaven." Viewed from this perspective, the practice of equality can be seen as no less than an expression of justice, the principle that is "best beloved" in the sight of God, rather than a grudging concession made in a response to persistent demands.[47] Understanding equality as an expression of justice removes the need for women to apologize for seeking it or to adopt manipulative techniques in their quest for it.

The oneness of humankind is a cardinal principle of the Bahá'í Faith. 'Abdu'l-Bahá reframes equality in such a way as to make the realization of oneness inseparable from acceptance of the fact of equality of the sexes. He states, "In proclaiming the oneness of mankind He [Bahá'u'lláh] taught that men and women are equal in the sight of God and that there is no distinction to be made between them."[48]

Thus the oneness of humankind can neither remain at the level of abstract principle nor be applied solely to the relationship between people of different races; it must of necessity also encompass the equality of the sexes.

In society at large there is a tendency to consider the rights of women as purely a "women's problem"—a matter to be addressed and solved exclusively by women. When the issue is relegated to the province of women, it can readily be discounted and regarded as tangential to the major issues facing humanity. Even when the importance of the issue is acknowledged, it is often accorded low priority and is considered worthy of attention only after other pressing social problems have been resolved.

'Abdu'l-Bahá's talks clearly indicate that men and women alike must confront the issue of equality. He specifies that the implementation of equality is a prerequisite to social progress and prosperity and to the establishment of peace. In relation to social progress, He asserts,

> . . . until woman and man recognize and realize equality, social and political progress . . . will not be possible. . . . Until these two members [woman and man] are equal in strength, the oneness of humanity cannot be established, and the happiness and felicity of mankind will not be a reality.[49]

And again He asserts, ". . . until both are perfected, the happiness of the human world will not be realized." With regard to war, 'Abdu'l-Bahá states, "There is no doubt that when women obtain equality of rights, war will entirely cease among mankind."[50] As can be seen from these brief extracts, the meaning of the rights of women and the importance of equality are redefined. The new "frame" 'Abdu'l-Bahá employs broadens the context by relating equality to universally desired goals of progress, happiness, and peace. The vision He presents is world-embracing rather than exclusively serving one element of society. The reframing, therefore, has important implications for the individual's willingness to make the effort to change and to make personal sacrifices for a worthy end. As the cause of equality acquires global significance, it becomes not merely acceptable but desirable for self and society; in the case of peace, the implementation of equality takes on a particular urgency, given the world situation.

In some parts of the Western world, calls for the equality of rights and opportunities for women have been interpreted to mean that the development of women must take priority over that of men, and, since the available resources are regarded as insufficient to meet the needs of both, men fear that they will thereby be disadvantaged. The perceived threat of potential loss of privilege tends to mobilize resistance to change, and the barriers to women's participation are reinforced.

'Abdu'l-Bahá recasts the issue of human development, lifting it out of the realm of personal development for narrow, selfish ends and removing the element of competition. He introduces the paradoxical notion that the highest development of man depends on that of woman, thus making cooperation between the sexes the most effective route to personal and social development. 'Abdu'l-Bahá's talks provide the following explanations:

> The world of humanity consists of two parts: male and female. Each is the complement of the other. Therefore, if one is defective, the other will necessarily be incomplete, and perfection cannot be attained. There is a right hand and a left hand in the human body, functionally equal in service and administration. If either proves defective, the defect will naturally extend to the other by involving the completeness

of the whole; for accomplishment is not normal unless both are perfect. If we say one hand is deficient, we prove the inability and incapacity of the other; for single-handed there is no full accomplishment. Just as physical accomplishment is complete with two hands, so man and woman, the two parts of the social body, must be perfect. It is not natural that either should remain undeveloped; and until both are perfected, the happiness of the human world will not be realized.[51]

As long as women are prevented from attaining their highest possibilities, so long will men be unable to achieve the greatness which might be theirs.[52]

Relating the practice of equality to personal development reduces the threat perceived by men, while it increases their understanding of the personal benefits deriving from equality and their willingness to support the development of women. Similarly, for women, the anxiety associated with the need to compete for resources is removed, since they can anticipate that resources will be shared.

'Abdu'l-Bahá's explanations of the importance of practicing the equality of men and women address the concerns and fears of both sexes that are associated with changes to stereotypic and traditional sex roles. For example, by providing new perspectives from which to understand the necessity of equality, 'Abdu'l-Bahá defuses the threat of disunity. He provides an enlarged vision that reduces anxiety about social disruption; the loss of position, security, and privilege; and concern about competition for opportunities and resources. These new "frames" lift the problem of equality into a broader, less personal, context and highlight the positive benefits that accrue to all individuals, both female and male, and to society. Redefined in this way, the practice of equality becomes an attractive, ennobling pursuit of global significance, an activity to which all can commit themselves.

CHALLENGING STEREOTYPIC THINKING

'Abdu'l-Bahá uses a range of strategies for challenging prevailing assumptions about, and attitudes toward, women. These strategies differ in the degree to which they confront the issue and the individual, and also in their psychological impact.

Use of Analogy. One approach 'Abdu'l-Bahá employs frequently is the use of analogy to establish the basic principle of equality and demonstrate the untenability of its absence. For example, He states,

> Throughout the kingdoms of living organisms there is sex differentiation in function, but no preference or distinction is made in favor of either male or female. In the animal kingdom individual sex exists, but rights are equal and without distinction. Likewise, in the plane or kingdom of the vegetable sex appears, but equality of function and right is evident. Inasmuch as sex distinction and preference are not observed in these kingdoms of inferior intelligence, is it befitting the superior station of man that he should make such differentiation and estimate, when as a matter of fact there is no difference indicated in the law of creation?[53]

Not only are discriminatory attitudes and behaviors inappropriate, but 'Abdu'l-Bahá indicates that they are unworthy of the "superior station" of a human being.

Use of Rhetorical Questions. Another strategy 'Abdu'l-Bahá uses to call attention to mistaken attitudes is that of a barrage of penetrating questions that expose the logic (or lack thereof) of a point of view. This approach is well demonstrated by His challenge to the assumptions about the superiority of traditional masculine qualities. Another example of this approach is as follows:

> Inasmuch as we find no ground for distinction or superiority according to the creative wisdom in the lower kingdoms, is it logical or becoming of man to make such distinction in regard to himself? The male of the animal kingdom does not glory in its being male and superior to the female. In fact, equality exists and is recognized. Why should man, a higher and more intelligent creature, deny and deprive himself of this equality the animals enjoy? His surest index and guide as to the creative intention concerning himself are the conditions and analogies of the kingdoms below him where equality of the sexes is fundamental.[54]

'Abdu'l-Bahá's analysis is incisive, His observations acute, His questions psychologically telling. Note His implicit reference to the male glorying in his superiority, a behavior that may sometimes be observed even in contemporary times.

Use of the Direct Challenge. There are innumerable examples of 'Abdu'l-Bahá directly challenging discriminatory attitudes. Typically, He clearly states the principle of equality and, at the same time, deprecates the contrary view, assessing it to be faulty, inappropriate, or unworthy. For example, He asserts, "To accept and observe a distinction which God has not intended in creation is ignorance and superstition." He also asserts that woman "was denied the right and privilege of education and left in her undeveloped state. Naturally, she could not and did not advance." 'Abdu'l-Bahá further indicates,

> Man, endowed with his higher reason, accomplished in attainments and comprehending the realities of things, will surely not be willing to allow a great part of humanity to remain defective or deprived. This would be the utmost injustice.[55]

And:

> In this Revelation of Bahá'u'lláh, the women go neck and
> neck with the men. In no movement will they be left behind.
> ...At the time of elections the right to vote is the inalienable
> right of women, and the entrance of women into all human
> departments is an irrefutable and incontrovertible question.
> No soul can retard or prevent it.[56]

In such examples 'Abdu'l-Bahá directly confronts views based
on ignorant superstition and injustice, on unexamined positions, and on entrenched attitudes, all of which stand in the
way of inevitable change.

Use of Examples from History. 'Abdu'l-Bahá also provides
a number of effective examples from history to counteract the
negative evaluation of women and to demonstrate their capacity. Drawing examples from religious and political history stressing that women have been, and must be, involved in important
undertakings, He states, "History records the appearance in the
world of women who have been signs of guidance, power and
accomplishment. Some were notable poets, some philosophers
and scientists, others courageous upon the field of battle."[57] He
also states,

> ...it is well established in history that where woman has not
> participated in human affairs the outcomes have never at-
> tained a state of completion and perfection. ... every influ-
> ential undertaking of the human world wherein woman has
> been a participant has attained importance. This is histori-
> cally true and beyond disproof even in religion.[58]

This perspective is consonant with the ideas expressed in the
writings of contemporary feminist historians such as Gerda
Lerner, who sets out the following view in the introduction to
The Creation of Patriarchy:

Women are and have been central, not marginal, to the making of society and to the building of civilization. . . .
. . . What women have done and experienced has been left unrecorded, neglected, and ignored in interpretation. Historical scholarship, up to the most recent past, has seen women as marginal to the making of civilization and as unessential to those pursuits defined as having historical significance.[59]

'Abdu'l-Bahá cites examples from religious history that not only illustrate the integral role of women but also the excellence of their participation:

Often in history women have been the pride of humanity—for example, Mary, the mother of Jesus. She was the glory of mankind. Mary Magdalene, Ásíyih, daughter of Pharaoh, Sarah, wife of Abraham, and innumerable others have glorified the human race by their excellences.[60]

'Abdu'l-Bahá also provides illustrations of women from both the East and the West who played important roles in the political arena. He specifically mentions Zenobia, "Queen of the East, whose capitol was Palmyra"; Catherine the Great of Russia; Queen Isabella of Spain; Cleopatra, Queen of Egypt; and Queen Victoria of England.[61] 'Abdu'l-Bahá not only describes the major contributions of these outstanding women, but He also identifies the skills and qualities that they demonstrated in executing their functions. It is interesting to note that the qualities He mentions in characterizing these women are typically associated with the traditional masculine role—e.g., intelligence, courage, administrative ability, military strategy, and justice. Thus history demonstrates that women are both capable of participating in the world at large and capable of manifesting qualities that are valued by society and stereotypically associated with men.

Use of Contemporary Examples. In addition to citing examples from history, 'Abdu'l-Bahá draws attention to contemporary Bahá'í women who have achieved distinction in activities that were previously regarded as exclusively male preserves. He praises women who have become renowned as poets and scholars, who have occupied prominent positions in government, or whose fortitude and strength of conviction were such that they accepted martyrdom for their faith. These women demonstrate, by their behavior, qualities that cut across sex-role stereotypes. For example, 'Abdu'l-Bahá states, "In this day there are women among the Bahá'ís who far outshine men. They are wise, talented, well-informed, progressive, most intelligent and the light of men. They surpass men in courage."[62] Clearly, since 'Abdu'l-Bahá praises women for demonstrating these qualities, there can be no doubt as to their appropriateness for both women and men.

The strategies 'Abdu'l-Bahá employs in challenging unexamined assumptions about women and men vary in the extent to which they directly confront outdated attitudes and behaviors. His methods rely on persuasion, logical analysis, and the marshaling of historical and current examples. While expressing the principle of the equality of men and women in unequivocal language, His challenge is directed toward attitudes and actions that are not appropriate to the new age. His approach influences both the minds and hearts of His audience. His sensitive perception of the issue, the weight of His argument, and His use of a variety of techniques to communicate His point of view leave the individual with no alternative but to reassess his or her position in relation to women.

ASSIGNING RESPONSIBILITIES

The example of 'Abdu'l-Bahá in fostering full recognition and practice of the equality of the sexes extends far beyond the example of His daily life and His authoritative interpretation of Bahá'u'lláh's teachings. He actively promoted the full involvement of women in the work of the Bahá'í community, including their involvement in highly responsible duties that went far beyond what was considered normal in either the East or the West at that time. He encouraged women to aspire to a level of attainment equal to, if not surpassing, that of men.

Although a comprehensive survey of the actions taken by 'Abdu'l-Bahá in this regard is beyond the scope of this book, focusing on a few examples clearly illustrates the manner in which 'Abdu'l-Bahá involved Bahá'í women in the most responsible elements of the work of the Faith.

ETHEL ROSENBERG

A painter trained at the Slade School in London, Ethel Rosenberg became a Bahá'í in 1899, thus acquiring the distinction of being the first Englishwoman to recognize Bahá'u'lláh as the Manifestation of God. When she visited 'Abdu'l-Bahá in 1901, it was apparent to Him that she was a person of unusual capacity and intellect, and she was permitted to remain with His household for several months. During this time she filled several notebooks with notes taken while 'Abdu'l-Bahá instructed her in the Bahá'í teachings and answered her questions; this material, as well as the information she obtained during her subsequent pilgrimages in 1904 and 1909, formed the basis of her exposition of the Bahá'í Faith that was published in 1910 and was used extensively in the spread of the Faith in Britain during those early years. In 1911, while 'Abdu'l-Bahá was in Paris, He called upon Ethel Rosenberg to convene a committee

of Bahá'ís centered in London to administer the British Bahá'í
community's expanding activities. It is significant to note that
He appointed a committee of seven believers, six of whom were
women. This committee was the embryo that would evolve,
eventually transforming into the National Spiritual Assembly
of that land in years to come. 'Abdu'l-Bahá devoted considerable time to training Ethel Rosenberg in the administrative principles that the committee should follow, including its functions
and its procedures for handling funds. Known initially as the
Bahá'í "Consultation Committee," it changed its name and
composition in 1915, becoming the Bahá'í Council, with eight
members, including six women, and with Ethel Rosenberg continuing to play a central role.

CORINNE TRUE

In the United States the initial development of the body that
would evolve later into the National Spiritual Assembly was
centered around a woman designated by 'Abdu'l-Bahá to play a
crucial role in its functioning. When in 1903 the American
Bahá'ís appealed successfully to 'Abdu'l-Bahá for permission to
embark upon the construction of a House of Worship, He wrote
to Mrs. Corinne True indicating that He wanted her to become
very much involved in this project despite her lack of experience in such traditionally male domains as real estate, architec-
ture, or property development. In 1906 she was instrumental
in organizing a petition, signed ultimately by nearly eight hundred Bahá'ís from all over the United States, calling for Temple
construction to begin, and she was commissioned to deliver it
to 'Abdu'l-Bahá in 'Akká. He made it clear to her that she should
devote herself entirely to this endeavor and warned her that her
work for it would involve suffering and hardship.

The American Bahá'ís in those early days had not grasped
the importance and implications of the Bahá'í principle of equal-

ity of the sexes, and the rudimentary administrative bodies such as the House of Spirituality in Chicago were restricted to men. Their narrow views were abruptly perturbed by 'Abdu'l-Bahá's designation of Corinne True as the recipient of His guidance about the Temple construction. Nathan Rutstein, in a biography of this outstanding woman, writes of this period:

> While Corinne True and her daughter were on their way home via Paris and London, Thornton Chase, Carl Scheffler and the Agnews were on pilgrimage, experiencing, at one point, something they hadn't expected. It was the Master's response to Mr Chase's questions regarding the Temple. "When you return consult with Mrs True—I have given her complete instructions."
>
> Mr Chase was startled. He simply wasn't prepared for what 'Abdu'l-Bahá had said. The Master had upset his notions about the role of women in the Faith. Had the Master doubted Thornton Chase's firmness in the Faith, He wouldn't have been so direct with him. What was said was obviously meant to broaden and deepen the American pilgrims' understanding of a certain aspect of the Bahá'í teachings.[63]

Corinne True immersed herself in the work of the Temple project, which subjected her to tension and clashes with other Bahá'ís. As Rutstein points out,

> It was understandable why some of the early Bahá'ís clashed with her, especially some of the more assertive men, who felt she craved power. They were unfamiliar with such a display of drive in a woman, not realizing that Corinne's all-consuming love for the Master was what drove her.[64]

As she continued to develop plans for this project, she concluded that it should be carried out by a national organization

that was representative of the entire American Bahá'í community. 'Abdu'l-Bahá endorsed this approach, called for a national
convention to elect such a body, and specified that women
should be eligible for membership on it. As a result the "Bahá'í
Temple Unity" was formed, with a nine-member executive board
that included three women, with Corinne True elected as its
financial secretary. When in 1922 this body was superseded by
an entity that adopted the designation of National Spiritual
Assembly, Corinne True was elected to the new body with the
highest number of votes and continued to function as its financial secretary. As the years advanced, her role in the Temple
construction inevitably diminished, but she was privileged to
attend the dedication of the completed building in May 1953
as a ninety-one year old on whom had been conferred the exalted rank of Hand of the Cause of God. Rutstein comments
on the importance of the role she played in the involvement of
women in the work of the American Bahá'í community:

> 'Abdu'l-Bahá chose her to do what He felt others more
> experienced in the ways of the world weren't capable of do-
> ing. He chose a woman to spearhead the development of the
> most important single project in the first fifty years of the
> Faith in America. But there were other things that she was
> destined to do for the Master; and she probably did them
> unaware at the time of what her exploits would eventually
> lead to. Through her efforts the Administrative Order, on a
> national scale, was started and developed.
>
> And 'Abdu'l-Bahá used her to break down the psycho-
> logical barriers against women in the American Bahá'í com-
> munity. That was a long and painful experience. Above all
> she stood firm in the Faith, regardless of the severity of the
> tests within the Bahá'í community. Nothing could unhinge
> her attachment to the Cause. It was that, more than any-

thing else, that endeared her to the Master and the Guardian. For it is upon that kind of rock that true Faiths are built.[65]

AGNES PARSONS

Many other women were assigned important responsibilities in the work of the Faith. 'Abdu'l-Bahá entrusted Mrs. Agnes Parsons, a prominent socialite and a well-known hostess in Washington, D.C., with the task of organizing interracial gatherings at a time when there was little social mixing between the races in the United States, especially in a city such as Washington. Mrs. Parsons had the bounty of using her new home to extend hospitality to 'Abdu'l-Bahá during His first visit to Washington in the spring of 1912 and to place at His disposal her summer residence in Dublin, New Hampshire.

During her second visit to the Holy Land in 1920, 'Abdu'l-Bahá gave Mrs. Parsons the following instruction: "I want you to arrange a Convention for unity of the colored and white races. You must have people to help you."[66] He called upon her as a devoted Bahá'í to use her social position and skills to foster awareness and acceptance of the oneness of humanity, a principle that was generally flouted by leaders of society at that time. She succeeded in gathering around her an able committee, and the convention was held. In a message to be read to the gathering, 'Abdu'l-Bahá wrote,

> Say to this Convention that never since the beginning of time has one more important been held. This Convention stands for the Oneness of Humanity; it will become the cause of the removal of hostility between races; it will be the cause of the enlightenment of America. It will—if wisely managed and continued—check the deadly struggle between these races which otherwise will inevitably break out.[67]

'Abdu'l-Bahá expressed satisfaction with the event and voiced
the hope that such gatherings would be established throughout
North America. He referred to the event organized by Mrs. Parsons and her helpers as "the mother convention" from which
many Amity Conventions would be born.[68]

ELLA COOPER AND HELEN GOODALL

Another example of 'Abdu'l-Bahá's encouragement of Bahá'í
women concerns two early believers of California, Mrs. Ella
Cooper and her mother, Mrs. Helen Goodall, and their role in
an outstanding event in the Bahá'í history of the West. The
event was the convocation of the first "International Bahá'í
Congress," which was held in conjunction with the Panama-
Pacific International Exposition in the spring of 1915 in San
Francisco to celebrate the completion of the Panama Canal.
Although initiated by the Local Spiritual Assembly of San Francisco, the Congress was under the official auspices of the
Panama-Pacific International Exposition. Mrs. Cooper, Mrs.
Goodall, and a number of other Bahá'ís formed the executive
committee of the Congress. They had seen the potential of such
a gathering to promulgate the Bahá'í teachings on the oneness
of humanity and world peace and had approached 'Abdu'l-Bahá
with their desire to arrange it. He readily gave His approval and
even selected the speakers.

The Congress took place between 19 and 25 April 1915 and
attracted large audiences to hear the Bahá'í teachings. The di-
rectorate of the exposition set April 24 as "International Bahá'í
Congress Day" and held an official reception at which a com-
memorative bronze medallion was presented to the Bahá'ís in
recognition of the Bahá'í program for universal peace.[69]

LUA GETSINGER

'Abdu'l-Bahá did not hesitate to call upon Bahá'í women to accomplish extremely arduous tasks. In 1902 He requested Lua Getsinger, an outstanding early Bahá'í woman, to travel from the United States to Paris, there to deliver to the shah of Persia, during his visit to that city, a petition from Him calling on the shah to restrain the Muslim clerics from persecuting the Iranian Bahá'ís. She accomplished this difficult task through her determination and perseverance over a period of several weeks, even ensuring that one of the two petitions presented to the shah was delivered into his own hands. It is significant that the persecutions in Iran diminished for several years following this action.

At a time when the very idea of a Western woman traveling to the East to teach religion was almost incomprehensible, 'Abdu'l-Bahá instructed Lua Getsinger to travel to India and the Middle East for the purpose of spreading the Bahá'í message. She did so with her characteristic energy and commitment, eventually passing away in Cairo in 1916 at the age of forty-five while engaged in this task.

AGNES ALEXANDER AND MARTHA ROOT

Among the other women who were called upon by 'Abdu'l-Bahá to attain heights of heroism in their services to the Faith were Agnes Alexander, who proceeded to Japan from Hawaii to become the first Bahá'í in that land, and Martha Root, who initiated her worldwide travels as a promoter of the Faith in response to 'Abdu'l-Bahá's summons to her:

As ears are awaiting the summons for Universal Peace, it is therefore advisable for thee to travel . . . to the different

parts of the globe, and roar like unto a lion of the Kingdom
of God. Wide-reaching consequences thou shalt witness and
extraordinary confirmations shall be exhibited unto thee.[70]

Miss Root's magnificent exploits are discussed more fully in
chapter 6.

It should not be imagined that 'Abdu'l-Bahá's assignment of
responsibilities was confined only to Western Bahá'í women.
Within the limits imposed by the social conditions of the time,
He drew upon the abilities of capable Eastern women also. As
an example, during World War I, when the Holy Land was
threatened with famine, 'Abdu'l-Bahá utilized the personal integrity and the organizational skills of Sakínih Sulṭán, a Persian
Bahá'í who was the widow of a martyr and who was serving in
the Holy Land for a period. 'Abdu'l-Bahá gave her the great
responsibility of administering the distribution of relief food
that He had stored or managed to acquire and ship to Haifa
and 'Akká. He communicated with her frequently, describing
the challenges of arranging transport, discussing the cost of
grain, and issuing detailed instructions about who was to receive aid and just how much each was to get.[71]

In evaluating the courageous services of Bahá'í women under the guidance and urging of 'Abdu'l-Bahá, one can well understand why, in the words of the Universal House of Justice,

'Abdu'l-Bahá has pointed out that "Among the miracles
which distinguish this sacred dispensation is this, that women
have evinced a greater boldness than men when enlisted in
the ranks of the Faith." Shoghi Effendi has further stated
that this "boldness" must, in the course of time, "be more
convincingly demonstrated, and win for the beloved Cause
victories more stirring than any it has as yet achieved."[72]

PROVIDING ENCOURAGEMENT

These distinctive services were rendered as a result of the constant encouragement the women received from 'Abdu'l-Bahá. He emphasized the importance of such encouragement and described it as a duty of the members of Spiritual Assemblies:

> The members of the Spiritual Assembly should do all they can to provide encouragement to the women believers. In this dispensation one should not think in terms of "men" and "women" all are under the shadow of the Word of God and, as they strive the more diligently, so shall their reward be the greater—be they men or women or the frailest of people.[73]

'Abdu'l-Bahá also warned of the consequences of failure to offer such encouragement:

> In brief, the assumption of superiority by man will continue to be depressing to the ambition of woman, as if her attainment to equality was creationally impossible; woman's aspiration toward advancement will be checked by it, and she will gradually become hopeless. On the contrary, we must declare that her capacity is equal, even greater than man's. This will inspire her with hope and ambition, and her susceptibilities for advancement will continually increase. She must not be told and taught that she is weaker and inferior in capacity and qualification. If a pupil is told that his intelligence is less than his fellow pupils, it is a very great drawback and handicap to his progress. He must be encouraged to advance by the statement, "You are most capable, and if you endeavor, you will attain the highest degree."[74]

Obviously, encouragement will only be effective if it is sincere and based on conviction of the validity of the concept of the equality of the sexes.

'Abdu'l-Bahá used a variety of means to encourage women. In some instances He directed their attention to the limitless spiritual power accessible to them as followers of Bahá'u'lláh, as in the following admonition:

> O loved handmaidens of God! Consider not your present merits and capacities, rather fix your gaze on the favours and confirmations of the Blessed Beauty, because His everlasting grace will make of the insignificant plant a blessed tree, will turn the mirage into cool water and wine; will cause the forsaken atom to become the very essence of being, the puny one erudite in the school of knowledge.[75]

'Abdu'l-Bahá acknowledges the feelings of incapacity and insecurity, but He is unyielding in His urging that they not surrender to such sentiments.

At other times He called upon women to aspire to a level of accomplishment equal to, or even surpassing, that of men by drawing on the power of the Faith. He states,

> In this wondrous Dispensation the favours of the Glorious Lord are vouchsafed unto the handmaidens of the Merciful. Therefore, they should, like unto men, seize the prize and excel in the field, so that it will be proven and made manifest that the penetrative influence of the Word of God in this new Dispensation hath caused women to be equal with men, and that in the arena of tests they will outdo others.[76]

It was clear, during the days of 'Abdu'l-Bahá, that women in the Western world had been able to accomplish much more than those in the East, and they were dispatched by Him on assignments all over the world. 'Abdu'l-Bahá encouraged the Eastern women to follow the example of their Western sisters, exhorting them as follows:

O ye leaves who have attained certitude! In the countries of Europe and America the maidservants of the Merciful have won the prize of excellence and advancement from the arena of men, and in the fields of teaching and spreading the divine fragrances they have shown a brilliant hand. Soon they will soar like the birds of the Concourse on high in the far corners of the world and will guide the people and reveal to them the divine mysteries. Ye, who are the blessed leaves from the East, should burn more brightly, and engage in spreading the sweet savours of the Lord and in reciting the verses of God. Arise, therefore, and exert yourselves to fulfil the exhortations and counsels of the Blessed Beauty, that all hopes may be realized and that the plain of streams and orchards may become the garden of oneness.[77]

It should not be imagined that the encouragement 'Abdu'l-Bahá offered was directed only to women in the East. In the following passage addressed to the Bahá'í women of California 'Abdu'l-Bahá wrote,

If you arise in accord with the exhortations and commands of the Blessed Perfection—may my life be a sacrifice to His beloved ones!—before long agreeable results will be obtained, the great newspapers of the world will all engage in praising you and such activity will be brought about in the West as will increase the motion and activity in the East.[78]

The full significance of 'Abdu'l-Bahá's actions in assigning important responsibilities to women and in encouraging the female members of the Bahá'í community will only become apparent in years to come, as an increasing number of Bahá'í women strive to take His words to heart and to follow the example of the courageous and dedicated women who exerted themselves so mightily in those early days. Bahá'ís of both sexes,

following 'Abdu'l-Bahá's example, will regard it as their duty to
find means by which they can foster the aspiration of women
for accomplishment, self-development, and service.

PROMOTING THE ENLIGHTENMENT OF WOMEN

The emphasis that the Bahá'í teachings place on the education of women and girls has been described in chapter 2, where
some of 'Abdu'l-Bahá's statements on this subject are set out.
This section examines some of the actions that were taken and
some of the processes that were set in motion during His ministry to further the education of women. Attention is directed
almost entirely to the Eastern world, since the facilities available there were far less than those in the West, and the cultural
barriers to female education were more formidable in that part
of the world.

From the earliest days of the small Bahá'í community centered around Bahá'u'lláh and 'Abdu'l-Bahá in the Holy Land,
the education of children—both boys and girls—was emphasized, within the limits imposed by the confinement of the family
and companions as prisoners of the Ottoman Turks, and by
the meager facilities available to them. The emphasis on education was constant. Lady Blomfield, an early Bahá'í, describes
how, when the family of 'Abdu'l-Bahá was evacuated tempo-
rarily from Haifa to the village of Abú-Sinán during the period
of World War I when Haifa was in danger of bombardment,
'Abdu'l-Bahá arranged for schools to be set up in that village to
ensure that the children's education was not neglected. Genevieve
Coy, herself an educator, writes, in an account of her 1920
pilgrimage, about the education of the granddaughters of
'Abdu'l-Bahá, one of whom had been sent to a college in Beirut
and was proceeding to Cairo for further studies, while another
was about to enter a college in England; one of these young
women expressed great regret that the schools in Haifa did not

provide educational facilities for students over fifteen years old. Another early Bahá'í, Marion Jack, was brought to 'Akká in 1908, around the time 'Abdu'l-Bahá was being released from confinement, for the purpose of teaching English to the grandchildren.[79]

'Abdu'l-Bahá formulated plans to establish a girls' school on Mount Carmel, and His wife, Munírih Khánum, gave it her enthusiastic support, as is evident from a letter she wrote to the believers, seeking their financial support for the project.[80] Although circumstances did not permit the plans to reach fruition, other facilities for the education of girls later became available there.

The principal focus of 'Abdu'l-Bahá's attention to the education of girls was Iran, a country where the educational opportunities for girls were negligible. It had, at the time, the largest Bahá'í community in the world. With His strong encouragement one of the Iranian women named Munírih Khánum (unrelated to her namesake, the wife of 'Abdu'l-Bahá) established the Tarbíyat school for girls in 1911.[81] Because she was the wife of the Hand of the Cause of God Ibn-i-Abhar and the daughter of the Hand of the Cause of God Hájí Ákhund, she occupied a prestigious position in the Bahá'í community, which would doubtless have been most valuable in overcoming cultural inhibitions about the participation of girls in this school and in others that were later established in a number of towns and villages throughout the country. These Bahá'í schools were renowned for their emphasis on moral and spiritual training, their attitude of respect and dedication to learning shared by students and teachers alike, as well as their high academic standard, their progressive curriculum, and their use of modern educational methods, including laboratory-based science classes and gymnastics.

To facilitate the establishment and acceptance of the Bahá'í
schools for girls in Iran and to make possible the introduction
of a progressive curriculum, 'Abdu'l-Bahá recruited highly qualified teachers from North America. Foremost among these teachers were Miss Lillian Kappes and Dr. Genevieve Coy. Miss
Kappes, who is honored by Shoghi Effendi as one of the "Disciples of 'Abdu'l-Bahá," left her home in the United States in
1911 to settle in Iran, where she served as the principal of the
Tarbíyat girls' school until her death in 1920.[82] Upon her passing, 'Abdu'l-Bahá revealed in her honor a Tablet that extols her
services and the sacrifices she made to further the education of
girls. The Tablet states,

> She left her native land and remained apart from family
> ties and brothers, enduring every trouble and distress and
> was content to accept the bitterness of separation for the
> love of teaching the children. And with enthusiasm educat-
> ing the girls she lived in distant cities during long years and
> periods and was patient in every difficulty. Morn and eve she
> was endeavoring to clarify the intellects of the innocent chil-
> dren of good families and failed not in giving out daily that
> which was required of her in that distant region. She gave
> her hand unwearied every night and day and at evening-tide
> and morning-tide to the service of the friends and taught the
> little ones who drew nourishment from the breast of Thy
> favor until her body gave out, her strength failed, her body
> disintegrated and her form dissolved. Then, supported by
> Thy favor, she returned to Thee, eager to behold Thee near
> by. Verily Thou art the sublime Refuge, the Faithful, All-
> sufficient, the Dear and Illustrious, the Most Supreme![83]

Miss Kappes was succeeded by Dr. Coy. As the schools began
to produce graduates, a number of distinguished Persian women,

inspired by the example of their teachers from the West, also became involved in the educational enterprise and began to make a significant contribution to its development. They included Ishráqíyyih Dhabíh and Rúhangíz Fath-'Azam.[84]

The recruitment of qualified teachers lent a credibility to the enterprise in the eyes of the Persian community. It also intensified the interest in women's education in the West and provided an avenue for the Western Bahá'ís to collaborate with their coreligionists in the East. It allowed them to demonstrate their commitment, through such means as encouragement and financial support, to implementing the important principle of equality.

The Bahá'í schools in Iran achieved a high standard of excellence and, until their closure in 1934 as a result of governmental action, were regarded as the best schools in the country. They attracted the children of many prominent families and trained a generation of leaders.[85]

The initiatives taken to promote the enlightenment of women during 'Abdu'l-Bahá's ministry and with His active encouragement went beyond the formal education of girls, important though it be. They included a number of other measures to train women for involvement in society to an extent far beyond that which was culturally acceptable at the time. In Iran in 1909 the Hand of the Cause Ibn-i-Abhar and his wife, Munírih Khánum, formed a special committee for the liberation of women and participated in its work as members. Another Hand of the Cause, Ibn-i-Asdaq, formed an institute in Tehran that was devoted to training Bahá'í women in methods of teaching the Faith.[86]

In both the East and the West, to involve women in the organizational and administrative activities of a religion was quite novel, and it was challenging to some of the male followers of the Faith in its early days to find that they belonged to a religion that was fully committed to the expression of equality. 'Abdu'l-Bahá's strong and persistent encouragement of women resulted in the formation in Tehran in 1910 of the Spiritual Assembly of the Bahá'í Women, whose members included Munírih Khánum and Fáṭimih Khánum, the wives of the two Hands of the Cause Ibn-i-Abhar and Mullá 'Alí-Akbar, respectively. This Assembly turned to the exclusively male Spiritual Assembly of Tehran for guidance on basic issues during the seven years of its existence.[87]

A similar development occurred in Chicago, where the House of Spirituality formed in 1901 was entirely male. Its formation stimulated the election of the Women's Auxiliary Board a little later that year; at its first meeting this board decided to write to Bahá'í women all over the United States, urging them to organize themselves in like manner. Several months later it changed its name to the Women's Assembly of Teaching at 'Abdu'l-Bahá's suggestion.[88]

It is significant to note that 'Abdu'l-Bahá remained patient with these early and imperfect attempts to establish the structural basis of the Bahá'í Administrative Order and that, for some time, He chose to tolerate their segregation into male and female organizing bodies. Not until 1909 did He make it absolutely clear that women and men should both be eligible to serve on the membership of local and national administrative bodies, a provision that was implemented without delay in the West, but somewhat later in the East, where social conditions for women were much more restrictive.[89]

It is impossible to overestimate the importance of 'Abdu'l-Bahá's call for the formation of what He describes in His writings as women's assemblages. These gatherings were confined to women and were held for the purposes of fostering enlightenment and what would be described in modern terminology as consciousness-raising.

In the time of 'Abdu'l-Bahá, women in the East generally
lacked both the opportunity for education and any kind of a
life outside their home. To compensate for this deprivation
'Abdu'l-Bahá called for these women's assemblages as a means
of increasing women's understanding of the Faith and raising
their level of general knowledge and personal competence. He
defined the purpose of such gatherings as "the promotion of
knowledge," and, in Tablets addressed to the Bahá'í women of
Iran, He set the agenda for these meetings and provided practical guidelines for their conduct.[90]

It is clear that 'Abdu'l-Bahá considered women's assemblages
as having the potential to contribute significantly to the development of women and the potential to raise their status within
the community. He viewed these gatherings as an important
training ground for women to deepen their knowledge of the
Faith and to acquire the intellectual skills and competencies
needed for participation in the evolving administrative institutions of the Cause. He underlined their uniqueness in the following terms:

> From the beginning of existence until the present day, in
> any of the past cycles and dispensations, no assemblies for
> women have ever been established and classes for the pur-
> pose of spreading the teachings were never held by them.
> This is one of the characteristics of this glorious Dispensa-
> tion and this great century. Ye should, most certainly, strive
> to perfect this assemblage and increase your knowledge of
> the realities of heavenly mysteries, so that, God willing, in a
> short time, women will become the same as men; they will
> take a leading position amongst the learned, will each have a
> fluent tongue and eloquent speech, and shine like unto lamps
> of guidance throughout the world.[91]

In His Tablets 'Abdu'l-Bahá therefore called upon women to make a serious study of the Faith, to discuss the application of the Bahá'í teachings to everyday life, especially to child-raising, to practice delivering speeches on aspects of the Faith and, generally, to gain firsthand experience in the organization and administration of aspects of social and community life.

Attesting to the importance of women's assemblages, 'Abdu'l-Bahá stresses that "discussions must be confined to educational matters" and sets out a number of specific subjects to be considered by the participants:

> ... those present should concern themselves with every means of training the girl children; with teaching the various branches of knowledge, good behavior, a proper way of life, the cultivation of a good character, chastity and constancy, perseverance, strength, determination, firmness of purpose; with household management, the education of children, and whatever especially applieth to the needs of girls—to the end that these girls, reared in the stronghold of all perfections, and with the protection of a goodly character, will, when they themselves become mothers, bring up their children from earliest infancy to have a good character and conduct themselves well.
>
> Let them also study whatever will nurture the health of the body and its physical soundness, and how to guard their children from disease.[92]

'Abdu'l-Bahá provides the following advice to those in attendance:

> The attracted leaves should not, when associating with each other, talk merely about the temperature of the weather, the coldness of the water, the beauty of the flowers and gar-

dens, the freshness of the grass and the flowing water. They should rather restrict their discussions to glorification and praise and the uttering of proofs and reasons, to quoting verses and traditions and putting forth clear testimonies, so that all the homes of the loved ones will be converted into gathering places for lessons on teaching the Cause.[93]

It is interesting to observe that 'Abdu'l-Bahá calls for more than the mere acquisition of knowledge. He places great emphasis on the development and use of analytical skills requiring the organization of information and the exercise of judgment and logic. Such skills had traditionally been regarded as the exclusive preserve of men.

To ensure the success of the women's assemblages, 'Abdu'l-Bahá provided guidance concerning the spirit in which they should be conducted. He stressed the need for harmony both in relation to men and between women. He states, "It should be done in such a way that differences will, day by day, be entirely wiped out, not that, God forbid, it will end in argumentation between men and women."[94] Furthermore, He underlines the importance of women's encouraging and supporting each other and taking each other seriously:

> When ye meet each other, convey the glad-tidings and impart hope to one another because of the confirmations and bounties of the Ancient and Ever-Living Lord. Let each set forth proofs and evidences, and talk about the mysteries of the Kingdom, so that the true and divine Spirit may permeate the body of the contingent world and the secrets of all things, whether of the past or of the future, may become openly manifest and resplendent.[95]

Women's assemblages were held throughout Iran and had a major impact on the lives of women, indeed, on the Bahá'í

community as a whole. For example, in the early 1920s the
Tarbíyat girls' school instituted a monthly conference for mothers and other women, who had no other opportunity for education, no organized activities, and no involvement outside the
home. The conferences were extremely popular, attracting three
to four hundred women. At these meetings teachers and students presented talks, plays, and demonstrations to illustrate a
theme, such as modern home management, and generally tried
to show parents how to apply Bahá'í principles in child-rear-
ing.[96]

It may well be argued that the need for such meetings for
women continues to exist in those parts of the world where
women have been socialized to be silent and deferential in the
presence of men, or where they have felt intimidated from expressing their views because of the presence of men who have
had the benefits of training and experience in the larger society.
In such gatherings women can gain experience and courage and
thus acquire skills to be used in the Bahá'í community wherein
men and women associate as equals, as well as in the wider society.

FOSTERING INTELLECTUAL DEVELOPMENT

Some of the statements of 'Abdu'l-Bahá calling upon women
to aspire to the highest levels of scholarship and to participate
in all aspects of professional life have been set out in chapter 2.
This section considers some examples of the practical actions
He took to encourage women in such activities.

'Abdu'l-Bahá recognized the intellectual ability of individual
women and their eagerness to learn and, in certain instances,
facilitated their scholarly study of the Bahá'í Faith. For example,
'Abdu'l-Bahá willingly gave Miss Laura Clifford Barney His "tired
moments" to answer her questions about the Bahá'í teachings.
These table talks, delivered between 1904 and 1906, were re-

corded and collected by Miss Barney. 'Abdu'l-Bahá, with His own pen, corrected the transcription of the talks, and in due course she translated them and had them published under the title of *Some Answered Questions*. This work not only served to deepen Miss Barney's knowledge of the Faith, but it established a precious legacy for the education of future generations.[97]

In 1900 'Abdu'l-Bahá arranged for Mrs. Emogene Hoagg, an American believer, to spend a month in Port Sa'íd, Egypt, to study the Bahá'í interpretation of the Bible with the renowned Persian teacher Mírzá Abu'l-Faḍl. In her description of the events that transpired during those days, Mrs. Hoagg records the following observation:

> Almost every evening five or six of the Bahá'í brothers would meet with us to hear Mírzá Abu'l-Faḍl's explanations. Those were wonderful days,—to think that I, an American woman, was able to meet with these Bahá'í brothers of a different nationality and in a foreign country, and to feel so perfectly at home, just as though I had been with my own family! Probably to them it was yet a more novel experience to be able to meet with an unveiled sister. All this has been brought about by the power of Bahá'u'lláh.[98]

A close friend of Mrs. Hoagg wrote later,

> These lessons set the pattern for all her future service to the Faith. She became henceforth a student of the Holy Scriptures, not only of the Bahá'í and Judeo-Christian Dispensations, but also of the other world religions so little known in the West at that time.[99]

It would appear, in this instance, that 'Abdu'l-Bahá was not only supporting the development of scholarship in women, but was also providing a lesson through the context in which this was to take place, creating an opportunity to modify entrenched social attitudes. Thus it afforded an opportunity for the West to appreciate the scholarship of the East and for the East to appreciate the intellectual ability of women.

'Abdu'l-Bahá also encouraged Ghodsia Ashraf, a Persian believer, to undertake study in North America. From her childhood she had manifested a great desire for learning. Her preliminary training was received in the Persian Girls' School, after which she spent two years in the American School in Tehran. Her father, Mírzá Fazl'u'lláh Khán, encouraged his daughter's pursuit of knowledge. 'Abdu'l-Bahá approved her coming to the United States to prepare herself for the teaching profession.

Ghodsia Ashraf arrived in the United States in 1911 and enrolled at the Lewis Institute in Chicago. While in North America she was an enthusiastic participant in Bahá'í activities, giving public talks on the Faith and generally helping to foster understanding of the importance of the education of women throughout the world. When she returned to Iran she established the "Woman's Society for Progress" in Tehran and expended her energy promoting the development of Persian women.[100]

'Abdu'l-Bahá stresses the importance of women's involvement in "all departments of life" and links this to the attainment of the "recognition of equality in the social and economic equation."[101] It is clear from His Tablets and from the example of His life that 'Abdu'l-Bahá recognized the value of professional training for women. For example, when the American believer Katherine True was deciding on her profession, she wrote to 'Abdu'l-Bahá about her desire to study medicine, asking for His counsel in this decision. His reply came in the following Tablet:

O beloved daughter!
Your letter dated December 29th, 1919 arrived. From it, it became known that with a firm resolution you were deter-

mined to serve the world of humanity. One of the Divine Teachings is that man should be the source of a benevolent cause amongst the creatures and if it be universal good, all the better.

The study of medicine is highly acceptable and praiseworthy. With all thy power endeavor that thou mayest attain the utmost proficiency in this art and thus serve the world of humanity. . . .[102]

'Abdu'l-Bahá not only encouraged women to use their skills in service to humanity, but He also drew upon their expertise for the promotion of the Cause and the development of the Bahá'í community. Miss Martha Root, designated by 'Abdu'l-Bahá as the "herald of the Kingdom" and "harbinger of the Covenant," capitalized on her knowledge, experience, and skills as a journalist in gaining opportunities to proclaim and teach the Faith (see chapter 6). Likewise, Miss Beatrice Irwin, an Englishwoman who was a talented lighting engineer, poet, and essayist, well known in professional and artistic circles, had access to many important platforms and leading personalities through her attainments. She was later described by Shoghi Effendi as an "indefatigable promoter" of the Faith.[103]

These pioneering efforts to support the intellectual development of women provided both the model and the impetus for Bahá'í women in later decades to demonstrate the equality of the sexes in the intellectual realm through their distinguished accomplishments.

THE POWER OF EXAMPLE

The events described in this chapter show that Bahá'u'lláh and 'Abdu'l-Bahá did not confine Themselves to the prescription of equality of the sexes and the elaboration of the implications and applications of this principle. It is clearly apparent, from a close scrutiny of Their daily activities, that They provided an example which remains a source of inspiration and instruction to Bahá'ís striving to put into practice the teachings of this Faith.

Attention here has been directed principally to 'Abdu'l-Bahá, since information about His activities is more readily available at this time, and since the removal of restrictions on His freedom in His later years enabled Him to move in the Western world as well as in the East.

As the body of Bahá'í historical materials is enriched in the future through the collection and translation of manuscripts, a vastly greater number of examples will emerge of the promotion of equality of the sexes, a principle for which Bahá'u'lláh and 'Abdu'l-Bahá labored so assiduously.

6

Implementing Equality: The Role of Shoghi Effendi and the Universal House of Justice

. . . the Bahá'ís . . . should initiate and implement programs which will stimulate and promote the full and equal participation of women in all aspects of Bahá'í community life, so that through their accomplishments the friends will demonstrate the distinction of the Cause of God in this field of human endeavor.

—The Universal House of Justice

THE FORMATIVE AGE OF THE BAHÁ'Í DISPENSATION

The passing of 'Abdu'l-Bahá in November 1921 signalized the termination of the Apostolic Age of the Bahá'í Dispensation, the first of the three Ages into which it is divided. Shoghi Effendi describes that point in time in the following terms:

> The Age that had witnessed the birth and rise of the Faith had now closed. The Heroic, the Apostolic Age of the Dispensation of Bahá'u'lláh, that primitive period in which its Founders had lived, in which its life had been generated, in which its greatest heroes had struggled and quaffed the cup of martyrdom, and its pristine foundations been established . . .[1]

With the conclusion of its Apostolic Age, the Faith entered its Formative Age, characterized by Shoghi Effendi as

> an Age of Transition to be identified with the rise and establishment of the Administrative Order, upon which the institutions of the future Bahá'í World Commonwealth* must needs be ultimately erected in the Golden Age† that must witness the consummation of the Bahá'í Dispensation.[2]

During the Apostolic Age the principle of the equality of men and women had been clearly enunciated by Bahá'u'lláh

---

* The future community of nations united by a system of government that will operate in conformity with the laws and principles of Bahá'u'lláh.

† The third and final Age of the Dispensation of Bahá'u'lláh, which is to last until the advent of the next Manifestation of God. The Golden Age will be associated with the establishment of the Bahá'í World Commonwealth and the founding of a world civilization.

and 'Abdu'l-Bahá. As the appointed Exemplar of the Bahá'í teachings, 'Abdu'l-Bahá had provided to the believers a peerless model of its expression in practice in both the Western world, where women enjoyed a certain measure of emancipation, and in the East, where they labored under formidable restrictions. Furthermore, the processes of implementation had been set in motion with the constant encouragement of women; with their involvement in the rudimentary forms of administrative functioning that existed in countries such as Britain, the United States, and Iran; with the establishment of facilities for women's education in areas of pressing need; and with the participation of women in highly responsible functions for the protection and promotion of the Faith.

The inception of the Formative Age gave rise to a highly significant new development in the Faith's continuing endeavor to bring about implementation of the equality of the sexes. The Formative Age is to be distinguished by the application of this principle in all parts of the world by the diverse peoples who are gathered within the embrace of Bahá'u'lláh's Revelation. A prerequisite for accomplishing this mighty endeavor is the establishment of the administrative institutions of the Faith throughout the planet and the use of these institutions as the vehicle for further spreading the Faith and progressively applying all of its principles, including that of the equality of the sexes.

The ministry of the Guardian from 1921 until his passing in November 1957 witnessed spectacular progress toward attaining this objective. Shoghi Effendi guided the Bahá'í community forward, clarified its teachings, translated those passages of its holy writings needed to establish Bahá'í belief on a foundation of authenticity and accuracy, set the basis for the formation of Local Spiritual Assemblies and National Spiritual Assemblies, and took the preliminary measures required for the

formation in April 1963 of the Universal House of Justice. The
processes to which the Guardian gave a mighty impetus continue and are now being further expanded by the Universal
House of Justice as the Formative Age continues to unfold.

A comprehensive account of the work of the Guardian and
of the Universal House of Justice is beyond the scope of this
book. This chapter focuses on those elements of their work
that relate directly to the equality of the sexes and to fostering
the development of women. It should be borne in mind, however, that this limited focus can lead to a distortion of perspective. The administrative institutions of the Bahá'í Faith are organic entities that must perform a broad range of mutually interdependent functions in a balanced manner to ensure that
any one of these several functions is carried out effectively. The
pursuit of equality, which is an important function of these
bodies, can best occur within the setting of institutional activity designed to advance all aspects of Bahá'í community life.

THE ROLE OF SHOGHI EFFENDI

To examine Shoghi Effendi's role in furthering the implementation of the equality of women and men, it is first necessary to
consider briefly the extent to which the Faith had spread and
the state of its development at the time of 'Abdu'l-Bahá's passing. When 'Abdu'l-Bahá passed away in 1921, the Faith had
spread to some thirty-five countries. The majority of Bahá'ís
were in the Middle East and North America, with relatively
few believers residing in other parts of the world. The institutions of the Bahá'í Administrative Order were, at best, embryonic, and the writings of the Faith, though carefully preserved,
were yet to be collected and translated.

Upon his appointment as Guardian of the Faith and authorized interpreter of the Bahá'í writings, Shoghi Effendi eluci-

dated still further the meaning of the principle of equality; explained its application, especially in relation to the laws of the Faith; and actively encouraged its implementation in the life of the Bahá'í community. As head of the Faith he also set about laying and strengthening the foundations for the erection of the Administrative Order as a preliminary to implementing the Divine Plan of 'Abdu'l-Bahá for the spread of the Faith throughout the world.* Through a prodigious flow of letters to the Bahá'ís in the East and the West, Shoghi Effendi carefully and patiently nurtured the community's understanding of this unique system of organization, and he trained the believers in the election and operation of Local and National Spiritual Assemblies. Once elected and basically consolidated, these Assemblies became the vehicles for the systematic promotion of the Faith and for the development of Bahá'í community life.

INTERPRETING THE TEACHINGS

Because the principle of the equality of the sexes is so clearly enunciated by Bahá'u'lláh and 'Abdu'l-Bahá, the need for interpretation by the Guardian lies mainly in the realm of application, and his major contribution is in its implementation, as we shall see.

Reference has already been made to several of Shoghi Effendi's interpretations, which were given principally in response to questions from individuals who were struggling to absorb the effect of this principle on various aspects of their daily lives, especially in such areas as the marriage laws. Reference has also

---

* The Divine Plan is the plan for the dissemination of the Bahá'í Faith throughout the world, conveyed by 'Abdu'l-Bahá to the Bahá'ís of North America in fourteen letters called the Tablets of the Divine Plan. The implementation of the Divine Plan was initiated by Shoghi Effendi and is now being pursued under the guidance of the Universal House of Justice.

been made to the Guardian's statement that chastity is equally binding on both men and women. Among the clarifications Shoghi Effendi provided in relation to marriage and divorce are those emphasizing that monogamy is prescribed; that absolute equality between men and women allows either one to propose marriage; and that, in marital breakdown, each partner has the right to initiate divorce action. By responding to questions on these and other subjects, the Guardian patiently helped the Bahá'ís attain a fuller understanding of the magnitude of the principle of equality which is so emphatically proclaimed in the Bahá'í teachings.

DEVELOPING THE ADMINISTRATIVE ORDER

From the very earliest days of his ministry Shoghi Effendi drew upon the capacities of women to an extent unprecedented in any other religion. Reference has already been made to his designation of Bahíyyih Khánum to supervise and manage the affairs of the Faith when he felt compelled to leave the Holy Land for a period shortly after his appointment as Guardian. That a woman was called upon to assume this responsibility, even if only for a short time, constituted an unmistakable indication of the recognition of the capacities of womanhood presented by the Faith.

Another example from the same period was the Guardian's summoning to the Bahá'í World Center a small and diverse band of experienced and knowledgeable believers for consultations about the future development of the Faith. Women constituted about half of the membership of this highly select group.

Shoghi Effendi directed much of his attention to the establishment of Local and National Spiritual Assemblies throughout the world. As was evident from the activities of women such as Corinne True and Ethel Rosenberg, there was no impediment to membership of women on these institutions in the Western world. However, the situation was quite different in the East, where deeply ingrained prejudices and restrictions presented a major barrier to women's involvement. The approach Shoghi Effendi adopted was that of progressive implementation, as had occurred in the Apostolic Age, together with the clear promulgation of the principle of equality and the fostering of the advancement of women.

In areas such as India and Burma, where the prevailing cultural tradition already allowed women some degree of freedom, Shoghi Effendi affirmed women's eligibility for Assembly membership. In a letter dated 27 December 1923 to the National Spiritual Assembly of the Bahá'ís of India and Burma, he offered the following guidance:

> I feel that the time is now ripe that those women who have already conformed to the prevailing custom in India and Burma by discarding the veil should not only be given the right to vote for the election of their local and national representatives, but should themselves be eligible to the membership of all Bahá'í Assemblies throughout India and Burma, be they local or national.
>
> This definite and most important step, however, should be taken with the greatest care and caution, prudence and thoughtfulness. Due regard must be paid to their actual capacity and present attainments, and only those who are best qualified for membership, be they men or women, and irrespective of social standing, should be elected to the extremely responsible position of a member of the Bahá'í Assembly.[3]

Mindful of the potential impact of this momentous decision on the continuing development of women, Shoghi Effendi stated,

... I trust [it] will prove to be a great incentive to the women
Bahá'ís throughout India and Burma who, I hope, will now
bestir themselves and endeavour to the best of their ability
to acquire a better and more profound knowledge of the
Cause, to take a more active and systematic part in the general affairs of the Movement, and prove themselves in every
way enlightened, responsible and efficient co-workers to their
fellow-men in their common task for the advancement of
the Cause throughout their country.

May they fully realize their high responsibilities in this
day, may they do all in their power to justify the high hopes
we cherish for their future, and may they prove themselves
in every respect worthy of the noble mission which the Bahá'í
world is now entrusting to their charge.[4]

One can well imagine the stirring effect the Guardian's statement must have had on these women as they prepared to fulfill
this new and challenging responsibility. While clearly communicating his understanding of the difficulty of the task, he was
voicing his confidence in their ability to undertake their noble
mission and was summoning them to action.

In Islamic countries such as Iran, the situation was much
more complex, and progress had necessarily to be gradual, taking cognizance of the Bahá'í community's vulnerability to mis-
representation and persecution at the hands of fanatic elements.
Bahá'í actions to emancipate and educate women were liable to
be stigmatized as encouraging immorality, and thus to be used
by those who opposed the Faith as excuses for reinstituting repressive measures.

In the 1920s Shoghi Effendi reiterated 'Abdu'l-Bahá's guidance about the need for continued use of the veil in Islamic
countries, although Bahá'í women were encouraged to discard

it in other areas of the world. In a general letter dated 27 February 1923 to the Bahá'ís in the East, Shoghi Effendi strongly urged the Bahá'í women in all Islamic countries to use the veil in accordance with the social and religious circumstances of the countries in which they found themselves. Nevertheless, the practice of Bahá'í women in these countries of continuing to wear the veil for a period should not be construed as an endorsement of this restriction on women. In a general letter dated 6 December 1928, Shoghi Effendi hailed "the growing unpopularity of the veil among almost every section of society" in Iran as one of the promising signs of improvement in the conditions of life in that country.⁵ During that period when wisdom decreed that use of the veil be maintained in Iran, women were urged not to lose sight of the objective of equality toward which they should strive. In a letter of 14 March 1933 written on behalf of the Guardian to a Bahá'í in India, we find,

> Even though the Master and now Shoghi Effendi have not asked the Persian ladies to discard the veil, they have been constantly urging them to work for the development of their sex and the elimination of the yoke imposed by man. They have to work for equality, which is a basic teaching of the Faith, but be mindful not to precipitate things.⁶

In the 1930s Bahá'í women in Iran found it possible to gradually abandon use of the veil, as traditional practices were being broken down in Iranian society generally. This most welcome development made it possible for women to participate more fully in the activities of the community and opened the way to a further degree of emancipation. In 1944 Shoghi Effendi identified "the disuse of the veil" as a welcome sign of the declining influence of the Iranian ecclesiastics.⁷

In 1944 the Bahá'ís in Iran formed a national committee for the progress of women, which was given the responsibility of organizing women's activities throughout the country. The work of this committee was greatly reinforced by the Iranian Bahá'í community's adoption of a Four Year Plan (1946–1950) for women, which aimed to bring about equality of the sexes in administrative service to the Faith.[8]

A 1954 report on the results of this plan states, in part,

> This aim was pursued under a four-year plan the result of which has been to find women elected to membership on Assemblies for the first time, thus overcoming a long historic disability. The service of men and women in these elective bodies represents the operation of the principle of equality of opportunity and status for men and women which the Bahá'í Faith has established in the new social pattern now unfolding throughout the world.
>
> Through special classes and discussions and by active participation in Bahá'í community affairs the Bahá'í women of Persia have fully demonstrated their capacity to assume responsibilities which had been reserved for men. . . .
>
> The Four-Year Plan provided facilities for the education of girls and special classes for adult women. A National Women's Progressive Committee was appointed, with regional committees acting under its supervision. A national convention for Bahá'í women was held annually, with the participation of the members of the National Women's Progressive Committee and twenty-two representatives of the regional committees. At these gatherings the women demonstrated their ability and aptitude for serving their Faith on an equality with the men. In addition, district conventions were held semi-annually, to consult on ways to carry education even to women in the villages. The program of education included oral instruction for the illiterate and those who had little schooling; an advanced class for graduates of sec-

ondary schools, and a higher class of more advanced education for women living in the larger centers. Finally, a periodical was circulated with contents covering topics of general history, Bahá'í history, science, literature, health, hygiene, housekeeping and care of children.

From Shoghi Effendi a message was received which stated: "The great barrier has now been completely removed and absolute equality is attained as the result of recent developments, as well as the glorious and continuing efforts rendered by the beloved Bahá'í sisters in that country and abroad."[9]

A similar development occurred in Egypt in 1951, when women were elected as members of Local Spiritual Assemblies for the first time, an action the Guardian described as a notable step forward in the progress of Bahá'í women of the Middle East.[10]

It would be difficult to overestimate the significance of these achievements in Iran and Egypt, which came after three decades of education, stimulus, and training under the guidance of the Guardian. In countries where the prevailing culture had imposed the severest restrictions on women's participation in any sphere of activity outside the home, Bahá'í community functioning had evolved to such a degree of equality that women could be elected to membership of administrative bodies having authority over both male and female members of the Faith. When in 1954 this victory was achieved in Iran, the Guardian announced to the Bahá'í world,

> Full rights have been accorded to Bahá'í women residing in the cradle of the Faith, to participate in the membership of both national and local Bahá'í Spiritual Assemblies, removing thereby the last remaining obstacle to the enjoyment

of complete equality of rights in the conduct of the administrative affairs of the Persian Bahá'í Community.[11]

In a 1954 message addressed to Bahá'í women in Iran, the Guardian urged them not to be content with achieving administrative equality. He called upon them to outdo men in such areas of service to the Faith as teaching and pioneering* and urged them to demonstrate greater courage, audacity, and detachment than their male counterparts. Their attention was directed to the example of the American Bahá'í women as a standard they should strive to reach or even exceed.[12]

The Bahá'í women of Iran have continued to follow the path of courage and heroic endeavor in the decades since the Guardian issued this call to them. Their record of accomplishment is an example of the power of the Faith to change long-established attitudes, and of the progressive approach it adopts toward implementation, such that the goal is approached in a spirit of unity and cooperation between men and women who share a common belief in the spiritual duty to give practical expression to the equality of the sexes.

In the latter years of his ministry as Guardian, Shoghi Effendi called into being international institutions of the Faith to further reinforce and advance the growing work of the Cause. The Hands of the Cause of God became a functioning institution in 1951 with the appointment of twelve Bahá'ís to this high rank, followed by the appointment of seven more a few months later. Both men and women were included in this institution. The Guardian also brought into being in 1951 the International Bahá'í Council through the appointment of eight Bahá'ís, add-

---

* Pioneering is the act of leaving one's hometown or country to take up residence elsewhere for the purpose of teaching the Bahá'í Faith.

ing another in 1955 to complete its membership; five of these nine members were women. The Faith had, in no more than five decades, made enormous progress since the early days of the twentieth century, when Corinne True and Ethel Rosenberg were making their contribution to the development of embryonic Bahá'í administrative bodies in the West and the Spiritual Assembly of Bahá'í Women was being formed in Tehran.

FOSTERING THE ADVANCEMENT OF WOMEN

As indicated above, Shoghi Effendi devoted much effort to establishing Local and National Spiritual Assemblies in many parts of the world and to using these institutions for the further spread of the Faith. The advancement of women was a significant component in such endeavors.

While the believers throughout the world were called upon to practice the equality of women and men in everyday life, the Guardian issued more detailed guidance to the countries in the East. For example, writing in 1926 to the Spiritual Assemblies throughout the East, Shoghi Effendi states that one of their major functions is "to promote the emancipation and advancement of women and support the compulsory education of both sexes." Further, in a 1928 letter to the Iran Central Spiritual Assembly, Shoghi Effendi stresses the importance of Bahá'í literacy classes and encourages the initiation of educational programs to prepare women for service on Local and National Spiritual Assemblies.[13]

The specific nature of the Guardian's encouragement appears to have depended, in part, on the prevailing social milieu and the ability of the women at that time to successfully discharge their God-given responsibility. In those instances in which women may have lacked certain skills and competencies, the Guardian sought first to help them overcome the existing deficit before assigning a particular function to them, thereby increasing the likelihood of their success and contributing to the greater acceptance, by both men and women, of women's participation in the Bahá'í community.

Bahá'í women in the West, who had benefited from access to more educational opportunities than their Bahá'í sisters in the East, and who were constrained by fewer barriers to participation in activities outside of the home, were, from the Faith's earliest days, at the forefront of teaching activities and served as elected members of Spiritual Assemblies. On the eve of a teaching endeavor in Latin America, Shoghi Effendi acknowledged their exemplary services, addressing to them the following encouragement:

> I am moved, at this juncture, as I am reminded of the share which, ever since the inception of the Faith in the West, the handmaidens of Bahá'u'lláh, as distinguished from the men, have had in opening up, single-handed, so many, such diversified, and widely scattered countries over the whole surface of the globe, not only to pay a tribute to such apostolic fervor as is truly reminiscent of those heroic men who were responsible for the birth of the Faith of Bahá'u'lláh, but also to stress the significance of such a preponderating share which the women of the West have had and are having in the establishment of His Faith throughout the whole world. *"Among the miracles,"* 'Abdu'l-Bahá Himself has testified, *"which distinguish this sacred Dispensation is this, that women have evinced a greater boldness than men when enlisted in the ranks of the Faith."* So great and splendid a testimony applies in particular to the West, and though it has received thus far abundant and convincing confirmation must, as the years roll away, be further reinforced, as the American believers usher in the most glorious phase of their teaching activities

under the Seven Year Plan. The *"boldness"*which, in the words of 'Abdu'l-Bahá, has characterized their accomplishments in the past must suffer no eclipse as they stand on the threshold of still greater and nobler accomplishments. Nay rather, it must, in the course of time and throughout the length and breadth of the vast and virgin territories of Latin America, be more convincingly demonstrated, and win for the beloved Cause victories more stirring than any it has as yet achieved.[14]

With regard to the promotion of peace, Shoghi Effendi re-affirmed the role of women as agents of change in this important enterprise. He underlined the potential of the Bahá'í administrative machinery in furthering peace activities and encouraged their active involvement in "this essential matter."[15]

In this regard, the Guardian stated in a letter written on his behalf,

> What 'Abdu'l-Bahá meant about the women arising for peace is that this is a matter which vitally affects women, and when they form a conscious and overwhelming mass of public opinion against war there can be no war. The Bahá'í women are already organized through being members of the Faith and the Administrative Order. No further organization is needed. But they should, through teaching and through the active moral support they give to every movement directed towards peace, seek to exert a strong influence on other women's minds in regard to this essential matter.[16]

Shoghi Effendi encouraged individual Bahá'ís and the Spiritual Assemblies to participate in activities that focused on women and peace. For example, in 1930 the National Spiritual Assembly of the Bahá'ís of India and Burma wrote to the Guardian, inquiring about the advisability of participating in an interna-

tional women's conference. In a letter written on his behalf the
Guardian responds,

> Concerning Bahá'í representation at the All-Asian Women's
> Conference: this is undoubtedly a most commendable thing
> to do especially as the Cause has so much concerning the
> position of women in society. Shoghi Effendi hopes that the
> National Assembly will do its best to win the admiration of
> all the assembled delegates for the teachings of the Cause
> along that line. We should always take such opportunities
> that present themselves. Maybe we would succeed to render
> some service to society and alleviate its ills.[17]

Shoghi Effendi not only endorsed Bahá'í participation in the
conference, but he also sent, via the National Spiritual Assembly, the following personal message of greeting to it:

CONVEY TO INDIAN ASIAN WOMEN'S CONFERENCE BEHALF GREAT-
EST HOLY LEAF 'ABDU'L-BAHÁ'S SISTER AND MYSELF EXPRESSION
OUR GENUINE PROFOUND INTEREST IN THEIR DELIBERATIONS. MAY
ALMIGHTY GUIDE BLESS THEIR HIGH ENDEAVOURS.[18]

One of the believers who was closely associated with the work
of the All-Asian Women's Conference was Mrs. Shirin Fozdar.
Born in 1905 in Bombay of Persian Zoroastrian parents who
had converted to the Bahá'í Faith, Shirin Fozdar was one of the
first Eastern Bahá'í women to speak in public in India. In 1922,
while still in her teens, she addressed a public meeting in the
town hall of Karachi, the center of Muslim influence in what
was then British India. Karachi's mayor presided at this historic
event. In 1931, Mrs. Fozdar was elected to the Executive Committee of the All-Asian Women's Conference, and by 1934 she
was its representative to the League of Nations. In this capacity

she pleaded with representatives of the great powers to proclaim a Universal Declaration of Women's Rights.
Throughout her long life of service Mrs. Fozdar was the
champion of Asian women. She traveled widely for this purpose, serving as an eloquent spokeswoman for their emancipation and working tirelessly to promote opportunities for their
education.[19]

INTERNATIONAL ASSIGNMENTS TO WOMEN

Like 'Abdu'l-Bahá before him, Shoghi Effendi called upon
the special skills and services of capable, intelligent, and practical women to undertake delicate international missions for the
Faith. Though it is far beyond the scope of this book to provide
a comprehensive survey of the activities of the many women
whose abilities the Guardian drew upon to carry out strenuous,
and in many instances heroic, services to advance the Faith,
attention will be directed to four significant examples: two
Western women who carried out unusually difficult assignments
in the East, and two other women whose services were so highly
meritorious that they were designated as Hands of the Cause of
God, the highest rank that can be conferred in the Bahá'í Administrative Order.

Shoghi Effendi often drew upon the talents of Western Bahá'í
women to undertake special missions in Iran. These assignments
demonstrated the Guardian's faith in the capacity of women,
and the presence of such women in Iran underlined the principle of equality and encouraged the female believers. Two of
these women, Miss Effie Baker and Mrs. Keith Ransom-Kehler,
are discussed here.

Effie Baker. In the early 1930s Shoghi Effendi tapped the
skills of Miss Effie Baker, a photographer and artist, to make a
photographic record of the Bahá'í historical sites in Persia. Miss

Baker, the first woman to embrace the Faith of Bahá'u'lláh in
Australia, had the privilege of serving at the Bahá'í World Center for eleven years. During this period she traveled from Haifa
to Persia by car, across Syria and Iraq, in territory where ban-
dits were common. At a time when it was unusual for a woman
to travel in Persia, when certain parts of the country were dangerous for any Westerner, male or female, to enter, Miss Baker,
shrouded in a chador for protection, undertook her assignment
with courage and determination. To reach the sites of historical
interest she went by car, on horseback, and sometimes on don-
key or mule. A collection of the photographs Miss Baker took
during this period is immortalized through its inclusion by
Shoghi Effendi in his translation of *The Dawn-Breakers*, Nabíl-
i-A'zam's chronicle of the early history of the Bahá'í Faith.[20]

The following extract from a letter written on behalf of
Shoghi Effendi to Miss Baker makes clear how greatly he appreciated her skill. The letter states,

> Often Shoghi Effendi remarks that if you were in Haifa, you
> would take some wonderful photos. He considers that no
> one has ever captured the beauty of the place as you did,
> and your photographs adorn his own rooms, and the ar-
> chives and the Mansion. . . .[21]

Keith Ransom-Kehler. Mrs. Keith Ransom-Kehler traveled
to Iran in 1932 to serve as the representative of the National
Spiritual Assembly of the Bahá'ís of the United States and
Canada. Chosen by the Guardian for this assignment, her challenging task was to intercede with the Persian government in an
attempt to have the ban on the entry and circulation of Bahá'í
literature in Iran lifted.

In a land where women were still largely secluded in the home,
Mrs. Ransom-Kehler was required to relate, at the highest level,

to government ministers and members of parliament in her
efforts to have the Bahá'í petition presented to the shah. Reflecting on her experience in a letter she wrote from Tehran to
her National Spiritual Assembly, she comments, "How strange
the ways of God, that I, a poor, feeble, old woman from the
distant West, should be pleading for liberty and justice in the
land of Bahá'u'lláh. . . ."[22]

For over a year Mrs. Ransom-Kehler encountered formidable
obstacles, broken promises, and conflicting advice from the
Persian government. In the end, the petition was never answered
by the officials. Yet despite such difficulties she persisted,
undeflected in bringing to bear her keen intelligence, great elo-
quence, wise and strategic judgment, and sensitivity to the task
at hand. Disappointed at the failure of her mission and ex-
hausted from her constant efforts to visit and address Bahá'í
gatherings throughout Persia, Mrs. Ransom-Kehler fell victim
to smallpox and passed away in Iṣfahán on 23 October 1933.
When Shoghi Effendi received the distressing news of her sud-
den passing, not only did he express appreciation for her efforts,
but he also clarified the true significance of her contribution.
In a cable dated 28 October 1933 he designated her as the "FIRST
AND DISTINGUISHED MARTYR" drawn from the American Bahá'í
community and bestowed upon her the rank of Hand of the
Cause of God. The cabled message reads,

KEITH'S PRECIOUS LIFE OFFERED UP SACRIFICE BELOVED CAUSE IN
BAHÁ'U'LLÁH'S NATIVE LAND. ON PERSIAN SOIL FOR PERSIA'S SAKE
SHE ENCOUNTERED CHALLENGED AND FOUGHT FORCES OF DARK-
NESS WITH HIGH DISTINCTION, INDOMITABLE WILL, UNSWERV-
ING EXEMPLARY LOYALTY. MASS OF HER HELPLESS PERSIAN BRETH-
REN MOURN THE LOSS THEIR VALIANT EMANCIPATOR. AMERICAN
BELIEVERS GRATEFUL AND PROUD MEMORY THEIR FIRST AND DIS-
TINGUISHED MARTYR. SORROW-STRICKEN I LAMENT EARTHLY SEPA-

RATION INVALUABLE COLLABORATOR UNFAILING COUNSELOR ES-
TEEMED AND FAITHFUL FRIEND. URGE LOCAL ASSEMBLIES BEFIT-
TINGLY ORGANIZE MEMORIAL GATHERINGS IN MEMORY ONE WHOSE
INTERNATIONAL SERVICES ENTITLE HER EMINENT RANK AMONG
HANDS OF CAUSE OF BAHÁ'U'LLÁH.[23]

Reports of her activities in Iran show that, in addition to her
valiant and determined efforts to relieve the difficulties under
which the Persian Bahá'ís were laboring, Mrs. Ransom-Kehler
played an important part in the upliftment of women. One
report states,

> Her work with women Bahá'ís and inquirers was extensive,
> and the Women's Program Committee arranged many meet-
> ings at which she discussed phases of the Administration,
> women's progress, child psychology and the like; it was felt
> that her presence gave tremendous impetus to the cause of
> Persian women, and those who heard her will not forget the
> thunder of her words. In . . . 1932 . . . the Women's Teaching
> Committee held two noteworthy meetings for her at each of
> which approximately one hundred women inquirers were
> present, and Keith spoke to them on the growing under-
> standing of Islám in the West, through the spread of the
> Bahá'í teachings; her stirring talks to the twenty-six mem-
> bers of the Women's Progress Committee dealt with the rôle
> that group will play in modern Persia.[24]

The following report of her journey to one part of Iran provides an indication of the excitement aroused by the travels of
this courageous American Bahá'í woman:

> In Sísán the friends built an auto road over five miles long
> for her reception, and some thousand Bahá'ís came out to
> meet her in holiday clothing. At Zanján Keith visited the

house of Ḥujját,* and astonished passers-by by kneeling in the ruins to pray and weep. An important incident of her Ma<u>shh</u>ad visit was her meeting with the chief Muslim ecclesiastic in that city, keeper of all the shrines of Imám Riḍá; this eminent divine entertained her at his home and escorted her through various secular institutions dedicated to the Imám, such as the famous school and the great new hospital. When after a delay occasioned by motor trouble Keith and her party reached 'Alíyábád-i-<u>Sh</u>áhí, it developed that the Bahá'ís of Sárí and Máhfurúẓak had not received her telegram and had camped two days in pouring rain on a near-by hill, waiting to welcome her. At Bandar-i-jaz a large crowd came to the railway station and accompanied Keith and her party on foot to the residence appointed for her; their numbers drew such attention that authorities in the neighboring town of Istirábád phoned Bandar-i-jaz to find out what had happened, and were told by the police that an American Bahá'í had come to visit the local Bahá'í community.[25]

At Shoghi Effendi's instruction and with her family's approval, Mrs. Ransom-Kehler's remains were interred in Iṣfahán in the vicinity of the grave of the distinguished early believer who had been designated by Bahá'u'lláh as the "King of Martyrs."[26]

As noted above, Mrs. Ransom-Kehler was designated a Hand of the Cause of God and was thus a member of that institution assigned the highest rank in the Bahá'í Administrative Order. The institution was ordained by Bahá'u'lláh, Who during His lifetime appointed four individuals to be concerned with the

---

* Ḥujját, a distinguished follower of the Báb; he was martyred in Zanján.

protection and propagation of His Faith. 'Abdu'l-Bahá in His
writings refers to four other outstanding believers as Hands of
the Cause, and His Will and Testament includes a provision
calling upon the Guardian to appoint Hands of the Cause at
his discretion. The Will and Testament of 'Abdu'l-Bahá also
provides for the selection of nine Hands whose function is to
work closely with the Guardian.* At first, Shoghi Effendi bestowed, posthumously, the rank of Hand of the Cause on ten
believers; during the latter years of his ministry he appointed
twelve initially, and a total of thirty-two Bahá'ís in all, from all
continents to this position.

In addition to Mrs. Keith Ransom-Kehler, another woman,
Miss Martha Root, was designated as a Hand of the Cause of
God at the time of her passing. Six women were appointed
during their lifetime: namely, Mrs. Dorothy Baker, Mrs. Amelia
Collins, Mrs. Clara Dunn, Mrs. Corinne True, Amatu'l-Bahá
Rúḥíyyih Khánum, and Miss Agnes Alexander. The distin-
guished services of all of these Hands of the Cause have been
described elsewhere.[27] We will refer briefly here to Miss Martha
Root and Mrs. Amelia Collins, whose endeavors received un-
usually high praise from Shoghi Effendi.

Martha Root. In *God Passes By* Shoghi Effendi describes Miss
Martha Root in the following terms:

> . . . that archetype of Bahá'í itinerant teachers and the fore-
> most Hand raised by Bahá'u'lláh since 'Abdu'l-Bahá's pass-
> ing, . . . Leading Ambassadress of His Faith and Pride of
> Bahá'í teachers, whether men or women, in both the East
> and the West.

---

* Hands of the Cause, provisions concerning their appointment by the
Guardian and for the selection of nine Hands of the Cause to work closely
with the Guardian, are set out on page 12 of the *Will and Testament of 'Abdu'l-
Bahá.*

The first to arise, in the very year the Tablets of the Divine Plan were unveiled in the United States of America, in response to the epoch-making summons voiced in them by 'Abdu'l-Bahá; embarking, with unswerving resolve and a spirit of sublime detachment, on her world journeys, covering an almost uninterrupted period of twenty years and carrying her four times round the globe . . . this indomitable soul has, by virtue of the character of her exertions and the quality of the victories she has won, established a record that constitutes the nearest approach to the example set by 'Abdu'l-Bahá Himself to His disciples in the course of His journeys throughout the West.[28]

During her travels for the Faith, Martha Root made contact with royalty, statesmen, and academics. She delivered lectures in over four hundred universities and colleges in both the East and the West; published innumerable articles in newspapers and magazines in practically every country she visited; placed Bahá'í books in private and state libraries; supervised the translation and production of a large number of versions of the early Bahá'í textbook *Bahá'u'lláh and the New Era*, by Dr. John Esslemont;[29] made a pilgrimage to the Bahá'í historic sites in Persia; and visited Adrianople (Edirne) in Turkey, where she searched out the houses in which Bahá'u'lláh had dwelled and the people whom He had met during His exile in that city.

Miss Root's travels were constant, arduous, and often hazardous. She had limited financial resources, often encountered political disturbances, and on more than one occasion she was exposed to perilous circumstances. Toward the end of her life she suffered from breast cancer, from which she died at the age of sixty-seven in Hawaii in 1939.

Assessing her contribution to the Cause of God, Shoghi Effendi singles out Martha Root's introduction of the Faith to Queen Marie of Rumania. He writes,

Of all the services rendered the Cause of Bahá'u'lláh by
this star servant of His Faith, the most superb and by far the
most momentous has been the almost instantaneous response
evoked in Queen Marie of Rumania to the Message which
that ardent and audacious pioneer had carried to her. . . .[30]

He states that Miss Root's life "may well be regarded as the
fairest fruit as yet yielded by the Formative Age of the Dispensation of Bahá'u'lláh" and designates her as "the foremost Hand
raised by Bahá'u'lláh since 'Abdu'l-Bahá's passing."[31]

Amelia E. Collins. Mrs. Amelia E. Collins was born in 1873
and embraced the Bahá'í Faith in 1919. Her appointment as a
Hand of the Cause of God was announced in 1951. She served
for many years as a member of the National Spiritual Assembly
of the United States and Canada.

Mrs. Collins made bountiful and generous financial contributions to the institutions of the Faith in North America and
the Holy Land. Shoghi Effendi refers to her as an "outstanding
benefactress of the Faith." Her contributions helped significantly
to make possible the purchase of sites for Bahá'í Houses of
Worship, including the Temple site on Mount Carmel; the construction of Bahá'í Temples in Kampala, Sydney, and Frank-
furt; the publication of Bahá'í literature; the embellishment of
the area surrounding the Shrine of Bahá'u'lláh at Bahjí; the construction of the superstructure of the Shrine of the Báb; and
the erection and furnishing of the International Bahá'í Archives
on Mount Carmel. The beautiful "Collins Gate," which is the
main gate leading to the Shrine of Bahá'u'lláh, was named in
her honor by Shoghi Effendi.[32]

Mrs. Collins traveled widely for the Faith, undertaking many
of her journeys at Shoghi Effendi's request. He entrusted to her
delicate tasks, which he knew she would carry out with the
greatest discretion and devotion. One such assignment, undertaken during World War II, was her journey to Buenos Aires in

1942 to arrange for the erection of a monument for the grave of Rúḥíyyih Khánum's mother, May Maxwell, who had passed away there and had been hailed by the Guardian as a martyr for the Faith.

Although Mrs. Collins was appointed by Shoghi Effendi as a Hand of the Cause of God in 1947, the designation was not made public until 1951, when the Guardian announced the first contingent of living Hands of the Cause of God. She was also appointed to serve as a member and as vice-president of the International Bahá'í Council, the precursor of the Universal House of Justice.

The uniqueness of Mrs. Collins's services to the Guardian and the distinction that singled her out from other Hands of the Cause are apparent in an extract from a letter written on behalf of Shoghi Effendi in 1947. This letter and the Guardian's postscript to it indicate that she was in the category of the nine Hands of the Cause, foreshadowed in 'Abdu'l-Bahá's Will and Testament, who would work closely with the Guardian:

> He wants to make clear to you that when he said, in his recent cable, that your example might well be emulated by the nine Hands of the Cause, who will in the future be especially chosen to serve the Guardian, he meant that the very services you have been recently rendering the Cause, because of their nature and their intimate association with him, are of the kind which one of these nine might well be called upon to render. So you see you are not only worthy to be a Hand of the Cause, but have rendered a service which ordinarily would be performed by this select body of nine.

Shoghi Effendi added a postscript in his own handwriting:

> With a heart overflowing with profound gratitude, I am now writing you these few lines to reaffirm the sentiments,

expressed lately on several occasions and in a number of telegrams, of heartfelt and unqualified admiration for your magnificent services, rendered in circumstances so exceptional and difficult as to make them doubly meritorious in the sight of God. You have acquitted yourself of the task I felt prompted to impose upon you in a manner that deserves the praise of the Concourse on high. The high rank you now occupy and which no Bahá'í has ever held in his own lifetime has been conferred solely in recognition of the manifold services you have already rendered, and is, by no means, intended to be a stimulus or encouragement in the path of service. Indeed the character of this latest and highly significant service you have rendered places you in the category of the Chosen Nine who, unlike the other Hands of the Cause, are to be associated directly and intimately with the cares and responsibilities of the Guardian of the Faith.[33]

Mrs. Collins's extensive travels and services to the Faith continued unabated until the end of her life in 1962.

THE ROLE OF
THE UNIVERSAL HOUSE OF JUSTICE

Following the passing of Shoghi Effendi in 1957, the Hands of the Cause of God acted as custodians of the Faith, guiding and encouraging the National Spiritual Assemblies and the members of Bahá'í communities all over the world in their endeavors to fulfill the goals of the Ten Year Plan formulated by the Guardian in 1953. The successful completion of that plan opened the way for the formation of the Universal House of Justice, an institution that had been ordained in the Bahá'í writings.

The Universal House of Justice, first elected in 1963, is the international governing body of the Bahá'í Faith, that coordinates and oversees the development of the Faith. It establishes priorities for the worldwide expansion of the Faith, fosters the enhancement of its community life, and encourages and directs its relationship with the world at large. Its duties are outlined in *The Constitution of the Universal House of Justice*.[34] The role of the House of Justice in promoting application of the principle of the equality of men and women is discussed below. It will become apparent from this survey of the work of the Universal House of Justice that it has continued and given further emphasis to the various processes initiated by Bahá'u'lláh, 'Abdu'l-Bahá, and Shoghi Effendi. It has also been able to take advantage of the growth in size and influence of the Faith to bring to the attention of the larger society the Bahá'í principle of equality of the sexes.

Because the implementation processes described here continue to expand rapidly, the account of their present state must necessarily be inadequate or even obsolete, such is the pace of change in the Bahá'í community all over the world.

ELUCIDATING THE TEACHINGS

Among the duties assigned to the Universal House of Justice in the Will and Testament of 'Abdu'l-Bahá is the following:

> It is incumbent upon these members (of the Universal House of Justice) to . . . deliberate upon all problems which have caused difference, questions that are obscure and matters that are not expressly recorded in the Book . . . and bear upon daily transactions. . . .[35]

In the process of carrying out this function the Universal House of Justice provides much authoritative guidance to the Bahá'í community on the application of the principle of equality of the sexes, often in response to questions.

In many instances the Universal House of Justice has been
the source of resolution of the misconceptions that must inevitably arise in Bahá'í communities endeavoring to emancipate
themselves from traditional patterns of thought and behavior.
This consistent reiteration of the teachings in answer to questions from believers endeavoring to accommodate in their frame
of reference the implications of the principle of equality is a
means by which Bahá'ís receive reassurance and develop confidence as they embark on the process of constructing a new
society centered around such equality.

Earlier chapters contain many examples of the clarifications
provided by the Universal House of Justice concerning the application of the principle of equality between men and women.
Several examples relate to domestic relations, including marital
decision-making without unjust domination by either partner;
the condemnation of domestic violence and sexual abuse; and
the distinction between administrative rank and spiritual station.

Of far-reaching significance is the statement of the Universal House of Justice that Bahá'í laws are equally applicable to
men and women unless the context renders this impossible.
This provides the correct orientation within which all formulations of Bahá'í law, including those set out in the Kitáb-i-Aqdas,
should be viewed.

In *The Promise of World Peace,* a statement on peace addressed
to the peoples of the world in 1985, the Universal House of
Justice drew attention to the fact that acceptance of the oneness
of humanity is the primary foundation for the attainment of
peace and world order. Such acceptance requires the abandonment of every form of prejudice, including that of sex, since
such prejudiced attitudes foster a sense of superiority that leads
to division and oppression.

Integral to the acceptance of the oneness of humankind is an appreciation of the equality of men and women. Indeed, the Universal House of Justice affirms that "The emancipation of women, the achievement of full equality between the sexes, is one of the most important, though less acknowledged prerequisites of peace" and that "Only as women are welcomed into full partnership in all fields of human endeavor will the moral and psychological climate be created in which international peace can emerge."[36]

ADVANCING THE PROCESS OF IMPLEMENTATION

Recognizing that formidable barriers of attitude and conduct must be overcome to bring about the full expression of the equality of men and women in the Bahá'í community, the Universal House of Justice has taken progressive measures to advance the process of implementation initiated by Bahá'u'lláh and developed further by 'Abdu'l-Bahá and Shoghi Effendi. These measures have been embarked upon in synchronism with the vast expansion of the Bahá'í community in the years since 1963 and with the extension of its influence and membership into all parts of the world.

The task is far from complete, but good progress has been made in response to the urging of the Universal House of Justice in statements such as the following excerpt from a 1984 message addressed to the entire worldwide Bahá'í membership:

> The equality of men and women is not, at the present time, universally applied. In those areas where traditional inequality still hampers its progress we must take the lead in practicing this Bahá'í principle. Bahá'í women and girls must be encouraged to take part in the social, spiritual and administrative activities of their communities.[37]

In addition to making such exhortations, the Universal House of Justice has called for specific measures designed to foster the emancipation of women from the fetters of traditional practice. Among these measures are such endeavors as the extension of literacy, the devising of programs aimed specifically at increasing women's participation in all aspects of community life, and the convening of women's conferences that play an important role in raising consciousness and developing bonds of mutual support and encouragement among Bahá'í women.

An account of progress in the advancement of Bahá'í women in Iran, where the cultural barriers to equality have been particularly strong, was set out in a 1973 report of the accomplishments of the Bahá'í committee specialized for this work. The account, published in a survey of activities in *The Bahá'í World*, volume 15, states,

> As a result of intensified activities the special Committee charged with this responsibility held special training classes; extracts from the Writings were compiled relating to such subjects as family life and the status of women; a highly popular magazine for Bahá'í women was produced regularly; circuit tours were made throughout the country to assist with women's programmes in various areas; all-women's conferences were held; and women were increasingly encouraged to play important roles as teachers, pioneers and administrators. It was reported that by Riḍván, 1973, the efforts of the Committee had to all intents and purposes effectively eradicated illiteracy among Bahá'í women under the age of forty throughout Írán.[38]

The development of the worldwide Bahá'í community proceeds through a series of plans, the duration and general features of which are prescribed by the Universal House of Justice, with detailed specification of goals to be carried out at national and local levels. A significant milestone in women's advancement in the Faith was the assignment by the Universal House of Justice in the Five Year Plan (1974–1979) of the goal for eighty National Spiritual Assemblies to arrange Bahá'í activities for women in countries where traditional restrictions on the freedom of women have been pronounced. In a letter addressed to all National Spiritual Assemblies in 1975, the Universal House of Justice elaborated on the importance of this assignment:

> Although obviously the entire Bahá'í world is committed to encouraging and stimulating the vital role of women in the Bahá'í community as well as in society at large, the Five Year Plan calls specifically on eighty National Spiritual Assemblies to organize Bahá'í activities for women. In the course of the current year which has been designated "International Women's Year" as a worldwide activity of the United Nations, the Bahá'ís, particularly in these eighty national communities, should initiate and implement programs which will stimulate and promote the full and equal participation of women in all aspects of Bahá'í community life, so that through their accomplishments the friends will demonstrate the distinction of the Cause of God in this field of human endeavor.[39]

The report prepared in 1979 at the end of the five-year period states, in part,

> This goal has been successfully pursued in many parts of the world. Bahá'í activities for women which have been initiated include greater participation in a wide range of endeavours to further the progress of the Cause through wom-

en's conferences, family life conferences, classes in child care, reading, nutrition and hygiene, arts and crafts, and many others. Particularly significant has been a great increase in regular children's classes, and the formation of women's teaching teams. Some of these latter have visited three islands in the New Hebrides following a women's conference there, opened new localities in the Dominican Republic, spent four months opening new localities in Guatemala, and from Panama embarked on a three-nation travel-teaching trip.[40]

The most striking accomplishment in the fulfillment of this Five Year Plan goal was the initiation of a series of Bahá'í women's conferences, which resulted in over 150 such gatherings at an international, national, and local level during that period. Such conferences may well be regarded as a further response to 'Abdu'l-Bahá's call for women's assemblages to be a potent factor in the enlightenment and advancement of women. These conferences directed attention to the statements in the Bahá'í writings on the equality of men and women and to statements on the vital role assigned to women in the progress of humanity, both within the family and in the larger society. Their programs included accounts of distinguished Bahá'í women such as Bahíyyih Khánum and Martha Root, sessions on the importance of the education of women, and discussions aimed at fostering greater participation by women in all spheres of activity. The aims of the conferences were reinforced in 1977 by a cable from the Universal House of Justice to all National Spiritual Assemblies, stating, in part, "PARTICULARLY CALL UPON BAHÁ'Í WOMEN, WHOSE CAPACITIES IN MANY LANDS STILL LARGELY UNUSED, AND WHOSE POTENTIAL FOR SERVICE CAUSE SO GREAT, TO ARISE AND DEMONSTRATE IMPORTANCE PART THEY ARE TO PLAY IN ALL FIELDS SERVICE FAITH."[41]

International conferences were held in India, El Salvador, Peru, and Liberia, but the bulk of the conferences were held at national or regional levels. That these conferences were, for some, a turning-point in the process of implementing the Bahá'í teachings on the equality of the sexes is evident in the following excerpt from a report:

> In many cases these conferences were the first regional or national Bahá'í activity in which women from the more remote villages participated, and often they were the first occasion on which native women arose to speak publicly. . . .
>
> . . . Particularly noteworthy is the fact that many of these conferences were held not in large cities but in villages and towns in remote areas, the home territory of indigenous Bahá'ís. Often the trip to and from the conference was an important step in bringing the Bahá'í women together as sisters. An account of the trip by participants in the first Bahá'í Women's Conference of Malaysia by launches and on foot to Kampong Temiang where the conference was held, tells of the friendly spirit as women gathered from eleven jungle communities:

>> It was a happy journey with news being exchanged and the Bahá'ís getting to know each other as the launch proceeded through the afternoon heat of the equatorial jungle . . . eventually we had to take to our feet and walk the last hour of our journey balancing on tree trunks neatly felled so that one can step from one to the other—a great deal easier than walking through swampy land . . . we were tired but so happy to arrive.

Bahá'í villagers from the Bouake, Man, and Danane regions of the Ivory Coast walked distances up to 400 miles overland to attend the International Bahá'í Women's Conference in Monrovia, Liberia. Village women such as these contributed actively to the success of these conferences throughout the world, speaking often for the first time before large gatherings and translating addresses into the native languages. Men as well as women contributed in a variety of ways to making these meetings a success: in many cases the men attending the conference prepared the food, washed the dishes, and cared for the children, in order to allow the women to concentrate on the discussion of their responsibilities and development within the Faith and the importance of their role as the first educators of the next generation of Bahá'ís. Such active and cheerful co-operation and service to the women by the men is particularly interesting as in most cases it was offered in marked contrast to social customs prevailing in the world around them. The enthusiasm created by these gatherings often resulted in women setting goals for themselves for their own deepening and the deepening of their families in the essential verities of the Faith, for the establishment of local classes for women and children, for teaching the Faith locally and as travel teachers, for the enrollment of entire families in the Faith, and for raising up Local Spiritual Assemblies. Often the women examined their local customs and habits in an effort to bring their lives more closely in line with the principles of their Faith and more consonant with their dignity as Bahá'í women.

Most important perhaps has been the fostering of a new spirit among the Bahá'í women who participated in the conferences, as their perception of their role in the progress of the Faith and of humanity in general was transformed by learning of 'Abdu'l-Bahá's revolutionizing statements on the importance of women to the progress of all humankind.[42]

The two new elements added to the implementation process during the Five Year Plan—the assignment of specific goals to National and Local Spiritual Assemblies for women's activities and the holding of women's conferences—have expanded in subsequent years. Thus, during the Seven Year Plan (1979–1986), over 400 national and regional conferences for women were held, and 116 national communities carried out specific activities geared toward the advancement of women.[43] Literacy programs also proliferated. Some National Spiritual Assemblies published special magazines for Bahá'í women while other Assemblies used their regular national news bulletins as a vehicle for articles designed to foster the progress of women.

Reviewing the application of the principle of the equality of the sexes within the Bahá'í community during recent years, the Universal House of Justice notes in a 1996 message to the Bahá'ís of the world, that

> Efforts at improving the status of women gathered momentum in a number of countries where, in addition to Bahá'í participation in projects sponsored by other organizations, the Bahá'í institutions set up committees and offices to attend to the interests of women.[44]

In messages addressed to various parts of the world in 1996, the Universal House of Justice underlines continuing deficits in relation to the practice of equality, and it identifies specific areas of opportunity for fostering the development of women in various regions. For example, in the message addressed to the Bahá'ís of the Indian subcontinent and adjacent areas, the Universal House of Justice states,

> ... we call upon you to give special attention to the advancement of women. In almost all of your region, women have traditionally played a secondary role in the life of society, a

condition which is still reflected in many Bahá'í communities. Effective measures have to be adopted to help women take their rightful place in the teaching and administrative fields. By teaching entire families, you can ensure that increasing numbers of women enter the Faith, thereby improving the balance in the composition of your communities and beginning in each family, from the moment of acceptance, a process through which the fundamental principle of the equality between men and women can be realized.[45]

Likewise, the Bahá'ís in the African continent are called upon to "Multiply plans and programs to raise the status of women and to encourage the active support of men in such endeavors."[46] And, to the countries of the Pacific region, the Universal House of Justice provides the following assessment and guidance:

> In many of the nations of your area, women have traditionally been restricted to a secondary role in the life of society. We call upon the Bahá'í women of these countries, assured of the support and encouragement of all elements of the Bahá'í community, to demonstrate the transforming power of this Revelation by their courage and initiative in the teaching work and their full participation in the administrative activities of the Faith.[47]

FOSTERING WOMEN'S PARTICIPATION IN BAHÁ'Í ADMINISTRATION

It is clear from the discussion in chapter 4 of women's service on Bahá'í institutions that the Bahá'í Faith calls for the full involvement of women in its administrative activities, and the foundational endeavors of Shoghi Effendi to bring this about have been described above. The Universal House of Justice continues the strengthening of this aspect of the equality of the sexes and has made it clear that, in areas where women are restricted by traditional practices, encouragement must be given to Bahá'í women and girls to take part in the administrative activities of their communities.

The Bahá'í Faith eschews the use of quotas or any other artificial means to bring about the appearance of equality in institutional composition. A central feature of the Bahá'í institutions is that the members of these bodies are expected to consider, in the light of the Bahá'í teachings, what is in the best interests of all members of the community, rather than only a segment. Thus it is expected that a Bahá'í institution's endeavor to practice justice will not be dependent on its composition, and its expression of equality of the sexes is not dependent on having an equal number of males and females in its membership. Moreover, each Spiritual Assembly is expected to make a continuing effort to become informed of the views and concerns of all members of the community, and it is expected to be receptive to considering suggestions and recommendations made to it either directly by individuals or through such Bahá'í gatherings as Nineteen Day Feasts and conventions or conferences.*

In voting for members of Local or National Spiritual Assemblies, Bahá'ís are expected to consider

without the least trace of passion and prejudice, and irrespective of any material consideration, the names of only those who can best combine the necessary qualities of un-

---

* The Nineteen Day Feast is a meeting of the Bahá'í community at a local level held on the first day of every Bahá'í month, each of which consists of nineteen days. The program of the Feast has devotional, consultative, and social elements.

questioned loyalty, of selfless devotion, of a well-trained mind, of recognized ability and mature experience. . . .[48]

It might be expected, from statistical considerations, that these "necessary qualities" will be distributed equally between male and female members of a Bahá'í community of reasonable size and that, as the community matures in its understanding and expression of equality of the sexes, the proportion of men and women on an Assembly will be comparable. For this reason, the proportion of women on Local and National Spiritual Assemblies is of interest and provides useful information about the progress of the Bahá'í community in its continuing quest to implement more fully the principle of equality.

Comparison with the wider society indicates the magnitude of the task with which the Bahá'í community is confronted. In the religious sphere of human endeavor throughout the world, the encouragement women receive does not extend generally to their inclusion in a decision-making role over a constituency that includes males, apart from occasional token gestures. Even in the secular realm of civil administration, the proportion of women in the world's legislative bodies is, as discussed below, far from ideal.

The process of fostering the greater participation of women in Bahá'í administrative service has been focused initially on the local level. As more women are involved in consultation at Nineteen Day Feasts, so their capacities are recognized and they are elected to Local Spiritual Assemblies or as delegates to the national convention at which the members of the National Spiritual Assembly are elected. In turn this leads to the involvement of women at a national level as elected members of the National Spiritual Assembly or through appointment to national committees. The election of the first woman to a National Spiritual Assembly is considered noteworthy and a cause for pleasure in a national community, but eventually it becomes commonplace and both men and women participate together on National Assemblies as a matter of course.

The effect of women's involvement in the administration of the Faith is described in a 1985 report of activities in India that states,

> The very act of becoming a Bahá'í is the first major personal decision for most women in rural areas. Then, as they are deepened in the Bahá'í teachings and the role they are expected to play in Bahá'í administrative activity, they are changed from being passive members of an existing social order into dynamic members of a new order. Because of their functions in serving on Bahá'í administrative bodies and in voting and in being voted for and elected, women have made great strides in a largely male dominated society. An increasing number of local Bahá'í assemblies have women as members and local assemblies with all women members have also been reported.[49]

A similar report from New Zealand indicates

> Women are truly exercising to the full their privileges and responsibilities in the work of the community. The success of their efforts is due to a sense of dignity, spiritual assurance, education and the recognition of the role of women in all avenues of society. Since many women are involved in all aspects of Bahá'í administration and community life, this appears to be the area where the principle of equality bears the most fruit.[50]

Steady progress has been reported in the increase of the proportion of women serving on Bahá'í administrative institutions, with well-designed surveys being carried out to measure this progress. In 1997 it was found that 32 percent of the members of 172 National Spiritual Assemblies are women, with Europe and the Americas having the largest proportion (40 percent) and Africa having the lowest proportion (17 percent). At a regional level within the various continents, the proportions ranged from 51 percent in North America to 14 percent in West Africa. These figures measure both the progress that has been made and the need for continued endeavors. They are best assessed by comparison with the figures for representation of women in national civil legislatures, the worldwide average of which is no more than 10 percent, ranging from Scandinavia with a 40 percent proportion of women to Middle Eastern countries where the participation of women is negligible. National legislatures in countries such as the United States, Russia, and Japan all have a female representation of less than 10 percent.[51]

An important role in the development of the Bahá'í community is played by institutions that are composed of believers appointed to provide advice, encouragement, and counseling to Spiritual Assemblies and individual Bahá'ís in their endeavors to practice the teachings of the Faith. These institutions include five Boards of Counselors for the continental areas of the world, the Auxiliary Board members, and the Assistants to the Auxiliary Board members. In some instances, where a particular need is deemed to exist, Auxiliary Board members will appoint assistants whose sole assignment is to stimulate greater involvement of women in the activities of the Faith. A recent survey showed that 34 percent of Counselors are women, while the proportion of women among the Auxiliary Board members and their assistants is around 47 percent.[52]

THE OFFICE FOR THE ADVANCEMENT OF WOMEN

The Bahá'í community has always sought fellowship and collaboration with groups and organizations in the larger society that are pursuing objectives congruous with the Bahá'í teachings. Its purpose in so doing is to offer its perspective on the attainment of these objectives and to reinforce the endeavors of such entities. Beyond that, it has not hesitated, when circumstances are propitious, to offer suggestions and advice on means by which the condition of society can be improved.

When 'Abdu'l-Bahá was in the United States in 1912, He addressed a Woman's Suffrage meeting in New York and also spoke to members of a Federation of Women's Clubs in Chicago. On both occasions He emphasized the need for equality. In New York, referring to man and woman, He stated, "It is not natural that either should remain undeveloped; and until both are perfected, the happiness of the human world will not be realized." In the Chicago meetings He proclaimed, "until woman and man recognize and realize equality, social and political progress here or anywhere will not be possible."[53]

In recent years the Bahá'í International Community has established an influential presence in association with various agencies. It was officially recognized as an international non-governmental organization (NGO) in 1948 and subsequently was granted consultative status with the United Nations Economic and Social Council (ECOSOC) as well as with the United Nations Children's Fund (UNICEF). It has used this presence to work for the advancement of women, collaborating with like-minded NGOs and submitting statements on various aspects of equality to United Nations conferences and agencies.

Bahá'í activities intended to promote the advancement of women became particularly prominent during the United Na-

tions Decade for Women, 1976–1985. Bahá'í representatives
participated in the major conferences held in Mexico City
(1975), Copenhagen (1980), and Nairobi (1985) and were involved in the special NGO activities held on these occasions. A
lengthy report was submitted to the 1985 conference, conveying the results of a comprehensive survey of the activities being
carried out by the Bahá'ís in all continents of the world to improve the status of women. One of the conclusions of the report was that

> Bahá'í communities, while realistic in their assessment of
> obstacles to be overcome, are dedicated to a change in atti-
> tudes, and are working systematically and in a practical way
> to win the goal of equality of the sexes. They are dedicated
> to the education of women, even in preference to that of
> men, since women, as mothers, have such an important bear-
> ing on the life of future generations. In addition, they see
> the importance of women's potential for the accomplishment
> of peace and world order as women increasingly participate
> in all areas of community life.[54]

The Bahá'í International Community has been particularly
effective in drawing the attention of United Nations agencies
to the importance of ameliorating the condition of the girl child.
A statement presented to the UNICEF Executive Board in 1991
expresses deep concern "at the blatant neglect of girl children,
justified in many parts of the world as part of the culture," and
urges UNICEF to "broaden its approach to maternal health to
include an attempt to alter factors that affect girl's and women's
health before maternity, including harmful traditional attitudes
and practices."[55] The statement goes on to emphasize the vital
role mothers are called upon to play:

Mothers can now be the primary agents for empowering individuals to transform society. They alone can inculcate in their children the self-esteem and respect for others essential for the advancement of civilization. It is clear, then, that the station of mothers, increasingly denigrated in many societies, is in reality of the greatest importance and highest merit.[56]

At the same time, however, the statement points out the need for involvement of the family:

It must be stressed, however, that this dual responsibility of developing the child's character and stimulating his intellect also belongs to the family as a whole, including the father and grandparents, and to the community.[57]

More than four decades of such activity at the United Nations reached its culmination in December 1992, when the Universal House of Justice announced its decision to establish an Office for the Advancement of Women as an agency of the Bahá'í International Community. In a letter dated 10 December 1992 to all National Spiritual Assemblies, the Universal House of Justice indicates that the purpose of the new office is to

promote the principles of the Faith through its interaction with international entities concerned with matters affecting the rights, status and well-being of women. It will also advise National Spiritual Assemblies regarding programs and projects in which the involvement of the community can encourage efforts towards the realization of the equality of men and women.[58]

The Universal House of Justice highlights the special significance of the new office in the following terms:

The inauguration of the Office for the Advancement of Women, as a companion of the other offices of the Bahá'í International Community in New York, is a further significant step in the administration of the external affairs of the Faith and, of course, provides our community with a visible instrument for the practical application of one of the cardinal principles of the Cause of Bahá'u'lláh.[59]

In making this announcement the Universal House of Justice draws attention to the fact that, since 1988, the Bahá'í International Community has served as the convenor of Advocates for African Food Security, a coalition of NGOs, United Nations agencies, and intergovernmental bodies formed in 1986 to raise awareness of women as producers of most of the domestic food in Africa. The Universal House of Justice also highlights the involvement of the Bahá'í International Community with the United Nations Development Fund for Women (UNIFEM).

Since its inception the Office for the Advancement of Women has given leadership to, and greatly enhanced the visibility of, the Bahá'í community's efforts to raise the status of women. Its director led the official Bahá'í delegation to the Fourth World Conference on Women in Beijing, China, in September 1995. The office also made a major contribution to planning and executing the NGO Forum on Women, which was a companion event, and it successfully mobilized five hundred Bahá'ís from throughout the world to lend their active support to this important gathering. A book titled *The Greatness Which Might Be Theirs*, published by the Office for the Advancement of Women for the Beijing conference, conveyed a Bahá'í perspective on a number of issues on the conference agenda.

Commenting on the need for the education of girls in a statement submitted in March 1995 to the thirty-ninth session of the United Nations Commission on the Status of Women, the

Office for the Advancement of Women applauds the commission's decision "to include under the priority theme of development a focus on educating girls and women," but asserts that the education needed is of three kinds: material education concerned with physical health and well-being; human education, which prepares one to participate in such activities of civilized society as commerce, science, arts, and public administration; and also spiritual education, which is concerned with values and character development. On the latter point it indicates that

> Spiritual or moral education is almost never seen outside of parochial schools or religious institutions, is shunned in most developed countries as irrelevant or intrusive to modern education, and is rarely funded by international donors. It is the one kind of education which asserts the dignity of the human spirit in all its diversity, and formalizes its relationship to the Divine. Such universal human values as trustworthiness, honesty, courtesy, generosity, respect and kindness are rapidly disappearing from our increasingly belligerent and fractured world. Through moral or character education, whether formalized in religious or secular programs or provided informally by wise and caring family or community members, that which is valued by society and gives meaning to life is transmitted to succeeding generations.[60]

Violence against women has been a particular concern of the Office for the Advancement of Women, which has made submissions on this subject to the World Conference on Human Rights in Vienna in June 1993 and to the United Nations Commission on Human Rights in Geneva in January 1995. The office states,

Domestic violence is a fact of life for many women throughout the world, regardless of race, class, or educational background. In many societies traditional beliefs that women are a burden make them easy targets of anger. In other situations, men's frustration is vented on women and children when economies shrink and collapse. In all parts of the world, violence against women persists because it goes unpunished.[61]

The office points out that

It is becoming increasingly evident, however, that all forms of violence against women degrade not only the victim but the perpetrator as well. Those who inflict violence on women are themselves among the casualties of power-based systems. When unbridled competition, aggression, and tyranny destroy the fabric of society, everyone suffers. In the Bahá'í view, "the harvest of force is turmoil and the ruin of the social order" and violence against women is a grave symptom of this larger disorder.[62]

Addressing the means of eradicating this violence, the office indicates that

Beliefs and practices that contribute to the oppression of women must be reexamined in the light of justice. When properly understood, the principle of the fundamental equality of men and women will eventually transform all social relations, allowing each person to develop his or her unique gifts and talents. The utilization of everyone's strengths will foster the maturation of society. As the principle of equality gains acceptance, the challenge of transmitting it to the next generation must be undertaken by parents, schools, governments and NGOs.[63]

The Office for the Advancement of Women also asserts,

> The persistence and growth of violence directed against women, both personal and institutional, is largely attributable to the traditional exclusion of women from processes of development and decision-making. A profound adjustment in humanity's collective outlook is needed, guided by the considerations of universal values and spiritual principles. Legislation is needed which lends practical expression to the equality of the sexes by dealing with the particular injustices which women face.[64]

The office also calls for the reeducation of men as well as women to achieve the elimination of violence against women:

> But the problem of violence cannot truly be resolved unless men are also educated to value women as equal partners. Any effort to protect women against male aggression which does not involve the early training of boys will necessarily be short-lived. Likewise, all attempts to understand the causes and consequences of violence against women which do not involve men are bound to fail.[65]

One of the most pernicious forms of violence perpetrated against women is that of female genital mutilation. In a statement presented at a conference on the commercial sexual exploitation of children that was held in New York in May 1996 under the auspices of UNICEF and the World Conference on Religion and Peace, the Office for the Advancement of Women reports that, in those areas where female genital mutilation is prevalent, the Bahá'í institutions regard themselves as having a duty to contribute to its eradication through "an ongoing program of education based on spiritual principles and sound scientific information."[66]

The establishment and functioning of the Bahá'í International Community Office for the Advancement of Women has given additional impetus to Bahá'í endeavors at a national level to bring to the attention of the wider society the Bahá'í principle of the equality of the sexes. In launching a Four Year Plan in 1996 for the activities of Bahá'ís throughout the world, the Universal House of Justice called for "the status of women" to be given particular emphasis in efforts "aimed at influencing the processes towards world peace" in the wider society; this may well be regarded as a continuation of the emphasis upon the role of women in attaining world peace.[67]

A number of National Spiritual Assemblies have established Offices for the Advancement of Women, functioning at a national level and drawing on advice from the international office, while, in Europe, the formation of the European Task Force for Women has been the agent for the promotion of conferences for women all over the continent and for the training of women as leaders in societal change. In addition, Bahá'í professional organizations and associations for Bahá'í studies have given emphasis to the advancement of women in their programs. Singapore has played a notable role, with a 1994 international report stating,

> In Singapore, the Bahá'í Women's Committee collaborated with the Singapore Council of Women's Organizations to produce a comprehensive survey of the women's movement, released in 1993 and entitled *Voices and Choices: The Women's Movement in Singapore*. One of the two most prominently featured women in the publication is Shirin Fozdar, a Bahá'í who founded the Singapore Council of Women in 1952, was a spokesperson for the Singapore Women's Committee in the 1950s and 1960s, and is regarded as a pioneering proponent of women's rights in Asia.[68]

The Bahá'í view, as stated in chapter 2, is that the denial to women of full equality with men has had a far-reaching effect on all areas of human activity. In a statement titled *The Prosperity of Humankind* issued by the Bahá'í International Community Office of Public Information in January 1995, the effect of equality of the sexes on global development is discussed in the following terms:

A commitment to the establishment of full equality between men and women, in all departments of life and at every level of society, will be central to the success of efforts to conceive and implement a strategy of global development.

Indeed, in an important sense, progress in this area will itself be a measure of the success of any development program. Given the vital role of economic activity in the advancement of civilization, visible evidence of the pace at which development is progressing will be the extent to which women gain access to all avenues of economic endeavor. The challenge goes beyond ensuring an equitable distribution of opportunity, important as that is. It calls for a fundamental rethinking of economic issues in a manner that will invite the full participation of a range of human experience and insight hitherto largely excluded from the discourse. The classical economic models of impersonal markets in which human beings act as autonomous makers of self-regarding choices will not serve the needs of a world motivated by ideals of unity and justice. Society will find itself increasingly challenged to develop new economic models shaped by insights that arise from a sympathetic understanding of shared experience, from viewing human beings in relation to others, and from a recognition of the centrality to social well-being of the role of the family and the community. Such an intellectual breakthrough—strongly altruistic rather than self-

centered in focus—must draw heavily on both the spiritual
and scientific sensibilities of the race, and millennia of experience have prepared women to make crucial contributions
to the common effort.[69]

On the occasion of the fiftieth anniversary of the United
Nations in October 1995, the Bahá'í International Community issued a statement entitled *Turning Point For All Nations,*
which contains a number of recommendations for improving
the effectiveness of the United Nations. Under the heading "Advancing the Status of Women" appears the following passage:

The creation of a peaceful and sustainable world civilization will be impossible without the full participation of
women in every arena of human activity. While this propo-
sition is increasingly supported, there is a marked difference
between intellectual acceptance and its implementation.

It is time for the institutions of the world, composed
mainly of men, to use their influence to promote the systematic inclusion of women, not out of condescension or
presumed self-sacrifice but as an act motivated by the belief
that the contributions of women are required for society to
progress. Only as the contributions of women are valued
will they be sought out and woven into the fabric of society.
The result will be a more peaceful, balanced, just and pros-
perous civilization.[70]

PROMOTING THE SOCIAL AND ECONOMIC
DEVELOPMENT OF WOMEN

Promoting the development of the human race in all aspects—spiritual, intellectual, social, and economic—has always
been an integral part of Bahá'í teachings and practice. As the
Universal House of Justice points out, "The oneness of man-

kind, which is at once the operating principle and ultimate goal of His [Bahá'u'lláh's] Revelation, implies the achievement of a dynamic coherence between the spiritual and practical requirements of life on earth."[71]

In recent years the growth in size of the Bahá'í community and its spread to even the most remote regions of the world have made it both possible and necessary for Bahá'ís to take a more prominent role in the social and economic development of the people in areas where they reside.[72]

The Bahá'í approach is distinctive in that a key component is the local Bahá'í community, which is distinguished by its spiritual motivation, by its endeavors to apply the principles of Bahá'u'lláh, and by its commitment to group decision-making through the process of Bahá'í consultation. While the Bahá'í Faith is quite properly interested in spreading the Bahá'í teachings and attracting a larger number of people to membership in the Faith, it is required by these teachings to adhere to an exalted standard of ethical conduct, which proscribes the use of material inducements in an effort to win new recruits.

The number and scope of Bahá'í social and economic development programs being carried out throughout the world is growing so rapidly that they cannot accurately be surveyed here. They include literacy programs; tutorial schools; primary, secondary, and tertiary educational institutions; agricultural and medical projects; educational radio stations; training institutes for income-producing crafts; and programs in rural development and village-level hygiene.

In this section attention will be focused only on a representative sample of projects in education, health care, and attitudinal change that have been directed principally at improving the condition of women. No attempt is made here to carry out a comprehensive survey, but rather to provide an indication of those aspects of this subject to which attention is being directed at the present time.

EDUCATION

The education of girls and women has been a priority of the
Faith since the first programs were initiated for this purpose in
Iran during 'Abdu'l-Bahá's ministry. Such education continues
to receive emphasis from the Universal House of Justice, which
states in a message of April 1996 to the Bahá'ís of Africa,

> Parents have a special responsibility to see that their chil-
> dren, both boys and girls, receive an education; and they
> must take care that the girls are not left behind, since well-
> educated girls are a guarantee of the excellence of future so-
> ciety; indeed, preference should, if necessary, be given to
> their education. Closely linked to this concern is the prin-
> ciple of the equality of men and women taught by Bahá'u'lláh.
> It is also highly desirable for adults, men and women, who
> are illiterate to participate in literacy programs, so that gradu-
> ally all Bahá'ís will be able to read the Word of God for
> themselves.[73]

There are innumerable examples of Bahá'í educational programs designed to raise the status of women. The women of
India, for example, face the double challenge of overcoming
caste prejudice and the inferior status assigned to women within
their culture. The Bahá'í institutes, schools, and community
learning centers gradually address these traditional prejudices
by first creating programs for women and girls that provide them
with domestic and crafts skills that are acceptable in the current
environment and which are valued because of their potential
for added income. During these courses additional topics such
as the education of daughters, the caste system, unity, family
planning, loyalty to one's government, and the nobility of each
human being are progressively introduced.[74]

Features of the Bahá'í approach to providing literacy training to women are illustrated by detailed examination of the

operation of the Faizi Vocational Institute for Rural Women, which promotes positive social change while teaching income-generating skills to women in the tribal areas around Indore, in southwestern Madhya Pradesh, India. Established in 1983, the institute operates in a tribal area that is economically deprived and socially disadvantaged—90 percent of the women are illiterate, a strong caste system exists among the various local tribes, the level of poverty is high, few health services are available, and there is a high female mortality rate, especially among girl children.[75]

The formal education program of the Vocational Institute for Rural Women provides an impetus to the processes of social transformation in the tribal areas from which it draws its participants. This powerful impetus results from giving attention to the spiritual dimension of existence and to the implementation of the principle of the equality of women and men. As an expression of the Bahá'í view that the advancement of women is essential for social transformation, the institute encourages women to develop the full range of their capacities—economic, intellectual, social, and moral. Trainees are assisted to see themselves as equal in capacity to men, to discover their innate abilities, and to see new ways of contributing to the welfare of the community. As educated mothers, they also gain a new sense of the importance of their role in reshaping tribal societies. At the institute, rural women can develop their intellectual capacities, strengthen their commitment to their families and communities, and learn useful crafts. Back in the villages, follow-up support ensures that the benefits of the training are sustained.

The courses provided at the institute are not confined to literacy training, essential as it is. They include training in income-generating activities, e.g., making candles, soap, chalk, handloom products, carpets, and handicrafts such as beadwork and embroidery; the programs also impart knowledge of health and the environment in the form of health care, basic first aid and awareness of environmental hazards, and information about useful village technologies such as fuel-efficient smokeless stoves, and means of filtering drinking water. Most important of all, participation in the institute provides the rural women with opportunities for spiritual development through devotions, chanting, and reading of inspirational materials, as well as through the discussion of spiritual and moral principles and their application to personal and contemporary social issues. It is also evident that the institute promotes within its participants attitudinal change through informal interactions intended to foster greater social awareness, a scientific orientation to issues, and participation in planning and decision-making activities.

An important element of the success of this institute lies in the fact that its programs are planned in consultation with the Spiritual Assemblies in the villages surrounding Indore from which the participants are drawn. Consultation fosters acceptance of new ideas and methods and generates both grassroots support for the participation of women in the training programs and appreciation for the contribution the trainees are able to make to their local communities after their training courses. Specifically, the Assemblies assist in selecting the candidates. They support the institute's activities, helping village men to understand the importance of women's education, and they encourage women to take part in the programs and to contribute their new knowledge and skills to the service of the Bahá'í community upon completing their courses.

It is clear that the programs of the Vocational Institute for Rural Women have had a significant impact on the lives of the village women. On a personal level, these women have gained self-respect and confidence, with which are associated their acquisition of skills and their heightened awareness of spiritual and moral principles. Beyond that, they are making a significant contribution to the process of overcoming the prejudice of caste, which continues to separate villagers in this part of India.

On a social level, the development of the women's income-earning capacity has raised their status in the eyes of their menfolk. Furthermore, education in literacy, health, and hygiene has not only helped to improve the material standard of their own lives but has also had a positive impact on village life. For example, a program undertaken by the institute's graduates to provide safe drinking water in the villages led to the eradication of the guinea worm in over three hundred villages in the area. In addition, male community members have begun to defend women's rights, to protect women's interests, and to promote the development of women's capacities.

Many other examples of Bahá'í programs for literacy are to be found in Africa, Latin America, and Australasia. When the participants are from a village area, it is not uncommon for literacy classes to be combined with training in the acquisition of skills such as cooking, basic hygiene, child care, and sewing. Income-generating skills may also be taught, as is done at the Faizi Institute in India. In other instances such as the Lar Linda Tanure Orphanage conducted by the Bahá'í community in Manaus, Brazil, literacy classes for women are part of an extensive education program arising from the education being provided to the children in the orphanage. In France, the Bahá'í community has offered literacy classes for Turkish-speaking women, and similar classes have been offered for new immigrants in the United States and in Australia.[76]

Bahá'í schools at a secondary level or beyond are generally coeducational. However, in certain places where the society has failed to provide opportunities for girls to continue their education beyond the primary level, the Bahá'ís are instituting special measures to meet the girls' educational needs as resources permit. An example is the Banani International Secondary School for Girls, opened in January 1993 in Zambia, where only 20 percent of girls have access to education. Praised by government officials for its high standards of education and its admirable moral tone, this school provides girls with a comprehensive educational program oriented toward practical training in the sciences and agriculture.[77]

Other Bahá'í educational programs for women have aimed at assisting them to acquire expertise in specialized fields of knowledge to which they have traditionally not had access. Typical of such programs is a five-day course for women conducted in Uganda by the Bahá'ís in collaboration with a women's association to enhance the participants' knowledge of financial management, marketing, and bookkeeping, as well as associated legal issues. Such specialized courses are likely to proliferate in the years ahead in those countries where women are particularly in need of such remedial assistance.[78]

HEALTH CARE

Measures to improve women's health in countries where it has received little attention have their origin in the actions 'Abdu'l-Bahá took to provide medical services for Iranian women. In recent years it has been possible for the Bahá'í community to give greater attention to this need in many parts of the world.[79]

In most cases, health education arises from a program in literacy or general education, such as that of the Faizi Institute in India. The Bahá'í contribution is twofold: It includes information, to which women have long lacked access, about such matters as hygiene, sanitation, and nutrition, but perhaps the more significant help provided by the Bahá'ís is in offering a more enlightened perspective on the world. By this means prejudices are broken down, and myths and fallacies about personal and family hygiene can be removed. The process involved here is based on perception of the harmony of religion and science, a foundational principle of the Faith.

One example of a Bahá'í health-education project is that conducted recently in Malaysia over the five-year period 1989–1994 to foster health-awareness among women in low-income areas. The first phase of the Health Awareness Project aimed to provide health and child-development education to mothers and families in selected areas and to expose mothers to health and child-development practices that are more beneficial than their existing customs. As an initial step, a program aimed at reducing the incidence of scabies, lice, and worm infestation among the families in these low-income areas was introduced. Besides providing a needed service, the program succeeded in establishing a good and lasting relationship with the local women so that the health-awareness project could be continued, and further development initiatives emerged naturally from the local community.

In the second phase the project was extended to ten areas, one in each state of the region. Within these areas were seven different majority and minority ethnic groups in low-income, isolated, or remote regions. Even in the most remote areas, the participation, especially of the women, increased as the project advanced; in one area about two hundred women, children, and men attended the initial gathering. Thereafter, there was willing participation in all activities pertaining to children's dental care, prenatal care, vitamins and their importance to physical and mental growth, child growth, safe motherhood, and breast-feeding.

The positive impact of the project can be seen in the improved cleanliness and personal hygiene of the people in the communities involved and in their increased interest in general health issues. Very often in the more remote and conservative areas women would ask questions related to myths, fallacies, and superstitions about health. Such questions not only demonstrated a trust in the health professionals but also evinced the desire to ascertain whether those beliefs were scientifically sound.

There was also an increased interest in education and child development. Women in the ten communities gained an appreciation of the contribution they could make simply by teaching their children through games and by interacting with them. Furthermore, the women themselves gained a greater awareness of their own potential and of the need to develop themselves, so that they began to come forward to participate, to offer ideas, to organize, and—most significant of all—to lead. Thus the project accomplished far more than simply raising awareness of health issues; it trained more local women as managers and enhanced the status of women. In addition, the project spurred other development activities in the area. Members of the community became aware of the need to do more for themselves and thus to take on for their own benefit other development projects such as paving a dirt track or holding literacy classes. Generally, the women began to show a greater interest in the education of their children.

Bahá'í endeavors have not been confined to hygiene and awareness of good health practices. In Africa, for example, women have been taught to use soybean products to obtain protein for the diet of their families in areas where conventional sources of protein are inaccessible due to cost. In many places women have been trained to plant trees, not only for the purpose of improving the environment but also for the health benefits that accrue from reducing soil erosion and dust.

ATTITUDINAL CHANGE

Central to the aims of the Bahá'í Faith is the accomplishment of a change in attitudes on the part of men and women, leading to a full recognition of the equality of the sexes. In reaching out to the larger society, Bahá'í communities in many countries are seeking, through example and discussion, to bring about such a fundamental change in the larger society.

Perhaps the most striking example of Bahá'í activity in this regard is a two-year project called "Traditional Media as Change Agent" conducted by the Bahá'í Office for the Advancement of Women in cooperation with UNIFEM in Bolivia, Cameroon, and Malaysia, with Bahá'í-sponsored extensions in Brazil and Nigeria.

A report on this project describes it as having three principal components:

- It seeks to involve the people directly in analyzing their own problems, by first training them in the use of modern analytic tools like focus groups and community surveys, as well as in Bahá'í consultation;
- It then gives direction to that analysis by stressing the importance of a positive moral principle, in this case the equality of women and men;
- It seeks finally to promote change in the community by communicating the results of that analysis through traditional media, such as theater, songs, and dance, which are relatively non-threatening.[80]

The process began with the training of a select group of Bahá'í
volunteers at a national level in Bahá'í consultation, the distinctive approach to nonadversarial group decision making discussed in chapter 3, and in data-gathering techniques such as
participatory surveys and focus groups. Training was also provided in assessment, record keeping, and organization. These
volunteers then returned to their home communities, where
they conducted similar training sessions at a local level, resulting in a core group of project volunteers in each village.

Working in close collaboration with the Local Spiritual Assembly in its area, each core group interviewed male and female members of the wider community about issues pertaining
to the role of women and then facilitated consultation on the
issues that were identified. In a typical instance, men and women
were asked to list their daily tasks, from which it became clearly
apparent that the list of women's duties was invariably at least
twice as long as that of the men.

Such survey results became the basis for consultation on their
problems and needs. Generally, three basic problems emerged:
illiteracy among women, the mismanagement of family funds
by men, and the unfair burden of work shouldered by women.
Through the consultative process the people in the wider community were assisted to devise means of stimulating attitudinal
change through the use of traditional media such as songs,
dances, stories and plays, all involving local artists and per-
formers. Performances were then presented to the entire population of the area at festivals, special evening programs, and
other community events.

The significance of the project lies in several factors: It does
not rely on literacy for conveying its message; it involves both
women and men in collecting and analyzing information and
devising constructive measures to produce change; and it ad-

dresses at a village level the basic problem of unequal distribution of labor among men and women.

Surveys have shown that this project has achieved spectacular success in giving rise to greater participation of women in family and community decision making, increased motivation of women and girls to seek education, and greater involvement by men in domestic chores that were previously left entirely to women.

A report on the project quotes a female participant as stating,

> At the beginning, the project did not mean anything to me. Later on I discovered the advantages of the project. Now I see that my husband, who was not helping me before the project, has now changed. We work together at home and in the field. My husband helps me more now with the housework that before he thought was the sole duty of woman. He carries the baby, cleans the dishes and clothes. I also learned the importance of children's education and that it is first my responsibility and now I try to take better care of them. I got those ideas through songs because through the songs I listened carefully to what was being said.[81]

A male who was involved in the project indicates,

> Here in the village men and women were not used to working together but through the project I was surprised to see that they are working hand in hand. I personally have witnessed a change in my way of life. Concerning the equality of man and woman I see also that there is a change in the attitude of men. Now they consult with their wives. And I do the same. Before the project it was very difficult to know what women do with their money, but now my wife consults with me. I also work with my wife in the same farm,

and I help with cleaning the house, for example; things I
have never done before.[82]

The success of this project has been so pronounced as to
merit its extension on a far wider scale. In addition a video
titled *Two Wings* has been produced on this project and has
been widely circulated as a means of attracting greater attention to this approach.[83]

SIGNIFICANCE OF THE EXAMPLES

Only a few examples have been discussed in this section,
and they will doubtless be superseded by other more extensive
models of Bahá'í social and economic development activity in
the near future. Nonetheless, they are offered as a means of
showing that the Bahá'í community exemplifies an evolutionary approach to bringing about fundamental changes in attitudes and behaviors, such that they progressively accord ever
more closely with an ideal, a vision of unity and equality that is
found in the writings of Bahá'u'lláh and is shared by those who
identify with His religion. The approach adopted illustrates a
commitment to fostering change over an extended period of
time and demonstrates the power of faith as an agent of change.
It is the spirit of faith that motivates and sustains the participants in the ongoing study activities within the Bahá'í community and that energizes the social and economic development
projects, thus leading to the accomplishment of their objectives.

The several programs of social and economic development
we have described provide evidence of the power of the Bahá'í
Faith, coupled with the determination of its followers and its
institutions, to bring about fundamental social change that can
transform traditional prejudices and long-held discriminatory
attitudes and practices in parts of the world where women have
been, at best, invisible and, more frequently, greatly oppressed.

7

Practicing Equality

*Change is an evolutionary process
requiring patience with one's self
and others, loving education and
the passage of time as the believers
deepen their knowledge of the
principles of the Faith, gradually
discard long-held traditional
attitudes and progressively conform
their lives to the unifying teachings
of the Cause.*
                    —The Universal House of Justice

THE MORAL IMPERATIVE

It is evident that the Bahá'í Faith occupies a distinctive position among the religions of the world in the strength of its commitment to the equality of men and women and in the uncompromising integration of this principle into the entire body of its teachings, with due allowance for the necessary differentiation of functions.

From a Bahá'í perspective, the purpose of religion is the spiritual transformation of human values and behavior on both an individual and social level. Consequently, the Bahá'í Faith places great emphasis on implementing its teachings, giving special attention to those teachings, such as equality of the sexes, that differ from prevailing custom or practice.

Chapters 5 and 6 described efforts made progressively under the direction of the Head of the Faith to bring about this implementation within the Bahá'í community and also, through example and encouragement, in the wider society. The distinguishing characteristics of this endeavor are consistency of effort and patience in recognizing the magnitude and implications of the attitudinal and behavioral changes that are being called for. Bahá'ís freely admit that the process is incomplete, as the habits of centuries must be changed, and the disruption to traditional practices addressed. Through the Bahá'í teachings, both men and women are being assisted to transform the most personal aspects of their domestic lives and the most intimate of their social relationships. Bahá'ís throughout the world can quite properly represent themselves as a community of people who are committed, by the explicit precepts of their religion, to the equality of men and women, a community of people who are making an earnest and sustained endeavor to put this principle into practice. Much has been accomplished, and the achievement thus far is most impressive, but much more remains to be done.

The central issue is the emancipation of one-half of the entire human race from the restrictions under which it has labored for countless centuries. To Bahá'ís this is far more than a matter of social amelioration or harmony, and its benefits transcend the release of vastly greater energy and capability for the advancement of civilization. Rather, Bahá'ís regard the issue as essentially one of morality, anchored in belief in the worth of the human soul and the necessity of liberating the spirit for the worship of God. Therefore the imperative that drives Bahá'ís to the practice of equality is that of their duty to their Creator and their eternal quest for spiritual development.

Here we are concerned with the role of the individual Bahá'í, as a member of a local Bahá'í community, in implementing the equality of the sexes in his or her daily life. Drawing heavily on earlier chapters, we will explore personal applications of the various elements of the Bahá'í teachings discussed in those chapters. The approach outlined here is essentially an application of the general method prescribed for putting into practice all of the principles of the Bahá'í Faith. We will first present a general treatment of the implementation of Bahá'í teachings, which will provide a suitable framework for focusing on applying the principle of the equality of men and women.

TRANSLATING THE BAHÁ'Í TEACHINGS
INTO PRACTICE

Analysis of the method by which a Bahá'í endeavors to express the Bahá'í teachings through personal conduct must take account of the essentially spiritual nature of this process. It must also give due consideration to the encouragement and reinforcement obtainable through constructive interaction with the community.

THE SPIRITUAL DIMENSION

Many principles of the Bahá'í Faith, including the oneness of humankind, the importance of universal education, the equality of the sexes, and the necessity for independent investigation of truth and for the eradication of prejudices, are nowadays far from unique to this religion. They are generally accepted as valid by that segment of the wider population which regards itself as enlightened, liberal, or forward-looking. For this reason, in exploring the application of Bahá'í teachings in practical behavior, we must address the question of what there is within the Bahá'í Faith that provides to its adherents a motivational energy for translating the teachings into practice, which surpasses that available to those who are not members. The response to this question may also be of interest to those who find much they consider admirable in the Bahá'í teachings but who have chosen not to become members of the religion, believing they can practice its teachings as completely without the constraints that appear to be inherent in joining an organized religious community.

Enrollment as a member of the Bahá'í Faith depends on one's acceptance of Bahá'u'lláh's claim to be the Manifestation of God Who has brought a Revelation that represents the Word of God for this period in history, which is thus a statement of divine truth. The Bahá'í principle of independent investigation of truth requires that such a claim not be accepted blindly, but rather that the inquirer be satisfied of its validity through examination of the pertinent evidence. The nature of this evidence will be different for each person but may well include the quality of Bahá'u'lláh's life, the nature of His teachings, His fulfillment of prophetic expectation, or the appropriateness of His precepts for the needs of the time. Belief is ultimately a matter of faith, which transcends rational analysis but does not contradict it. Hence acceptance of Bahá'u'lláh's claim is not based on blind faith, but follows as a consequence of an investigative process in which the power of reason usually plays a most valuable role.

A Bahá'í is motivated to follow the teachings of Bahá'u'lláh because of the conviction that they are derived from the Will of God. This conviction provides a far stronger motivation than the wish to create a society that is more equitable or just, or the desire to secure human rights. A believer is impelled to pursue the challenging task of translating the Bahá'í teachings into practice from the knowledge that they represent the path to spiritual development, to the liberation of the human spirit, and to the achievement of a true sense of happiness and fulfillment. The Universal House of Justice writes,

> Just as there are laws governing our physical lives, requiring that we must supply our bodies with certain foods, maintain them within a certain range of temperatures, and so forth, if we wish to avoid physical disabilities, so also there are laws governing our spiritual lives. These laws are revealed to mankind in each age by the Manifestation of God, and obedience to them is of vital importance if each human being, and mankind in general, is to develop properly and harmoniously.[1]

Such a perspective is crucial in providing the will to persevere, as implementation is often difficult, requiring that prejudices be overcome and that new patterns of thought, attitude, and practical activity be acquired and sustained.

A survey of the spiritual dimension would be incomplete without mention of its most mysterious aspect, the energizing factor described in religious literature, and especially in that of the Bahá'í Faith, as the power of the Holy Spirit. Modern science recognizes and provides some understanding of invisible force fields that act over a distance—for example, electromagnetism, gravity, and the forces at work within the nucleus of an atom. The Bahá'í writings indicate that the power of the Holy Spirit operates within the world of creation. 'Abdu'l-Bahá states, "We understand that the Holy Spirit is the energizing factor in the life of man." He also explains, "It is only by the breath of the Holy Spirit that spiritual development can come about." He describes the Holy Spirit as that which gives "light and life to the souls of men."[2] From these and other passages in the Bahá'í writings it is clear that this power provides a source of motivation and energy for putting into practice the teachings, far beyond that associated with human power alone. Bahá'ís believe that their acceptance of Bahá'u'lláh's claim to be the Manifestation of God for this age, together with their sincere endeavors to practice these teachings, gives them access to a fresh outpouring of the power of the Holy Spirit. Consciousness of the reality and potential of this power is the source of that optimism about the ability of human beings to change their attitudes and values which characterizes the Bahá'í perspective on the future condition of humanity.

INDIVIDUAL CONDUCT

The Bahá'í writings provide clear guidance on the manner in which the individual should proceed in the process of transforming personal values and conduct, which is the central purpose of the Bahá'í Faith. The process begins with an effort to put its teachings into practice. As mentioned before, the very act of striving itself attracts the power of the Holy Spirit, which reinforces and magnifies the initial effort, no matter how puny it may have been. Shoghi Effendi writes, through his secretary, that "the very act of striving to serve, however unworthy one may feel, attracts the blessings of God and enables one to become more fitted for the task." Shoghi Effendi also writes, through his secretary, "The harder you strive to attain your goal, the greater will be the confirmations of Bahá'u'lláh, and the more certain you can feel to attain success."[3]

The process of personal transformation is essentially cyclic, occurring through the constructive interaction between effort and spiritual powers. The initial effort attracts energizing power, whose influence enables the individual to make a greater effort, thus attracting a larger measure of spiritual power and conducing to even greater effort, and so on. More detailed scrutiny of the Bahá'í writings indicates that the process is somewhat more complicated than set out here, due to such factors as tests and setbacks, and the operation of the spiritual and material natures in human makeup, but its basic feature is as described.

For this reason, the individual Bahá'í is enjoined to make a start in the implementation process, with full confidence that this beginning will, with perseverance, lead to great change in the course of time. The intrinsically devotional practices of the Bahá'í teachings—including prayer, an annual nineteen-day period of fasting, and reading the sacred words of the Manifestation of God daily*—all serve the vital purpose of providing the believer with a measure of the spiritual power necessary to transform individual conduct. A letter written on behalf of the Guardian states,

---

* See Shahin Vafai, *The Path Toward Spirituality: Sacred Duties and Practices of the Bahá'í Life* (Riviera Beach, Fla.: Palabra Publications, 1996).

The power of God can entirely transmute our characters and make of us beings entirely unlike our previous selves. Through prayer and supplication, obedience to the divine laws Bahá'u'lláh has revealed, and ever-increasing service to His Faith, we can change ourselves.[4]

An important component in this process of spiritual growth and development is that of a constructive periodic review and assessment. 'Abdu'l-Bahá expresses this need in graphical and poetic terms:

> Therefore I say that man must travel in the way of God. Day by day he must endeavor to become better, his belief must increase and become firmer, his good qualities and his turning to God must be greater, the fire of his love must flame more brightly; then day by day he will make progress, for to stop advancing is the means of going back. The bird when he flies soars ever higher and higher, for as soon as he stops flying he will come down. Every day, in the morning when arising you should compare today with yesterday and see in what condition you are. If you see your belief is stronger and your heart more occupied with God and your love increased and your freedom from the world greater then thank God and ask for the increase of these qualities. You must begin to pray and repent for all that you have done that is wrong and you must implore and ask for help and assistance that you may become better than yesterday so that you may continue to make progress.[5]

Such periodic assessment is not confined to a daily cycle. The devotional activities of Bahá'í life include the observance, at various times in the year, of Bahá'í holy days that commemorate significant Bahá'í anniversaries. On nine of these holy days, work is to be suspended whenever possible, and it is usual for each Bahá'í community to hold devotional meetings on such occasions. These special days provide a useful opportunity for all Bahá'ís to interrupt the routine of their daily lives and to reflect on their endeavors to progress spiritually.

Another important cyclic event in Bahá'í devotional life is that of the nineteen-day period of fasting, from sunrise to sunset, in March every year. The significance of this practice is explained by the Guardian in a letter written on his behalf in January 1936:

> It is essentially a period of meditation and prayer, of spiritual recuperation, during which the believer must strive to make the necessary readjustments in his inner life, and to refresh and reinvigorate the spiritual forces latent in his soul. Its significance and purpose are, therefore, fundamentally spiritual in character. Fasting is symbolic, and a reminder of abstinence from selfish and carnal desires.[6]

There are, of course, hazards associated with the prescription for periodic self-assessment. It is a private and intensely personal matter in a religion that is devoid of priesthood, confession of sins, or ecclesiastical authority. The individual must avoid both the extreme of complacent review, which could lead to smug self-satisfaction and passivity, and the other extreme, a ruthless and condemnatory self-assessment, which could give rise to self-defeating feelings of discouragement and hopelessness.

Again, the Bahá'í teachings attach great importance to effort, since it attracts the reinforcing spiritual powers, the blessings of God. This emphasis on effort is highly significant. When the primary value is placed on achievement rather than effort, the way is open for individuals to conclude that they have attained an exalted state of spiritual development and that they are no longer required to exert themselves to effect further improvement in their condition; the consequence is often arrogance or sanctimoniousness. The emphasis on effort offers reassurance and encouragement to those believers who mistakenly feel that past irreligious acts render their condition hopeless beyond redemption; they may legitimately take comfort in knowing that their commitment to effort satisfies the primary Bahá'í needs. This does not mean that achievement is unimportant; rather, the emphasis on effort is an example of the process orientation of the Bahá'í teachings, and of the confidence conveyed in these teachings, that sustained effort, reinforced by the power of the Holy Spirit, will succeed in effecting transformation.

The entire range of Bahá'í teachings on personal conduct make up an integrated and interdependent whole, and a Bahá'í is naturally expected, as a follower of Bahá'u'lláh, to endeavor sincerely to put them all into practice without reservation. It would be a logical contradiction for a Bahá'í to decide, for example, to defer any attempt to practice racial equality until he or she has succeeded in overcoming delinquency in other areas of behavior. In like manner no Bahá'í can properly decide not to make a commitment to practice the equality of the sexes until other aspects of personal behavior have been rectified. In this connection it is interesting to read the response given by the Guardian in a letter written on his behalf to an individual who was apparently inquiring what would be his spiritual condition before God if he were to maintain delinquency in one aspect of his behavior, in this case sexual misconduct, while striving to follow other aspects of the Bahá'í teachings:

> God judges each soul on its own merits. The Guardian cannot tell you what the attitude of God would be towards a person who lives a good life in most ways, but not in this

way. All he can tell you is that it is forbidden by Bahá'u'lláh, and that one so afflicted should struggle and struggle again to overcome it. We must be hopeful of God's Mercy but not impose upon it.[7]

The Bahá'í principles of personal conduct describe the attributes that a believer is expected to strive to express in daily life. They do not set out precise rules of behavior to be followed in a mechanical and inflexible manner. There is room to express individual personality differences and cultural diversity, but within the limits prescribed by the teachings; racial discrimination or prejudiced behavior toward women can never be justified on the basis that they are part of a time-honored cultural tradition. Using the Bahá'í teachings as a reference standard, a believer will naturally develop powers of good judgment in the process of making everyday decisions about personal conduct. In response to a request from a Bahá'í for a precise set of regulations to cover one aspect of Bahá'í conduct, the Universal House of Justice states, in a letter written on its behalf,

It is neither possible nor desirable for the Universal House of Justice to set forth a set of rules covering every situation. Rather it is the task of the individual believer to determine, according to his own prayerful understanding of the Writings, precisely what his course of conduct should be in relation to situations which he encounters in his daily life. If he is to fulfil his true mission in life as a follower of the Blessed Perfection, he will pattern his life according to the Teachings. The believer cannot attain this objective merely by living according to a set of rigid regulations. When his life is oriented toward service to Bahá'u'lláh, and when every conscious act is performed within this frame of reference, he will not fail to achieve the true purpose of his life. Therefore, every believer must continually study the sacred Writings and the instructions of the beloved Guardian, striving always to attain a new and better understanding of their import to him and to his society. He should pray fervently for Divine Guidance, wisdom and strength to do what is pleasing to God, and to serve Him at all times and to the best of his ability.[8]

Both observation and experience confirm that the endeavor to apply the Bahá'í teachings on personal behavior is spiritually and intellectually liberating and that it leads to a richness of experience and insight far removed from the fettered thinking, narrow outlook, and limited experience so often associated with the observance of religious precepts in the wider society.

INTERACTION WITH SOCIETY

In contrast to the prevailing view of many religions, the Bahá'í Faith does not regard the spiritual development of the individual as something that is best accomplished in seclusion. Its prescription for spiritual advancement does not call for isolation from the world of social intercourse and commerce, nor does it advocate withdrawal to remote locations for the purpose of total absorption in devotional pursuits.

Rather, the Bahá'í teachings inform us that the individual can best accomplish the goal of personal transformation through involvement in human society and through continued interaction with others in a community. This view rests on the recognition of the interconnection between the external and the internal, the wider social and physical environment interacting with the inner spiritual development. Shoghi Effendi addresses this fundamental issue in a letter written on his behalf, stating,

We cannot segregate the human heart from the environment outside us and say that once one of these is reformed everything will be improved. Man is organic with the world. His inner life moulds the environment and is itself also deeply affected by it. The one acts upon the other and every abiding change in the life of man is the result of these mutual reactions.

No movement in the world directs its attention upon both these aspects of human life and has full measures for their improvement, save the teachings of Bahá'u'lláh. And this is its distinctive feature. If we desire therefore the good of the world we should strive to spread those teachings and also practise them in our own life. Through them will the human heart be changed, and also our social environment provides the atmosphere in which we can grow spiritually and reflect in full the light of God shining through the revelation of Bahá'u'lláh.[9]

The aim of the Bahá'í teachings is to create conditions under which this interaction between individual and society is constructive and mutually beneficial, leading simultaneously to individual progression, the advance of civilization, the growth of social cohesion, and the best use of the physical environment. Indeed the features of this interactive relationship provide a useful framework in which to consider the wide scope of these teachings and to examine the diverse aspects of Bahá'í activity and plans.

The interdependence of the individual and society is mentioned by the Universal House of Justice in reference to personal obedience to the laws the Manifestation of God gives to humanity:

These laws are revealed to mankind in each age by the Manifestation of God, and obedience to them is of vital importance if each human being, and mankind in general, is to develop properly and harmoniously. Moreover, these various aspects are interdependent. If an individual violates the spiritual laws for his own development he will cause injury not only to himself but to the society in which he lives. Similarly, the condition of society has a direct effect on the individuals who must live within it.[10]

A Bahá'í striving to put the teachings into practice can well expect the Bahá'í community to provide a welcoming and accepting environment in which each member can initiate attempts to implement behaviors that may be novel or socially unpopular, as in the efforts to eradicate racial prejudice, to treat minorities with the respect and courtesy due to them, and to practice the equality of the sexes. As the community matures and develops, it more closely approaches the ideal of providing an environment of mutual encouragement in which experiences can be shared, the example of others drawn upon, and courage and motivation augmented. Responding to a question addressed to him, Shoghi Effendi explains in a letter written on his behalf that

> The Bahá'í community life provides you with an indispensable laboratory, where you can translate into living and constructive action the principles which you imbibe from the Teachings. By becoming a real part of that living organism you can catch the real spirit which runs throughout the Bahá'í Teachings. To study the principles, and to try to live according to them, are, therefore, the two essential mediums through which you can ensure the development and progress of your inner spiritual life and of your outer existence as well.[11]

No consideration of the approach to be used by the individual in putting into practice the Bahá'í teachings on personal conduct is complete without addressing this interaction with the community. The Bahá'í teachings characterize the community, at its various levels—local, national, and international—as an organic unit that is, in the words of the Universal House of Justice,

> united in its aspirations, unified in its methods, seeking assistance and confirmation from the same Source, and illumined with the conscious knowledge of its unity. Therefore, in this organic, divinely guided, blessed and illumined body the participation of every believer is of the utmost importance, and is a source of power and vitality as yet unknown to us.[12]

The formula for progressively attaining this glorious condition is provided by the Universal House of Justice:

> . . . the friends should love each other, constantly encourage each other, work together, be as one soul in one body, and in so doing become a true, organic, healthy body animated and illumined by the spirit. In such a body all will receive spiritual health and vitality from the organism itself, and the most perfect flowers and fruits will be brought forth.[13]

In a growing Bahá'í community that seeks to welcome into its midst people at all stages of development, there will arise occasionally flagrant examples of individual malfunctioning and failure to follow the Bahá'í teachings. A religion such as the Bahá'í Faith, which places its primary emphasis on effort, which is oriented to process and to evolutionary change, and which is founded on a realistic perspective of the complexities of human nature, regards as natural the struggle to accomplish spiritual objectives and the shortcomings that occur in the course of this endeavor.

The response of a Bahá'í to the awareness that a fellow believer appears to be failing to make a reasonable effort to follow the teachings must always be devoid of backbiting. The Guardian states in a letter written on his behalf that

> ... one of the first essentials insisted on by Bahá'u'lláh and 'Abdu'l-Bahá is that we resist the natural tendency to let our attention dwell on the faults and failings of others rather than on our own. Each of us is responsible for one life only, and that is our own. Each of us is immeasurably far from being "perfect as our heavenly father is perfect" and the task of perfecting our own life and character is one that requires all our attention, our will-power and energy. . . .
>
> On no subject are the Bahá'í teachings more emphatic than on the necessity to abstain from faultfinding and backbiting while being ever eager to discover and root out our own faults and overcome our own failings.[14]

In many instances, a Bahá'í should endeavor not to dwell on the apparent inadequacy of the behavior of fellow believers, much less become preoccupied with it. One should strive to follow the Guardian's admonition, in a letter written on his behalf, that "The greater the patience, the loving understanding and the forbearance the believers show towards each other and their shortcomings, the greater will be the progress of the whole Bahá'í Community at large."[15] This calls for a nonjudgmental and uncensorious attitude animated by a recognition that we are all children of God, striving to overcome attitudes and behaviors acquired in the past that are inconsistent with the Bahá'í teachings. We can very often best assist others through the power of personal example, when it is presented without a sense of superiority, and through prayer for ourselves and others proceeding along the stony path of spiritual development.

Magnanimity is required when a Bahá'í detects in other believers attitudes that cause concern, such as unconscious prejudice or subtle discrimination. To preserve the unity of the community so that it can continue to attract spiritual powers generally mandates a response of forbearance and charity when it is clear that the offending behavior is unintentional and is not motivated by disdain for the precepts of the Faith.

In some instances, close friendship and good rapport may allow a believer to draw to the attention of another Bahá'í, in a tactful and discreet manner, the need or opportunity for further development through modification of a specific aspect of behavior, provided this can be done without conveying the impression of prying into another's private affairs or of presuming to tell others how they should conduct their lives. It may be possible, sometimes, to draw attention to relevant Bahá'í principles in a general community discussion in the hope that the individual who is apparently in need will be reminded and thus impelled toward renewed endeavor; here, also, wisdom, sensitivity, and purity of motive are needed to avoid remarks that are so pointed as to make evident the target to which they are being directed.

There remain instances in which the range of responses set out above is inadequate. A believer's conduct may appear to be a blatant and flagrant violation of explicit Bahá'í teachings, which is inimical to the welfare and best interests of the Faith or which adversely affects the reputation of the Bahá'í community in the larger society. Another instance is when a Bahá'í experiences unwarranted distress because of the manner in which he or she is being treated by another Bahá'í, perhaps through intentional belittling or discrimination or because of some other moral or ethical delinquency. In such cases the avenue for rectifying the situation is for the believer troubled by the misconduct to take the matter to the Spiritual Assembly, motivated by a desire to protect the welfare of the community or to seek justice from that Bahá'í institution charged with the responsibility to maintain and safeguard justice. This action should not be misconstrued as backbiting, because it is a report made to an institution of the Faith and is not disseminated among the rank and file of the community. It is not an affront to the unity of the Bahá'í community but is, on the contrary, a measure taken to preserve that unity; in the Bahá'í teachings, unity rests on the strong foundation of adherence to principle and not on the shifting sands of compromise and pretense. A Spiritual Assembly also has the function of intervening when a believer appears not to be making a sincere effort to conform to the Bahá'í standard of conduct and is having a harmful effect on others.

APPLYING THE PRINCIPLE OF EQUALITY OF THE SEXES

A sustained endeavor by all Bahá'ís is necessary for the expression in practice of the principle of the equality of the sexes. In addition efforts are needed to incorporate fully the practice of this principle in marriage and family relationships and in Bahá'í community functioning.

At the Individual Level

Earlier chapters of this book emphasize the great importance attached to the application in daily life of the principle of the equality of the sexes, as well as the progressive measures undertaken by the Head of the Faith to bring about this implemention. The approach to be used at the individual level to achieve this objective is summarized in the following passage written on behalf of the Universal House of Justice:

The principle of the equality between women and men, like the other teachings of the Faith, can be effectively and universally established among the friends when it is pursued in conjunction with all the other aspects of Bahá'í life. Change is an evolutionary process requiring patience with one's self and others, loving education and the passage of time as the believers deepen their knowledge of the principles of the Faith, gradually discard long-held traditional attitudes and progressively conform their lives to the unifying teachings of the Cause.[16]

The approach to be adopted by the individual can well be viewed within the general framework set out above, and the considerations discussed there are as applicable to this principle of the Faith as to any other Bahá'í precept.

As mentioned earlier, an important feature of individual effort is the periodic review of one's actions and attitudes. In their efforts to implement the principle of equality of the sexes, both men and women must strive to accomplish this objective, and both should carry out this periodic review. In so doing they could well examine whether they have unconsciously adopted prejudices that are prevalent in the larger society, reflecting attitudes derived from the past and taken for granted. Stereotypic thinking based on unwarranted generalizations about women and about men should be carefully identified and progressively eliminated, while recognizing that the equality expressed in the Bahá'í teachings accommodates the inherent physiological differences between men and women and some appropriate differentiations of function. Periodic self-assessment should not exclude habits of speech and conduct unwittingly derived from attitudes of inequality that may have become part of one's behavior. Particular attention should be given to the use of humor; while it does have a legitimate, and indeed valuable, role in social intercourse, it can also inflict humiliation or wounds when used inappropriately or unthinkingly. A regrettable feature of the quest for equality of the sexes in the larger society has been the argumentation and contention that have at times arisen between men and women, leading to a polarization of attitudes and mutual recrimination. It is essential that Bahá'í men and women exercise restraint to prevent such destructive attitudes from entering Bahá'í discourse. 'Abdu'l-Bahá asserts, "Divine Justice demands that the rights of both sexes should be equally respected since neither is superior to the other in the eyes of Heaven. Dignity before God depends, not on sex, but on purity and luminosity of heart. Human virtues belong equally to all!" In His advice to some Bahá'í women, 'Abdu'l-Bahá writes, "I appeal to you to obliterate this contention between men and women," while He also warns that "the assumption of superiority by man will continue to be depressing to the ambition of woman, as if her attainment to equality was creationally impossible; woman's aspiration toward advancement will be checked by it, and she will gradually become hopeless."[17]

During a period when the suffragette movement was creating agitation in England, 'Abdu'l-Bahá stated that "Demonstrations of force, such as are now taking place in England, are neither becoming nor effective in the cause of womanhood and equality." However, He also pointed out that "When men own the equality of women there will be no need for them to struggle for their rights!"[18]

The Bahá'í Faith looks with respect and appreciation at the cultural diversity of humankind and does not seek to establish the dominance of any particular culture, much less to create a sterile uniformity of cultural expression. It is, nonetheless, unyielding in asserting that cultural traditions that contradict fundamental Bahá'í principles such as the equality of the sexes must give way to the Bahá'í teachings, which are accepted by the followers of Bahá'u'lláh as the Message of God for this time in history. Thus the Universal House of Justice, in a letter to the Bahá'ís in the Pacific region, states,

> In many of the nations of your area, women have traditionally been restricted to a secondary role in the life of society. We call upon the Bahá'í women of these countries, assured of the support and encouragement of all elements of the Bahá'í community, to demonstrate the transforming power of this Revelation by their courage and initiative in the teaching work and their full participation in the administrative activities of the Faith.[19]

The Bahá'ís of the Indian subcontinent are addressed in these terms:

> . . . we call upon you to give special attention to the advancement of women. In almost all of your region, women have traditionally played a secondary role in the life of society, a condition which is still reflected in many Bahá'í communities. Effective measures have to be adopted to help women take their rightful place in the teaching and administrative fields.[20]

It would be a distortion of the Bahá'í teachings for either men or women to regard the achievement of equality as a matter of concern only to the members of the opposite sex rather than a need calling for sustained cooperative action on the part of both sexes. Encouragement plays an important role; the Universal House of Justice, in a 1979 message to the Bahá'ís of the world, calls for "the encouragement of Bahá'í women to exercise to the full their privileges and responsibilities in the work of the community," while a similar message in 1984 reiterates that "Bahá'í women and girls must be encouraged to take part in the social, spiritual and administrative activities of their communities."[21] Clearly, such encouragement can only be effective if it is sincere and springs from genuine conviction; a mechanical recital of positive statements will have little effect. The peerless example of 'Abdu'l-Bahá provides both an inspiration and a model to those who wish to encourage women in their development.

Not only should men commit themselves to encouraging women in their aspirations and exertions, but so also should women receive encouragement from other women, most especially from those who have been successful in their endeavors. The enlarged context within which 'Abdu'l-Bahá sets the principle of equality of men and women provides a useful basis from which a genuine commitment to the encouragement of women can be derived. Of particular significance are His statements affirming that the full development of men cannot be accomplished without the full development of women, and that this mutual development is a prerequisite for happiness in the world. It is also apparent that He was well aware how great must be the effort made by women to achieve that level of development consistent with the expression of equality, and that He summoned women to arise and make the necessary exertions and to strive to overcome their fears and apprehensions in the process.

WITHIN MARRIAGE AND FAMILY

No more dramatic demonstration of the transformation wrought by the Bahá'í teachings can be found than in the creation of Bahá'í marriage and family relationships that illustrate the equality of the sexes. The expression of equality in these most personal of human relationships with a marriage partner who is fully familiar with one's true feelings, attitudes, and values sets Bahá'í practice apart from the superficial assertions of equality that prevail in the larger society and which reduce to hypocrisy when subject to scrutiny in the domestic setting.

We have in earlier chapters surveyed the Bahá'í teachings on marriage and family relationships and described the pertinent Bahá'í laws. The challenge to every Bahá'í married couple is to apply these teachings to create a marriage in which equality is expressed. The magnitude of this task should not be underestimated, for it requires the development of a relationship far different from that found in any existing religious or cultural tradition, all of which are derived from the inequality of ages past. Meeting the challenge requires scrutiny of behavioral patterns that might otherwise be taken for granted and entails mutual encouragement and support in gradually adopting new modes of conduct.

Central to the endeavor to create such a marriage are the statements in the Bahá'í writings about consultative decision making in which neither husband nor wife has a dominant role. This is even more important with couples who have wide differences in knowledge, experience, education, or stature in the wider society. The call to avoid domination does not preclude according due weight to the expertise one partner may have on a particular subject, but requires mutual respect and consideration as well as the avoidance of such destructive practices as the use of psychological pressure, subtle forms of humiliation, or statements that might lower the self-esteem and self-confidence of one's spouse.

The Bahá'í teachings exclude a rigid definition of sex roles, although certain primary responsibilities are assigned. Personal circumstances and time constraints due to employment, study, health, or interests will determine the extent to which each marriage partner participates in domestic duties within the home and in the activities of the external society. Such matters should be determined through consultation so that neither partner feels as if he or she has been treated unfairly; this also paves the way for varying arrangements as circumstances change. It is important that there not be introduced into the initial phase of this consultation any constraints that have no basis in the Bahá'í teachings, such as the restriction of women to being occupied only with domestic functions, which is contrary to the authoritative texts of the Faith. A letter written on behalf of the Universal House of Justice states in response to a question, ". . . the decision concerning the amount of time a mother may spend in working outside the home depends on circumstances existing within the home, which may vary from time to time. Family consultation will help to provide the answers. . . ."[22] Likewise the Bahá'í teachings place no constraint on the participation of men in the performance of domestic functions as conditions dictate; mention has been made of the words of Bahíyyih Khánum about Bahá'u'lláh Himself helping Navváb with cooking and other domestic duties, and 'Abdu'l-Bahá's involvement in even the most mundane aspects of work in the home is well documented.

Even more important than the actual division of work in the marriage is the value attached to the functions performed within the home, which have traditionally been dismissed as requiring minimal skills and having negligible status. In stark contrast to such attitudes, the Universal House of Justice writes, in a letter prepared on its behalf in response to a question about the Bahá'í admonition that all must perform useful work in society, "Homemaking is a highly honourable and responsible work of fundamental importance for mankind. . . ."[23] Bahá'ís must necessarily strive to conform their own perspective on domestic work to that of the Faith, thus acquiring a heightened apprecia-

tion of the complex functions of management, resource allocation, counseling, and forward planning that are typically part
of present-day homemaking.

A vital feature of the practice of equality of the sexes within
the family is the restoration of motherhood to a position of
honor and respect, as described in chapter 3, where we explored
the relationship of the practice of such equality in the family
setting to the attainment of peace.

A statement prepared in 1997 by the National Spiritual Assembly of the Bahá'ís of the United States draws attention to
the implications of such an appreciation for motherhood:

> Reverence for, and protection of, motherhood have often
> been used as justification for keeping women socially and
> economically disadvantaged. It is this discriminatory and
> injurious result that must change. Great honor and nobility
> are rightly conferred on the station of motherhood and the
> importance of training children. Addressing the high station
> of motherhood, the Bahá'í Writings state, "O ye loving moth-
> ers, know ye that in God's sight, the best of all ways to wor-
> ship Him is to educate the children and train them in all the
> perfections of humankind. . . ." The great challenge facing
> society is to make social and economic provisions for the
> full and equal participation of women in all aspects of life
> while simultaneously reinforcing the critical functions of
> motherhood.[24]

As society moves gradually toward accomplishing this change
in attitudes toward motherhood, it is important to avoid building an adversarial relationship between those mothers who
choose to devote themselves fully to bringing up their children
and those who, for various reasons, seek part-time or full-time
remunerative employment outside the home.

In a Bahá'í family that is striving to implement the equality of the sexes, the nature of the children's education, both informal and formal, requires attention and monitoring. This process of implementation is necessarily progressive, occurring over an extended period of many generations; however, rapid progress can be made in a single generation by taking measures to prevent inadvertently transmitting harmful attitudes to the new generation. Both fathers and mothers should take care that their sons do not adopt an attitude of superiority toward females; such an attitude may well result, for example, if the sons are given privileges, attention, and praise much greater than that accorded to the daughters, or if the girls are trained to defer always to their brothers. Parents should also ensure that their daughters' legitimate aspirations are encouraged and that their desire for education and for accomplishment in the arts, crafts, and sciences is fostered when suitable opportunities are available. Adherence to the Bahá'í principle that, when circumstances restrict the accessibility of educational resources, priority be given to girls, will do much to bring about progress and enlightenment over time.

WITHIN THE COMMUNITY

The constructive interaction that takes place between the individual and the Bahá'í community as the principles of the Faith are implemented has been discussed above. The measure of support to be provided by the community regarding the equality of the sexes is found in a 1975 message of the Universal House of Justice to all National Spiritual Assemblies that states, ". . . the entire Bahá'í world is committed to encouraging and stimulating the vital role of women in the Bahá'í community as well as in society at large. . . ." So unequivocal a statement can well be regarded as a reiteration of 'Abdu'l-Bahá's categoric pronouncement that "The members of the Spiritual Assembly should do all they can to provide encouragement to the women believers."[25] There are many ways in which the Bahá'í community can fulfill this aspect of its functions. Clearly, much will depend on the particular needs and circumstances in each region of the world, but it is possible to identify some generally applicable lines of action.

The study programs that form part of Bahá'í community life are enriched if the range of topics studied incorporates exploration of the application in daily life of the principle of the equality of men and women. Such courses are enhanced by including within their compass the study of the lives of Bahá'í women who have performed heroic services to the Faith and whose courage, indomitable faith, and strength of will enabled them to overcome whatever barriers they encountered.

The Spiritual Assembly can render an important service by monitoring the conduct and characteristics of its community to determine what actions will advance the process of implementing the equality of the sexes. It may find that encouragement should be given to help change attitudes that are detrimental to the pursuit of equality. Positive measures may be required to prevent the women of the community from being relegated to no more than a stereotypic role in community affairs; the Assembly would be well advised to actively seek ways to create new opportunities for women to acquire experience in diverse aspects of community activity and to allow women to demonstrate their capabilities. In designating its representatives on public occasions, in selecting the members of its committees, and in encouraging universal participation in Nineteen Day Feast consultation, the Spiritual Assembly can make a distinctive contribution to the development of human resources in the community and to the advancement of women.

The Spiritual Assembly can also be a most useful source of advice and encouragement to Bahá'í women in their endeavors to discharge their responsibilities in teaching the Faith to others. As 'Abdu'l-Bahá states,

> Women must make the greatest effort to acquire spiritual power and to increase in the virtue of wisdom and holiness until their enlightenment and striving succeeds in bringing about the unity of mankind. They must work with a burning enthusiasm to spread the Teaching of Bahá'u'lláh among the peoples, so that the radiant light of the Divine Bounty may envelop the souls of all the nations of the world![26]

Since the mother is specified to be the first educator of the child, the role of the Spiritual Assembly includes providing whatever assistance is needed to carry out this essential function. 'Abdu'l-Bahá writes,

> It is incumbent upon the Spiritual Assemblies to provide the mothers with a well-planned program for the education of children, showing how, from infancy, the child must be watched over and taught. These instructions must be given to every mother to serve her as a guide, so that each will train and nurture her children in accordance with the Teachings.[27]

Involving women in this primary educative role provides a useful springboard from which to foster a greater involvement of women in a wider range of developmental activities. A letter written on its behalf conveys the guidance that "The House of Justice regards the need to educate and guide women in their primary responsibility as mothers as an excellent opportunity for organizing women's activities. Your efforts should focus on helping them in their function as educators of the rising generation. . . ."[28]

The importance of the education of women and girls has already been discussed in chapter 2. The Spiritual Assembly can, when necessary, provide encouragement to Bahá'í parents to see that their daughters are educated and can assist them in identifying resources that will aid the process. In some instances, the required action may be the provision of basic literacy classes to those in need, including adult women who were deprived of opportunities when they were girls.

By means such as those identified here, the organic life of the Bahá'í community is strengthened, its distinctive character is clarified, and progress toward its goal is accelerated.

FACING THE FUTURE WITH CONFIDENCE

The exploration of the equality of the sexes presented in this book emphasizes the spiritual equality of men and women, which has been an unchanging feature of every revealed religion in the history of humanity. Because of the circumstances in the past, including the nature of society in which physical force and warfare played so dominant a role, it was not possible for women to obtain social equality in status, freedom, and opportunities. The situation was greatly complicated by the departure of the religions of the past from the purity of their original teachings and by the consequent oppressive conditions which very often denied women the spiritual equality to which they were entitled.

The vast process of social evolution, occurring over thousands of years, has now reached its climax with the inauguration of a new period in history that is to be distinguished by justice, unity, and freedom. An essential feature of this new period is the attainment and perpetuation of the equality of the sexes in all of its aspects. The Bahá'í Faith provides the spiritual impulse designed to bring about the transformation of values and attitudes together with the consequent new forms of individual and social behavior that will reinforce and sustain this evolutionary process.

Such a fundamental change in the nature of human life and relationships cannot be accomplished instantaneously, especially if it is to endure and become an established part of the world of the future. The chapters of this book devoted to implementation of the principle of the equality of the sexes show how its implications have progressively been clarified and applied during the several decades of the Bahá'í Faith. It is clearly recognized that progressive application carries with it the danger of procrastination or unwarranted deferral, which are avoided in the Bahá'í Faith because of its cohesive organization under the guidance of a central head, the Universal House of Justice, to which all Bahá'ís must turn.

Adherents of this religion are required, as a matter of belief, to commit themselves to accepting all of the principles ordained by Bahá'u'lláh, including that of the equality of men and women. This begins a lifelong process of implementation, which is carried out in a mutually reinforcing manner at individual, family, and community levels. The record of Bahá'í achievement shows continuing progress toward the ideal, together with a steady increase in the influence in the wider society both of Bahá'í example and of the advice on social development and progress offered by Bahá'í institutions.

Those who are familiar with the record of religious practice in past ages might well inquire whether the Bahá'í Faith is doomed to suffer a similar fate of deviation from its initial values with the passage of time. Upon what basis can Bahá'ís assert that the purity and integrity of their religious teachings, including that of the equality of the sexes, will not be compromised in the course of decades and centuries? How can they be sure that the denial of freedom and human rights for women will not reemerge? The answers to these questions are to be found in the explicit provisions of the Bahá'í teachings—which have neither precedent nor parallel in any other religion—pertaining to the Covenant by which the authority, unity, and purity of the teachings are preserved. In the clarity and comprehensiveness of its provisions and their unambiguous derivation from explicit statements of Bahá'u'lláh is to be found the ironclad guarantee needed for Bahá'ís to feel fully confident about the future of this religious community and its principles.

Because of this Covenant, progressive implementation can be permitted without fear that practice will be frozen at an intermediate stage short of total fulfillment. The Covenant is the basis for the inversion of past historical practice; here, the successive generations are more able to free themselves from the unconsciously acquired attitudes and practices of the wider society, and so they more closely approach the Bahá'í ideal, which the Covenant protects from corruption or compromise. The preservation of the invariant standard of the Bahá'í teachings also provides freedom for diversity of expression within the boundaries imposed by the principles of the Faith.

By virtue of these considerations Bahá'ís face the future with unshakable confidence. Much remains to be done to complete the God-given task of establishing the equality of the sexes. But there is, to Bahá'ís, no doubt that it will be accomplished and that the aims of the Bahá'í community will be fully realized. The Universal House of Justice assures the members of the Bahá'í Faith that ". . . the Covenant of Bahá'u'lláh will aid them and the institutions of His World Order to see the realization of every principle ordained by His unerring Pen, including the equality of men and women, as expounded in the Writings of the Cause."[29]

Appendix

TWO WINGS OF A BIRD:
THE EQUALITY OF
WOMEN AND MEN

A STATEMENT ISSUED BY THE NATIONAL SPIRITUAL
ASSEMBLY OF THE BAHÁ'ÍS OF THE UNITED STATES

The emancipation of women, the achievement of full equality
between the sexes, is essential to human progress and the transformation of society. Inequality retards not only the advancement of women but the progress of civilization itself. The persistent denial of equality to one-half of the world's population
is an affront to human dignity. It promotes destructive attitudes and habits in men and women that pass from the family
to the workplace, to political life, and, ultimately, to international relations. On no grounds, moral, biological, or traditional, can inequality be justified. The moral and psychological climate necessary to enable our nation to establish social
justice and to contribute to global peace will be created only
when women attain full partnership with men in all fields of
endeavor.[1]

The systematic oppression of women is a conspicuous and
tragic fact of history. Restricted to narrow spheres of activity in
the life of society, denied educational opportunities and basic
human rights, subjected to violence, and frequently treated as
less than human, women have been prevented from realizing
their true potential. Age-old patterns of subordination, reflected
in popular culture, literature and art, law, and even religious
scriptures, continue to pervade every aspect of life. Despite the
advancement of political and civil rights for women in America
and the widespread acceptance of equality in principle, full
equality has not been achieved.

The damaging effects of gender prejudice are a fault line beneath the foundation of our national life. The gains for women rest uneasily on unchanged, often unexamined, inherited assumptions. Much remains to be done. The achievement of full equality requires a new understanding of who we are, what is our purpose in life, and how we relate to one another—an understanding that will compel us to reshape our lives and thereby our society.

At no time since the founding of the women's rights movement in America has the need to focus on this issue been greater. We stand at the threshold of a new century and a new millennium. Their challenges are already upon us, influencing our families, our lifestyles, our nation, our world. In the process of human evolution, the ages of infancy and childhood are past. The turbulence of adolescence is slowly and painfully preparing us for the age of maturity, when prejudice and exploitation will be abolished and unity established. The elements necessary to unify peoples and nations are precisely those needed to bring about equality of the sexes and to improve the relationships between women and men. The effort to overcome the history of inequality requires the full participation of every man, woman, youth, and child.

Over a century ago, for the first time in religious history, Bahá'u'lláh, the Founder of the Bahá'í Faith, in announcing God's purpose for the age, proclaimed the principle of the equality of women and men, saying: "Women and men have been and will always be equal in the sight of God."[2] The establishment of equal rights and privileges for women and men, Bahá'u'lláh says, is a precondition for the attainment of a wider unity that will ensure the well-being and security of all peoples. The Bahá'í Writings state emphatically that, "When all mankind shall receive the same opportunity of education and the equality of men and women be realized, the foundations of war will be utterly destroyed."³

Thus the Bahá'í vision of equality between the sexes rests on the central spiritual principle of the oneness of humankind. The principle of oneness requires that we "regard humanity as a single individual, and one's own self as a member of that corporeal form," and that we foster an unshakable consciousness that, "if pain or injury afflicts any member of that body, it must inevitably result in suffering for all the rest."⁴

Bahá'u'lláh teaches that the divine purpose of creation is the achievement of unity among all peoples:

> Know ye not why We created you all from the same dust? That no one should exalt himself over the other. Ponder at all times in your hearts how ye were created. Since We have created you all from one same substance it is incumbent on you to be even as one soul, to walk with the same feet, eat with the same mouth and dwell in the same land, that from your inmost being, by your deeds and actions, the signs of oneness and the essence of detachment may be made manifest.⁵

The full and equal participation of women in all spheres of life is essential to social and economic development, the abolition of war, and the ultimate establishment of a united world. In the Bahá'í Scriptures the equality of the sexes is a cornerstone of God's plan for human development and prosperity:

> The world of humanity is possessed of two wings: the male and the female. So long as these two wings are not equivalent in strength, the bird will not fly. Until womankind reaches the same degree as man, until she enjoys the same arena of activity, extraordinary attainment for humanity will

not be realized; humanity cannot wing its way to heights of real attainment. When the two wings . . . become equivalent in strength, enjoying the same prerogatives, the flight of man will be exceedingly lofty and extraordinary.[6]

The Bahá'í Writings state that to proclaim equality is not to deny that differences in function between women and men exist but rather to affirm the complementary roles men and women fulfill in the home and society at large. Stating that the acquisition of knowledge serves as a "ladder for [human] ascent," Bahá'u'lláh prescribes identical education for women and men but stipulates that, when resources are limited, first priority should be given to the education of women and girls.[7] The education of girls is particularly important because, although both parents have responsibilities for the rearing of children, it is through educated mothers that the benefits of knowledge can be most effectively diffused throughout society.

Reverence for, and protection of, motherhood have often been used as justification for keeping women socially and economically disadvantaged. It is this discriminatory and injurious result that must change. Great honor and nobility are rightly conferred on the station of motherhood and the importance of training children. Addressing the high station of motherhood, the Bahá'í Writings state, "O ye loving mothers, know ye that in God's sight, the best of all ways to worship Him is to educate the children and train them in all the perfections of humankind. . . ."[8] The great challenge facing society is to make social and economic provisions for the full and equal participation of women in all aspects of life while simultaneously reinforcing the critical functions of motherhood.

Asserting that women and men share similar "station and rank" and "are equally the recipients of powers and endowments from God," the Bahá'í teachings offer a model of equality based on the concept of partnership.[9] Only when women become full participants in all domains of life and enter the important arenas of decision-making will humanity be prepared to embark on the next stage of its collective development.

Bahá'í Scripture emphatically states that women will be the greatest factor in establishing universal peace and international arbitration. "So it will come to pass that when women participate fully and equally in the affairs of the world, when they enter confidently and capably the great arena of laws and politics, war will cease; for woman will be the obstacle and hindrance to it."[10]

The elimination of discrimination against women is a spiritual and moral imperative that must ultimately reshape existing legal, economic, and social arrangements. Promoting the entry of greater numbers of women into positions of prominence and authority is a necessary but not sufficient step in creating a just social order. Without fundamental changes in the attitudes and values of individuals and in the underlying ethos of social institutions full equality between women and men cannot be achieved. A community based on partnership, a community in which aggression and the use of force are supplanted by cooperation and consultation, requires the transformation of the human heart.

The world in the past has been ruled by force, and man has dominated over woman by reason of his more forceful and aggressive qualities both of body and mind. But the balance is already shifting; force is losing its dominance, and mental alertness, intuition, and the spiritual qualities of love and service, in which woman is strong, are gaining ascendancy. Hence the new age will be an age less masculine and more permeated with the feminine ideals . . . an age in which the masculine and feminine elements of civilization will be more evenly balanced.[11]

Men have an inescapable duty to promote the equality of women. The presumption of superiority by men thwarts the ambition of women and inhibits the creation of an environment in which equality may reign. The destructive effects of inequality prevent men from maturing and developing the qualities necessary to meet the challenges of the new millennium. "As long as women are prevented from attaining their highest possibilities," the Bahá'í Writings state, "so long will men be unable to achieve the greatness which might be theirs."[12] It is essential that men engage in a careful, deliberate examination of attitudes, feelings, and behavior deeply rooted in cultural habit that block the equal participation of women and stifle the growth of men. The willingness of men to take responsibility for equality will create an optimum environment for progress: "When men own the equality of women there will be no need for them to struggle for their rights!"[13]

The long-standing and deeply rooted condition of inequality must be eliminated. To overcome such a condition requires the exercise of nothing short of "genuine love, extreme patience, true humility, consummate tact, sound initiative, mature wisdom, and deliberate, persistent, and prayerful effort."[14] Ultimately, Bahá'u'lláh promises, a day will come when men will welcome women in all aspects of life. Now is the time to move decisively toward that promised future.

Notes

CHAPTER 2 / DEFINING EQUALITY

1. See Rosalind Miles, *The Women's History of the World* (London: Michael Joseph, 1988).

2. 'Abdu'l-Bahá, quoted in J. E. Esslemont, *Bahá'u'lláh and the New Era: An Introduction to the Bahá'í Faith,* 5th rev. ed. (Wilmette, Ill.: Bahá'í Publishing Trust, 1980), p. 149.

3. Juanita H. Williams, *Psychology of Women: Behavior in a biosocial context* (New York: W. W. Norton, 1977), p. 2.

4. See Bonnie S. Anderson and Judith P. Zinsser, *A History of Their Own: Women in Europe from Prehistory to the Present* (New York: Harper and Row, 1988), vol. 1, pp. 22–23, 28.

5. 'Abdu'l-Bahá, in *Women: A compilation of extracts from the Bahá'í Writings,* rev. ed. (London: Bahá'í Publishing Trust, 1990), no. 28.

6. 'Abdu'l-Bahá, *Selections from the Writings of 'Abdu'l-Bahá* (Wilmette, Ill.: Bahá'í Publishing Trust, 1997), no. 38.3.

7. 'Abdu'l-Bahá, *The Promulgation of Universal Peace: Talks Delivered by 'Abdu'l-Bahá during His Visit to the United States and Canada in 1912,* new ed. (Wilmette, Ill.: Bahá'í Publishing Trust, 1982), p. 133; 'Abdu'l-Bahá, in *Women,* no. 8; 'Abdu'l-Bahá, *Promulgation,* p. 455.

8. Saint Augustine, quoted in *History of Ideas on Woman: A Source Book,* [ed. Rosemary Agonito], (New York: Perigee Books, 1977), p. 77.

9. 'Abdu'l-Bahá, *Some Answered Questions,* comp. and trans. Laura Clifford Barney (Wilmette, Ill.: Bahá'í Publishing Trust, 1984), p. 123.

10. 'Abdu'l-Bahá, *Some Answered Questions,* pp. 123, 120, 125–26.

11. Saint Thomas Aquinas, quoted in *History of Ideas on Woman,* p. 85.

12. Ibid.

13. Fatima Mernissi, *Women and Islam: An Historical and Theological Enquiry,* trans. Mary Jo Lakeland (Oxford: Blackwell, 1991), pp. 49–61, 64–72.

14. See Mernissi, *Women and Islam,* pp. 62–84.

15. See Maulānā Muḥammad 'Ali, *The Religion of Islām: A Comprehensive Discussion of the Sources, Principles and Practices of Islam* (Lahore, Pakistan: Aḥmadiyya Anjuman Ishā'āt Islam, 1971), pp. 246–48.

16. Letter dated 24 January 1993 written on behalf of the Universal House of Justice to an individual, in *The American Bahá'í* 24, no. 17 (23 Nov. 1993): pp. 10–11.

17. Bahá'u'lláh, in *Women*, nos. 58, 3, 58.

18. 'Abdu'l-Bahá, *Selections*, no. 38.3.

19. 'Abdu'l-Bahá, in *Women*, no. 10.

20. Ibid.

21. The Universal House of Justice, *The Promise of World Peace: To the Peoples of the World* (Wilmette, Ill.: Bahá'í Publishing Trust, 1985), p. 26; Bahá'u'lláh, in *Women*, no. 2; 'Abdu'l-Bahá, *Paris Talks: Addresses Given by 'Abdu'l-Bahá in 1911* (London: Bahá'í Publishing Trust, 1995), nos. 40.33, 50.10.

22. The Universal House of Justice, *Promise of World Peace*, p. 27.

23. Ibid., p. 26; 'Abdu'l-Bahá, *Promulgation*, p. 133.

24. Ibid., p. 135.

25. Ibid., pp. 136–37.

26. Ibid., p. 300.

27. Ibid.

28. Ibid.

29. The Universal House of Justice, *Promise of World Peace*, p. 27.

30. Bahá'u'lláh, *The Kitáb-i-Aqdas: The Most Holy Book,* ps ed. (Wilmette, Ill.: Bahá'í Publishing Trust, 1993), n76; see *Messages from the Universal House of Justice, 1963–1968: The Third Epoch of the Formative Age,* comp. Geoffry W. Marks (Wilmette, Ill.: Bahá'í Publishing Trust, 1996), no. 166.2; the Universal House of Justice, *Promise of World Peace*, p. 27.

31. See [Agnes Akosua Aidoo], *The Girl Child: An Investment in the Future* (New York: UNICEF, 1990), pp. 14–15.

32. 'Abdu'l-Bahá, in *Women*, no. 52.

33. 'Abdu'l-Bahá, *Promulgation*, pp. 175, 281.

34. 'Abdu'l-Bahá, quoted in Esslemont, *Bahá'u'lláh and the New Era,* p. 147.

35. 'Abdu'l-Bahá, *Promulgation*, pp. 135, 283.

36. The Universal House of Justice, *Promise of World Peace*, pp. 26–27.

37. 'Abdu'l-Bahá, *Promulgation*, pp. 135, 175.

38. The Universal House of Justice, Introduction to *Kitáb-i-Aqdas*, by Bahá'u'lláh, p. 8.

39. 'Abdu'l-Bahá, *Selections*, no. 227.18.

40. 'Abdu'l-Bahá, *Promulgation*, p. 134.

CHAPTER 3 / FAMILY DYNAMICS AND PEACE

1. 'Abdu'l-Bahá, *Promulgation*, p. 157.

2. Ibid., p. 230.

3. The Universal House of Justice, *Promise of World Peace*, p. 26.

4. See Betty A. Reardon, *Sexism and the War System* (New York: Teachers College Press, 1986).

5. See Gerda Lerner, *The Creation of Patriarchy*, vol. 1 of *Women and History* (New York: Oxford University Press, 1986), p. 239; the Universal House of Justice, *Promise of World Peace*, p. 26.

6. Jean Baker Miller, M.D., *toward a new psychology of women*, 2d ed. (Boston: Beacon Press, 1986), pp. 6–7.

7. Lerner, *Creation of Patriarchy*, pp. 217–18. Reprinted with permission.

8. See Shan Guisinger and Sidney J. Blatt, "Individuality and Relatedness: Evolution of a Fundamental Dialectic," *American Psychologist* 49, no. 2 (Feb. 1994): pp. 104–11.

9. 'Abdu'l-Bahá, *Promulgation*, p. 134.

10. 'Abdu'l-Bahá, *Paris Talks*, no. 40.33.

11. See *Developing a National Agenda to Address Women's Mental Health Needs: A Conference Report* (Washington, D.C.: American Psychological Association, 1985), p. 29.

12. The Universal House of Justice, *Promise of World Peace*, p. 26.

13. See John Scanzoni and Greer Litton Fox, "Sex Roles, Family and Society: The Seventies and Beyond," *Journal of Marriage and the Family* 42 (Nov. 1980): pp. 743–56.

14. Riane Eisler, David Loye, and Kari Norgaard, *Women, Men, and the Global Quality of Life: A Report of the Gender Equity and Quality of Life Project of the Center for Partnership Studies* (Pacific Grove, Calif.: Center for Partnership Studies, 1995), pp. 40–41. Reprinted by permission of the Center for Partnership Studies.

15. Susan Moller Okin, *Justice, Gender, and the Family* (New York: BasicBooks, 1989), pp. 17–18.

16. Riane Eisler, "Human Rights: The Unfinished Struggle," *International Journal of Women's Studies* 6, no. 4: p. 329.

17. 'Abdu'l-Bahá, *Promulgation*, p. 375.

18. Shoghi Effendi, quoted in a letter dated 24 January 1993 written on behalf of the Universal House of Justice to an individual, in *The American Bahá'í* 24, no. 17 (23 Nov. 1993): p. 10.

19. 'Abdu'l-Bahá, *Promulgation*, p. 168.

20. Shoghi Effendi, quoted in letter dated 28 December 1980 written on behalf of the Universal House of Justice to the National Spiritual Assembly of the Bahá'ís of New Zealand, *Messages from the Universal House of Justice, 1963–1986*, no. 272.4.

21. Letter dated 28 December 1980 written on behalf of the Universal House of Justice to the National Spiritual Assembly of the Bahá'ís of New Zealand, *Messages from the Universal House of Justice, 1963–1986*, no. 272.4.

22. Bahá'u'lláh, *Kitáb-i-Aqdas*, ¶48; letter dated 28 December 1980 written on behalf of the Universal House of Justice to the National Spiritual Assembly of the Bahá'ís of New Zealand, *Messages from the Universal House of Justice, 1963–1986*, no. 272.6.

23. Letter dated 23 August 1984 written on behalf of the Universal House of Justice to an individual, *Messages from the Universal House of Justice, 1963–1986*, no. 407.3.

24. 'Abdu'l-Bahá, *Selections*, no. 98.2.

25. 'Abdu'l-Bahá, in *Compilation of Compilations: Prepared by the Universal House of Justice 1963–1990*, vol. 1 (Maryborough: Bahá'í Publications Australia, 1991), no. 1159.

26. See Guisinger and Blatt, "Individuality and Relatedness," *American Psychologist*, 49, no. 2: p. 109; see also Laurie Hayes, "Men

in Transition: Changing Sex Roles," *Guidepost* 30, no. 12 (1988): pp. 1–3.

27. Letter dated 28 December 1980 written on behalf of the Universal House of Justice to the National Spiritual Assembly of the Bahá'ís of New Zealand, *Messages from the Universal House of Justice, 1963–1986,* no. 272.4.

28. Extract from a letter dated 16 May 1982 written on behalf of the Universal House of Justice to an individual, in *Women,* no. 76.

29. Extract from a letter dated 1 August 1978 written on behalf of the Universal House of Justice to an individual, in *Women,* no. 73.

30. Letter dated 28 December 1980 written on behalf of the Universal House of Justice to the National Spiritual Assembly of the Bahá'ís of New Zealand, *Messages from the Universal House of Justice, 1963–1986,* no. 272.5e.

31. Extract from a letter dated 16 May 1982 written on behalf of the Universal House of Justice to an individual, in *Women,* no. 76.

32. Letter dated 28 December 1980 written on behalf of the Universal House of Justice to the National Spiritual Assembly of the Bahá'ís of New Zealand, *Messages from the Universal House of Justice, 1963–1986,* no. 272.4; extract from a letter dated 11 January 1988 written on behalf of the Universal House of Justice to an individual, used with the permission of the Universal House of Justice.

33. Extract from a letter dated 6 July 1952 written on behalf of Shoghi Effendi to an individual, in *Women,* no. 69.

34. 'Abdu'l-Bahá, *Selections,* no. 85.1.

35. Bahá'u'lláh, *Gleanings from the Writings of Bahá'u'lláh,* trans. Shoghi Effendi, 1st ps ed. (Wilmette, Ill.: Bahá'í Publishing Trust, 1983), p. 286.

36. 'Abdu'l-Bahá, in *Women,* no. 46.

37. 'Abdu'l-Bahá, *Selections,* no. 95.1.

38. Ibid.

39. 'Abdu'l-Bahá, *Promulgation,* p. 175.

CHAPTER 4 / WOMEN AND BAHÁ'Í LAW

1. The Universal House of Justice, letter dated 24 July 1975 to an individual, *Messages from the Universal House of Justice, 1963–1986,* no. 166.2.

2. The Universal House of Justice, Introduction to *Kitáb-i-Aqdas,* by Bahá'u'lláh, p. 3.

3. Extract from a letter written on behalf of Shoghi Effendi in 1935 to a National Spiritual Assembly, quoted in Universal House of Justice, Introduction to *Kitáb-i-Aqdas,* by Bahá'u'lláh, p. 7.

4. Bahá'u'lláh, *Gleanings,* p. 215.

5. 'Abdu'l-Bahá, quoted in Universal House of Justice, Introduction to *Kitáb-i-Aqdas,* by Bahá'u'lláh, p. 5.

6. The Universal House of Justice, Introduction to *Kitáb-i-Aqdas,* by Bahá'u'lláh, p. 5.

7. Ibid., pp. 7–8.

8. Bahá'u'lláh, *Kitáb-i-Aqdas,* ¶75, ¶74; see *Kitáb-i-Aqdas,* n106, n20.

9. Ibid., ¶32; the Universal House of Justice, Introduction to *Kitáb-i-Aqdas,* by Bahá'u'lláh, p. 8.

10. Extract from a letter dated 5 September 1938 written on behalf of Shoghi Effendi to an individual, quoted in Universal House of Justice, letter dated 6 February 1973 to all National Spiritual Assemblies, *Messages from the Universal House of Justice, 1963–1986,* no. 126.7a.

11. 'Abdu'l-Bahá, *Promulgation,* p. 166.

12. Extract from a letter dated 5 September 1938 written on behalf of Shoghi Effendi to an individual, quoted in Universal House of Justice, letter dated 6 February 1973 to all National Spiritual Assemblies, *Messages from the Universal House of Justice, 1963–1986,* no. 126.7a.

13. Bahá'u'lláh, *Kitáb-i-Aqdas,* ¶159.

14. Letter dated 24 January 1993 written on behalf of the Universal House of Justice to an individual, in *The American Bahá'í* 24, no. 17 (23 Nov. 1993): p. 10.

15. Bahá'u'lláh, *Kitáb-i-Aqdas*, ¶63; 'Abdu'l-Bahá, quoted in Esslemont, *Bahá'u'lláh and the New Era*, p. 147.

16. Bahá'í International Community, "Moral and Ethical Concerns of the Bahá'í International Community in the Face of the Widespread Sexual Exploitation of Children," (paper presented at the meeting of the World Conference on Religion and Peace and UNICEF, New York, March 1996).

17. Extract from a letter dated 5 September 1938 written on behalf of Shoghi Effendi to an individual, quoted in Universal House of Justice, letter dated 6 February 1973 to all National Spiritual Assemblies, *Messages from the Universal House of Justice, 1963–1986*, no. 126.7a.

18. Letter dated 24 January 1993 written on behalf of the Universal House of Justice to an individual, in *The American Bahá'í* 24, no. 17 (23 Nov. 1993): p. 10.

19. See, for example, Agnes Ghaznavi, *Sexuality, Relationships and Spiritual Growth* (Oxford: George Ronald, 1995).

20. 'Abdu'l-Bahá, *Selections*, no. 86.2.

21. Shoghi Effendi, *God Passes By*, rev. ed. (Wilmette, Ill.: Bahá'í Publishing Trust, 1974), p. 214.

22. Bahá'u'lláh, *Kitáb-i-Aqdas*, ¶63, ¶174.

23. Based on unpublished Tablets of 'Abdu'l-Bahá, summarized with the permission of the Universal House of Justice.

24. 'Abdu'l-Bahá, extract from an authorized translation of an unpublished Tablet, quoted with the permission of the Universal House of Justice.

25. 'Abdu'l-Bahá, quoted in *Kitáb-i-Aqdas*, n89.

26. Based on an unpublished Tablet of 'Abdu'l-Bahá, summarized with the permission of the Universal House of Justice.

27. See *Kitáb-i-Aqdas*, n93.

28. See *Kitáb-i-Aqdas*, p. 150.

29. Extract from a message dated 17 July 1979 written on behalf of the Universal House of Justice to an individual, in *Preserving Bahá'í Marriages: A Memorandum and Compilation prepared by the Universal House of Justice*, ([Haifa]: Bahá'í World Centre, 1991), no. 38.

30. Bahá'u'lláh, in *Women*, no. 58.

31. Letter dated 24 January 1993 written on behalf of the Universal House of Justice to an individual, in *The American Bahá'í* 24, no. 17 (23 Nov. 1993): p. 10.

32. Ibid.

33. Shoghi Effendi, quoted in *Kitáb-i-Aqdas*, n100; Bahá'u'lláh, *Kitáb-i-Aqdas*, ¶68.

34. Based on a letter dated 11 February 1986 written on behalf of the Universal House of Justice to the National Spiritual Assembly of the Bahá'ís of the United States, used with the permission of the Universal House of Justice.

35. *Encyclopædia Britannica*, 15th ed., s.v. "Family Law."

36. 'Abdu'l-Bahá, *Promulgation*, p. 283.

37. Bahá'u'lláh, *Kitáb-i-Aqdas*, ¶109; 'Abdu'l-Bahá, from unpublished Tablets, quoted with the permission of the Universal House of Justice.

38. Bahá'u'lláh, *Kitáb-i-Aqdas*, "Questions and Answers," no. 69; 'Abdu'l-Bahá, from an unpublished Tablet, quoted with the permission of the Universal House of Justice.

39. Extract from a letter written on behalf of Shoghi Effendi, quoted in *Kitáb-i-Aqdas*, n38.

40. See Mernissi, *Women and Islam*, pp. 49–61.

41. Bahá'u'lláh, *Kitáb-i-Aqdas*, ¶30, ¶52.

42. 'Abdu'l-Bahá, quoted in Universal House of Justice, letter dated 31 May 1988 to the National Spiritual Assembly of the Bahá'ís of New Zealand.

43. Extract from a letter dated 28 July 1936 written on behalf of Shoghi Effendi to an individual, quoted in Universal House of Justice, letter dated 31 May 1988 to the National Spiritual Assembly of the Bahá'ís of New Zealand.

44. The Universal House of Justice, letter dated 31 May 1988 to the National Spiritual Assembly of the Bahá'ís of New Zealand.

45. 'Abdu'l-Bahá, *Selections*, no. 38.4; extract from a letter dated 17 September 1952 written on behalf of Shoghi Effendi to an individual, quoted in Universal House of Justice, letter dated 24

July 1957 to an individual, *Messages from the Universal House of Justice, 1963–1986,* no. 166.6b; extract from a letter dated 9 August 1984 written on behalf of the Universal House of Justice to an individual, quoted with the permission of the Universal House of Justice.

46. The Universal House of Justice, letter dated 31 May 1988 to the National Spiritual Assembly of the Bahá'ís of New Zealand.

47. Extract from a letter dated 23 June 1987 written on behalf of the Universal House of Justice to an individual, quoted with the permission of the Universal House of Justice.

48. The Universal House of Justice, letter dated 31 May 1988 to the National Spiritual Assembly of the Bahá'ís of New Zealand.

49. The Universal House of Justice, letter dated 27 March 1978 to all National Spiritual Assemblies, in *The Continental Boards of Counselors: Letters, Extracts from Letters, and Cables from The Universal House of Justice / An Address by Counselor Edna M. True,* comp. National Spiritual Assembly of the Bahá'ís of the United States (Wilmette, Ill.: Bahá'í Publishing Trust, 1981), p. 60.

50. Shoghi Effendi, *God Passes By,* p. 386.

51. Extract from a letter dated 23 June 1987 written on behalf of the Universal House of Justice to an individual, quoted with the permission of the Universal House of Justice.

CHAPTER 5 / IMPLEMENTING EQUALITY: THE MINISTRIES OF BAHÁ'U'LLÁH AND 'ABDU'L-BAHÁ

1. Bahá'u'lláh, *Tablets of Bahá'u'lláh revealed after the Kitáb-i-Aqdas,* comp. Research Department of the Universal House of Justice, trans. Habib Taherzadeh et al., 1st ps ed. (Wilmette, Ill.: Bahá'í Publishing Trust, 1988), p. 50.

2. 'Abdu'l-Bahá, *The Secret of Divine Civilization,* trans. Marzieh Gail and Ali-Kuli Khan, 1st ps ed. (Wilmette, Ill.: Bahá'í Publishing Trust, 1990), pp. 71–72.

3. Bahá'u'lláh, *Tablets,* p. 130; Bahá'u'lláh, *Gleanings,* p. 93.

4. Bahá'u'lláh, in *Women*, no. 2.

5. Ibid., no. 58.

6. See Irene Franck and David Brownstone, *Women's World: A Timeline of Women in History* (New York: Harper Perennial, 1995), pp. 128–34.

7. Bahá'u'lláh, in *Women*, no. 99.

8. Ibid., no. 57.

9. Bahá'u'lláh, *Tablets*, pp. 254, 255.

10. Ibid., p. 256.

11. Ibid., p. 252.

12. Ibid., pp. 254–55.

13. Ibid., p. 255.

14. Bahá'u'lláh, in *Women*, no. 4.

15. Bahíyyih Khánum, quoted in Lady Blomfield (Sitárih Khánum), *The Chosen Highway* (Wilmette, Ill.: Bahá'í Publishing Trust, 1967), p. 47.

16. See Baharieh Rouhani Maʻani, *Ásíyih Khánum: The Most Exalted Leaf entitled Navváb* (Oxford: George Ronald, 1993), p. 57.

17. Bahá'u'lláh, quoted in Shoghi Effendi, letter dated 21 December 1939, in *Messages to America: Selected Letters and Cablegrams Addressed to the Bahá'ís of North America, 1932–1946*, new ed. (Wilmette, Ill.: Bahá'í Publishing Trust, forthcoming).

18. Bahá'u'lláh, quoted in *Bahá'í Holy Places at the World Centre* (Haifa: Bahá'í World Centre, 1968), p. 77.

19. Bahá'u'lláh, in *Bahíyyih Khánum: The Greatest Holy Leaf*, comp. Research Department at the Bahá'í World Centre (Haifa: Bahá'í World Centre, 1982), p. 4.

20. Shoghi Effendi, *Bahá'í Administration: Selected Messages, 1922–1932*, 7th ed. (Wilmette, Ill.: Bahá'í Publishing Trust, 1974), pp. 188–89.

21. Shoghi Effendi, in *Bahíyyih Khánum*, p. 3.

22. See Adib Taherzadeh, *The Revelation of Bahá'u'lláh: Mazra'ih & Bahjí, 1877–92*, [vol. 4] (Oxford: George Ronald, 1987), p. 429.

23. 'Abdu'l-Bahá, *Memorials of the Faithful* (Wilmette, Ill.: Bahá'í Publishing Trust, 1997), no. 67.5.

24. See Adib Taherzadeh, *The Revelation of Bahá'u'lláh: Baghdád, 1853–63,* [vol. 1], rev. ed. (Oxford: George Ronald, 1976), pp. 12–13.

25. Bahá'u'lláh, quoted in H. M. Balyuzi, *Bahá'u'lláh: The King of Glory* (Oxford: George Ronald, 1980), p. 117.

26. Taherzadeh, *Revelation of Bahá'u'lláh,* vol. 1, p. 13.

27. Nabíl-i-A'zam, in *Stories of Bahá'u'lláh,* comp. and ed. 'Alí-Akbar Furútan, trans. Katayoon and Robert Crerar et al. (Oxford: George Ronald, 1986), pp. 26–27.

28. Shoghi Effendi, *The World Order of Bahá'u'lláh: Selected Letters,* new ed. (Wilmette, Ill.: Bahá'í Publishing Trust, 1991), p. 134.

29. Shoghi Effendi, *Bahá'í Administration,* p. 192.

30. 'Abdu'l-Bahá, in *Bahíyyih Khánum,* p. 8.

31. Ibid., p. 11.

32. Ibid., p. 10.

33. Bahíyyih Khánum, in *Bahíyyih Khánum,* p. 100.

34. Shoghi Effendi, *Bahá'í Administration,* p. 25.

35. Munírih Khánum, quoted in Blomfield, *Chosen Highway,* p. 89.

36. Ibid., pp. 89–90.

37. Bahíyyih Khánum, quoted in Myron H. Phelps, *The Master in 'Akká,* rev. ed. (Los Angeles: Kalimát Press, 1985), p. 118.

38. 'Abdu'l-Bahá, quoted in Genevieve L. Coy, "A Week in 'Abdu'l-Bahá's Home," in *In His Presence: Visits to 'Abdu'l-Bahá* (Los Angeles: Kalimát Press, 1989), p. 146.

39. *Munírih Khánum: Memoirs and Letters,* trans. Sammireh Anwar Smith (Los Angeles: Kalimát Press, 1986), pp. 85–86.

40. Shoghi Effendi, cable dated 28 April 1938, in *Messages of Shoghi Effendi to the Indian Subcontinent, 1923–1957,* comp. and ed. Írán Fúrútan Muhájir, rev. ed. (New Delhi: Bahá'í Publishing Trust, 1995), p. 168; letter dated 7 July 1938 written on behalf of Shoghi Effendi to Siyyid Mustafa, in *Messages of Shoghi Effendi to the Indian Subcontinent,* p. 171.

41. Munírih Khánum, quoted in Phelps, *The Master in 'Akká,* pp. 75–76.

42. Robert Weinberg, *Ethel Jenner Rosenberg: The Life and Times of England's Outstanding Bahá'í Pioneer Worker* (Oxford: George Ronald, 1995), p. 56.

43. Ṭúbá Khánum, quoted in Blomfield, *Chosen Highway,* p. 101.

44. See Jessie E. Revell, "A Bahá'í Pioneer of East and West— Doctor Susan I. Moody (The Handmaid of the Most High), Amatu'l-A'lá," in *The Bahá'í World: A Biennial International Record, Volume 6, 1934–1936,* comp. National Spiritual Assembly of the Bahá'ís of the United States and Canada (New York: Bahá'í Publishing Committee, 1937), pp. 483–86.

45. 'Abdu'l-Bahá, *Promulgation,* p. 133.

46. Ibid., p. 283.

47. 'Abdu'l-Bahá, *Paris Talks,* no. 50.10; Bahá'u'lláh, *The Hidden Words,* trans. Shoghi Effendi (Wilmette, Ill.: Bahá'í Publishing Trust, 1990), Arabic, no. 2.

48. 'Abdu'l-Bahá, *Promulgation,* p. 174.

49. Ibid., p. 77.

50. Ibid., pp. 134, 175.

51. Ibid., p. 134.

52. 'Abdu'l-Bahá, *Paris Talks,* no. 40.33.

53. 'Abdu'l-Bahá, *Promulgation,* pp. 280–81.

54. Ibid., pp. 75–76.

55. Ibid., pp. 76, 133, 374–75.

56. 'Abdu'l-Bahá, *Paris Talks,* no. 59.5.

57. 'Abdu'l-Bahá, *Promulgation,* p. 74.

58. Ibid., p. 134.

59. Gerda Lerner, *The Creation of Patriarchy* (New York: Oxford University Press, 1986), p. 4; for another contemporary expression of such ideas, see, for example, Riane Eisler, *The Chalice and The Blade: Our History, Our Future,* (San Francisco: Harper and Row, 1987).

60. 'Abdu'l-Bahá, *Promulgation,* pp. 174–75.

61. Ibid., p. 135; see also pp. 135–36, 281–82.

62. Ibid., p. 175.

63. Nathan Rutstein with Edna M. True, *Corinne True: Faithful Handmaid of 'Abdu'l-Bahá* (Oxford: George Ronald, 1987), p. 71.

64. Ibid., p. 75.

65. Ibid., pp. 206–07.

66. 'Abdu'l-Bahá, quoted in Mariam Haney, "Mrs. Agnes Parsons," in *The Bahá'í World: A Biennial International Record, Volume 5, 1932–1934,* comp. National Spiritual Assembly of the Bahá'ís of the United States and Canada (New York: Bahá'í Publishing Committee, 1936), p. 413.

67. Ibid.

68. Ibid., p. 414.

69. See "Ella Goodall Cooper," in *The Bahá'í World: A Biennial International Record, Volume 12, 1950–1954,* comp. National Spiritual Assembly of the Bahá'ís of the United States (Wilmette, Ill.: Bahá'í Publishing Trust, 1956), pp. 681–84.

70. 'Abdu'l-Bahá, quoted in M. R. Garis, *Martha Root: Lioness at the Threshold* (Wilmette, Ill.: Bahá'í Publishing Trust, 1983), pp. 87–88.

71. See H. M. Balyuzi, *'Abdu'l-Bahá: The Centre of the Covenant of Bahá'u'lláh* (Oxford: George Ronald, 1974), pp. 418–19, 534–35.

72. The Universal House of Justice, letter dated 25 May 1975 to all National Spiritual Assemblies, *Messages from the Universal House of Justice, 1963–1968,* no. 162.32.

73. 'Abdu'l-Bahá, in *Women,* no. 19.

74. 'Abdu'l-Bahá, *Promulgation,* pp. 76–77.

75. 'Abdu'l-Bahá, in *Women,* no. 104.

76. Ibid., no. 103.

77. Ibid., no. 100.

78. 'Abdu'l-Bahá, quoted in Ramona Allen Brown, *Memories of 'Abdu'l-Bahá: Recollections of the Early Days of the Bahá'í Faith in California* (Wilmette, Ill.: Bahá'í Publishing Trust, 1980), p. 92.

79. See Blomfield, *Chosen Highway,* p. 190; see Coy, *In His Presence,* p. 95; see National Spiritual Assembly of the Bahá'ís of Canada, *Marion Jack, Immortal Heroine* (Thornhill, Ont: Bahá'í Canada Publications), p. 2.

80. See *Munírih Khánum*, pp. 77–81.

81. See H. M. Balyuzi, *Eminent Bahá'ís in the Time of Bahá'u'lláh with Some Historical Background* (Oxford: George Ronald, 1985), p. 268; see also Taherzadeh, *Revelation of Bahá'u'lláh*, vol. 4, p. 312.

82. *The Bahá'í World: A Biennial International Record, Volume 3, 1928–1930*, comp. National Spiritual Assembly of the Bahá'ís of the United States and Canada (New York: Bahá'í Publishing Committee, 1930), p. 85.

83. 'Abdu'l-Bahá, in *Star of the West* 12, no. 19 (2 Mar. 1922): pp. 307–08.

84. See Dorothea Morrell Reed, "Genevieve Lenore Coy," in *The Bahá'í World: A Biennial International Record, Volume 14, 1963–1968*, comp. Universal House of Justice (Haifa: Universal House of Justice, 1974), pp. 326–28; see "Ishráqíyyih Dhabíh," in ibid., pp. 517–18; see "Ruhangíz Fath-'Azam," in *The Bahá'í World: An International Record, Volume 17, 1976–1979*, comp. Universal House of Justice (Haifa: Bahá'í World Centre, 1981), pp. 467–70.

85. For information about the high reputation of the Tarbíyat schools, see Moojan Momen, *The Bábí and Bahá'í Religions: 1844–1944: Some Contemporary Accounts* (Oxford: George Ronald, 1981), pp. 475–79, and the article by Vahid Rafati titled "Bahá'í Schools," in *Encyclopædia Iranica*, vol. 3, pp. 467–70.

86. See Taherzadeh, *Revelation of Bahá'u'lláh*, vol. 4, pp. 312, 304; see also Balyuzi, *Eminent Bahá'ís*, p. 174.

87. See Taherzadeh, *Revelation of Bahá'u'lláh*, vol. 4, p. 312.

88. See Robert H. Stockman, *The Bahá'í Faith in America: Early Expansion, 1900–1912*, vol. 2 (Oxford: George Ronald, 1995), pp. 47, 49–50, 53–54.

89. See ibid., p. 323.

90. 'Abdu'l-Bahá, in *Women*, no. 13.

91. Ibid., no. 104.

92. Ibid., no. 13; 'Abdu'l-Bahá, *Selections*, no. 94.2–94.3.

93. 'Abdu'l-Bahá, in *Women*, no. 102.

94. Ibid., no. 13.

95. Ibid., no. 104.

96. See Genevieve L. Coy, "Educating the Women of Persia," *Star of the West* 17, no. 1 (April 1926): pp. 50–55.

97. 'Abdu'l-Bahá, quoted in Laura Clifford Barney, Preface to *Some Answered Questions*, by 'Abdu'l-Bahá, p. xvii; see Publisher's Foreword to 1964 Edition of ibid., p. xv.

98. Ella Goodall Cooper, "Henrietta Emogene Martin Hoagg," in *The Bahá'í World: A Biennial International Record, Volume 10, 1944–1946,* comp. National Spiritual Assembly of the Bahá'ís of the United States and Canada (Wilmette, Ill.: Bahá'í Publishing Committee, 1949), pp. 520–21.

99. Amine De Mille, "Emogene Hoagg, an exemplary pioneer," *Bahá'í News,* no. 511 (Oct. 1973): p. 7.

100. See *Star of the West* 2, no. 3 (28 April 1911): p. 6; *Star of the West* 2, no. 7–8 (1 Aug. 1911): pp. 7–9; *Star of the West* 16, no. 9 (Dec. 1925): p. 650.

101. 'Abdu'l-Bahá, quoted in Esslemont, *Bahá'u'lláh and the New Era,* p. 147; 'Abdu'l-Bahá, *Promulgation,* p. 283.

102. 'Abdu'l-Bahá, quoted in Edna M. True, "Katherine Knight True," in *Bahá'í World,* vol. 14, p. 383.

103. 'Abdu'l-Bahá, quoted in Shoghi Effendi, *God Passes By,* p. 308; Shoghi Effendi, quoted in Marion Hofman, "Beatrice Irwin," in *The Bahá'í World: An International Record, Volume 13, 1954–1963,* comp. Universal House of Justice (Haifa: Universal House of Justice, 1970), p. 882.

CHAPTER 6 / IMPLEMENTING EQUALITY: THE ROLE OF SHOGHI EFFENDI AND THE UNIVERSAL HOUSE OF JUSTICE

1. Shoghi Effendi, *God Passes By,* p. 324.

2. Ibid., p. 325.

3. Shoghi Effendi, extract from a letter dated 27 December 1923 to the National Spiritual Assembly of the Bahá'ís of India and Burma, in *Women,* no. 114.

4. Ibid.

5. Shoghi Effendi, letter dated 6 December 1928 to the beloved of the Lord and the handmaids of the Merciful throughout the West, *Bahá'í Administration*, p. 148.

6. Letter dated 14 March 1933 written on behalf of Shoghi Effendi to an individual, quoted with the permission of the Universal House of Justice.

7. Shoghi Effendi, *God Passes By*, p. 229.

8. See Vahid Rafati, "The Bahá'í Community of Iran," in *Encyclopædia Iranica* (London: Routledge, Kegan Paul, 1989), vol. 3, pp. 454–60.

9. "Review of Various National Events," in *The Bahá'í World*, vol. 12, p. 65.

10. See ibid., p. 66.

11. Shoghi Effendi, extract from a letter dated April 1954, in *Messages to the Bahá'í World, 1950–1957*, rev. ed. (Wilmette, Ill.: Bahá'í Publishing Trust, 1971), p. 65.

12. See Baharieh Rouhani Ma'ani, "The Interdependence of Bahá'í Communities: Services of North American Bahá'í Women to Iran," *Journal of Bahá'í Studies* 4, no. 1 (1991): p. 42.

13. Shoghi Effendi, extract from a letter dated 30 January 1926 to the Spiritual Assemblies throughout the East, in *Trustworthiness: A compilation of extracts from the Bahá'í Writings*, comp. Research Department of the Universal House of Justice (London: Bahá'í Publishing Trust, 1987), no. 69; based on a letter dated 2 November 1928 from Shoghi Effendi to the Iran Central Spiritual Assembly, summarized with the permission of the Universal House of Justice.

14. Shoghi Effendi, *The Advent of Divine Justice*, 1st ps ed. (Wilmette, Ill.: Bahá'í Publishing Trust, 1990), pp. 68–69.

15. Extract from a letter dated 24 March 1945 written on behalf of Shoghi Effendi to an individual, in *Women*, no. 93.

16. Ibid.

17. Extract from a letter dated 10 November 1930 written on behalf of Shoghi Effendi to the National Spiritual Assembly of the Bahá'ís of India and Burma, in *Women*, no. 92.

18. Shoghi Effendi, cablegram dated 30 December 1930 to an individual, quoted with the permission of the Universal House of Justice.

19. National Spiritual Assembly of the Bahá'ís of Singapore, *Eulogy, Shirin Fozdar, 1 March 1905–2 February 1992: Champion of Asian Women* (Singapore: National Spiritual Assembly of the Bahá'ís of Singapore, 1992).

20. Nabíl-i-A'ẓam [Nabíl-i-Zarandí], *The Dawn-Breakers: Nabíl's Narrative of the Early Days of the Bahá'í Revelation,* trans. Shoghi Effendi (Wilmette, Ill.: Bahá'í Publishing Trust, 1974).

21. Extract from a letter dated 27 August 1951 written on behalf of Shoghi Effendi to Effie Baker, quoted in James Heggie, "Effie Baker," in *Bahá'í World,* vol. 14, p. 321.

22. Keith Ransom-Kehler, letter dated 3 March 1933 to the National Spiritual Assembly of the Bahá'ís of the United States and Canada, in *Bahá'í World,* vol. 5, p. 402.

23. Shoghi Effendi, cable dated 28 October 1933, in *Messages to America* (forthcoming).

24. Dr. Lutfu'lláh S. Hakím and Mardíyyih N. Carpenter, "Part Three—Persia," in "Current Bahá'í Activities in the East and West," in *Bahá'í World,* vol. 5, p. 121.

25. Ibid., p. 122.

26. "In Memoriam," in *Bahá'í World,* vol. 5, p. 398.

27. See Barron Deems Harper, *Lights of Fortitude: Glimpses into the Lives of the Hands of the Cause of God* (Oxford: George Ronald, 1997).

28. Shoghi Effendi, *God Passes By,* pp. 386–87.

29. J. E. Esslemont, *Bahá'u'lláh and the New Era: An Introduction to the Bahá'í Faith,* 5th rev. ed. (Wilmette, Ill.: Bahá'í Publishing Trust, 1980).

30. Shoghi Effendi, *God Passes By,* p. 389.

31. Ibid., p. 388, 386.

32. Shoghi Effendi, quoted in Beatrice Ashton, "Amelia E. Collins," in *Bahá'í World,* vol. 13, p. 837; see ibid., pp. 834–41.

33. Letter received in January 1947 written on behalf of Shoghi Effendi to Amelia Collins, quoted in Beatrice Ashton, "Amelia E. Collins," in *Bahá'í World,* vol. 13, p. 838; Shoghi Effendi, postscript

to letter received in January 1947 written on behalf of Shoghi Effendi to Amelia Collins, quoted in Beatrice Ashton, "Amelia E. Collins," in *Bahá'í World*, vol. 13, p. 839.

34. The Universal House of Justice, *The Constitution of the Universal House of Justice* (Haifa: Bahá'í World Centre, 1972).

35. 'Abdu'l-Bahá, *Will and Testament of 'Abdu'l-Bahá* (Wilmette, Ill.: Bahá'í Publishing Trust, 1944), p. 20.

36. The Universal House of Justice, *Promise of World Peace*, pp. 26–27.

37. The Universal House of Justice, letter dated Riḍván 1984 to the Bahá'ís of the World, *Messages from the Universal House of Justice, 1963–1986*, no. 394.7.

38. "International Survey of Current Bahá'í Activities, 1968–1973," in *Bahá'í World*, vol. 15, p. 248.

39. The Universal House of Justice, letter dated 25 May 1975 to all National Spiritual Assemblies, *Messages from the Universal House of Justice, 1963–1986*, no. 162.32.

40. *The Five Year Plan, 1974–1979, Statistical Report, Riḍván 1978* (Haifa: Bahá'í World Centre, 1978), pp. 33–34.

41. The Universal House of Justice, letter dated 24 March 1977 to all National Spiritual Assemblies, *Messages from the Universal House of Justice, 1963–1986*, no. 190.5.

42. Rachel Collins, "Survey of Activities of Baha'i Women in the Five Year Plan," in *Bahá'í World*, vol. 17, pp. 210–12.

43. *The Seven Year Plan, 1979–1986, Statistical Report*, [n.p.: n.d.], p. 107.

44. The Universal House of Justice, letter dated Riḍván 153 [1996] to the Bahá'ís of the World, *The Four Year Plan: Messages of the Universal House of Justice* (Riviera Beach, Fla.: Palabra Publications, 1996), no. 3.9.

45. The Universal House of Justice, letter dated Riḍván 153 [1996] to the Followers of Bahá'u'lláh in the Andaman and Nicobar Islands, Bangladesh, India, Nepal and Sri Lanka, *Four Year Plan*, no. 10.11.

46. The Universal House of Justice, letter dated 153 [1996] to the Followers of Bahá'u'lláh in Africa, *Four Year Plan*, no. 4.13.

47. The Universal House of Justice, letter dated Riḍván 153 [1996] to the Followers of Bahá'u'lláh in Australia, the Cook Islands, the Eastern Caroline Islands, the Fiji Islands, French Polynesia, the Hawaiian Islands, Indonesia, Japan, Kiribati, Korea, the Mariana Islands, the Marshall Islands, New Caledonia and the Loyalty Islands, New Zealand, Papua New Guinea, the Philippines, Samoa, the Solomon Islands, Tonga, Tuvalu, Vanuatu, and the Western Caroline Islands, *Four Year Plan*, no. 8.5.

48. Shoghi Effendi, letter dated 3 June 1925 to the beloved of God and the handmaids of the Merciful, the delegates and visitors to the Bahá'í Convention, Green Acre Maine, *Bahá'í Administration*, p. 88.

49. "Achievements of the Bahá'í Community in Advancing the Status of Women," in *The Bahá'í World: An International Record, Volume 19*, comp. Universal House of Justice (Haifa: Bahá'í World Centre, 1994), p, 401.

50. Ibid., p. 402.

51. See Bahá'í International Community Office for the Advancement of Women, "The Status of Women in the Bahá'í Community," in *The Greatness Which Might Be Theirs* (n.p.: Bahá'í International Community, 1995), pp. 81–87.

52. Ibid.

53. 'Abdu'l-Bahá, *Promulgation*, pp. 134, 77.

54. "Achievements of the Bahá'í Community in Advancing the Status of Women," in *Bahá'í World*, vol. 19, p. 399.

55. Bahá'í International Community, "The Girl Child: A Critical Concern," in *The Greatness Which Might Be Theirs* (n.p.: Bahá'í International Community, 1995), pp. 77–78.

56. Ibid., p. 78.

57. Ibid.

58. The Universal House of Justice, letter dated 10 December 1992 to all National Spiritual Assemblies.

59. Ibid.

60. Bahá'í International Community, "Educating Girls: An Investment in the Future," in *The Greatness Which Might Be Theirs*, pp. 8–9.

61. Bahá'í International Community, "Protection of Women's Rights," in *The Greatness Which Might Be Theirs*, p. 64.

62. Bahá'í International Community, "Ending Violence Against Women," in *The Greatness Which Might Be Theirs,* p. 28.

63. Bahá'í International Community, "Protection of Women's Rights," in *The Greatness Which Might Be Theirs,* p. 64.

64. Ibid., pp. 63–64.

65. Bahá'í International Community, "Ending Violence Against Women," in *The Greatness Which Might Be Theirs,* p. 29.

66. Bahá'í International Community, "Moral and Ethical Concerns of the Bahá'í International Community in the Face of the Widespread Sexual Exploitation of Children," (paper presented at the meeting of the World Conference on Religion and Peace and UNICEF, New York, March 1996).

67. The Universal House of Justice, letter dated Riḍván 153 [1996] to the Bahá'ís of the World, in *Four Year Plan,* no. 3.33.

68. Ann Boyles, "Towards the Goal of Full Partnership: One Hundred and Fifty Years of the Advancement of Women," in *The Bahá'í World, 1993–94: An International Record* (Haifa: Bahá'í World Centre, 1994), p. 266.

69. Bahá'í International Community Office of Public Information, *The Prosperity of Humankind* (Wilmette, Ill.: Bahá'í Publishing Trust, 1995), pp. 21–22.

70. Bahá'í International Community, *Turning Point For All Nations: A Statement of the Bahá'í International Community on the Occasion of the 50th Anniversary of the United Nations* (New York: Bahá'í International Community, 1995) p. 18.

71. The Universal House of Justice, letter dated 20 October 1983 to the Bahá'ís of the World, *Messages from the Universal House of Justice 1963–1986,* no. 379.2.

72. See *The Bahá'í World, 1995–96* (Haifa: Bahá'í World Centre, 1997), pp. 317–20.

73. The Universal House of Justice, letter dated Riḍván 153 [1996] to the Followers of Bahá'u'lláh in Africa, in *Four Year Plan,* no. 4.9.

74. Based on information provided by the Bahá'í World Center's Office of Social and Economic Development.

75. See Boyles, "Towards the Goal of True Partnership: One

Hundred and Fifty Years of the Advancement of Women," in *Bahá'í World, 1993–94*, p. 257.

76. See ibid.; for further information about the Lar Linda Tanure orphanage, see "Profile: Association for the Coherent Development of the Amazon," in *Bahá'í World, 1995–96*, pp. 301–05.

77. See Boyles, "Towards the Goal of Full Partnership: One Hundred and Fifty Years of the Advancement of Women," in *Bahá'í World, 1993–94*, p. 255.

78. *The Six Year Plan, 1986–1992: Summary of Achievements* (Haifa: Bahá'í World Centre, 1993), p. 81.

79. See "Simple Methods, simple training are keys to primary health care in villages," *One Country* 1, no. 3 (June–August 1989): pp. 1, 8–9; see also *Six Year Plan*, pp. 76–79.

80. "UNIFEM/Bahá'í Project Raises Community Consciousness" (an article originally published in *One Country* 5, no. 3 [Oct.–Dec. 1993]: p. 9), in *The Greatness Which Must Be Theirs*, p. 56.

81. Quoted in Boyles, "Towards the Goal of Full Partnership," in *Bahá'í World, 1993–94*, p. 262.

82. Ibid.

83. See "The Bahá'í International Community: Activities 1994–95," in *Bahá'í World, 1994–95* (Haifa: Bahá'í World Centre, 1995), p. 145; Bahá'í International Community Office for the Advancement of Women, *Two Wings: Changing Behavior and Attitudes—Story of the Bahá'í International Community's Traditional Media as Change Agent Project* (New York: Bahá'í International Community Office for the Advancement of Women, 1994), videocassette 25:35 minutes.

CHAPTER 7 / PRACTICING EQUALITY

1. The Universal House of Justice, letter dated 6 February 1973 to all National Spiritual Assemblies, *Messages from the Universal House of Justice, 1963–1986*, no. 126.2.

2. 'Abdu'l-Bahá, *Paris Talks*, nos. 51.7, 40.35, 17.7.

3. Extract from a letter dated 4 May 1942 written on behalf of

Shoghi Effendi to an individual, in *The Power of Divine Assistance: Extracts from the Writings of Bahá'u'lláh, the Báb, 'Abdu'l-Bahá and Shoghi Effendi . . . and Selected Prayers,* comp. Research Department of the Universal House of Justice (n.p.: National Spiritual Assembly of the Bahá'ís of Canada, 1982), pp. 53, 50.

4. Extract from a letter dated 22 November 1941 written on behalf of Shoghi Effendi to an individual, in *Compilation of Compilations,* vol. 2, no. 1770.

5. 'Abdu'l-Bahá, in *Star of the West* 8, no. 6 (24 June 1917): p. 68.

6. Extract from a letter dated 10 January 1936 written on behalf of Shoghi Effendi to the National Spiritual Assembly of the Bahá'ís of the United States, in *Lights of Guidance: A Bahá'í Reference File,* comp. Helen Hornby, 3d rev. ed. (New Delhi: Bahá'í Publishing Trust, 1994), nos. 775, 1223.

7. Extract from a letter dated 26 March 1950 written on behalf of Shoghi Effendi to an individual, in *Lights of Guidance,* no. 1223.

8. Extract from a letter dated 17 October 1968 written on behalf of the Universal House of Justice to an individual, in *Compilation of Compilations,* vol. 1, no. 118.

9. Extract from a letter dated 17 February 1933 written on behalf of Shoghi Effendi to an individual, in *Compilation of Compilations,* vol. 1, pp. 84–85.

10. The Universal House of Justice, letter dated 6 February 1973 to all National Spiritual Assemblies, *Messages from the Universal House of Justice, 1963–1986,* no. 126.2.

11. Extract from a letter dated 2 November 1933 written on behalf of Shoghi Effendi to an individual, in *Compilation of Compilations,* vol. 1, no. 475.

12. The Universal House of Justice, letter dated September 1964 to the Bahá'ís of the World, *Messages from the Universal House of Justice, 1963–1986,* no. 19.4.

13. Ibid., no. 19.6.

14. Extract from a letter dated 12 May 1925 written on behalf of Shoghi Effendi to an individual, in *Compilation of Compilations,* vol. 2, no. 1272.

15. Extract from a letter dated 27 February 1943 written on behalf of Shoghi Effendi to an individual, in *Compilation of Compilations*, vol. 2, no. 1289.

16. Extract from a letter dated 25 July 1984 written on behalf of the Universal House of Justice to an individual, *Messages from the Universal House of Justice, 1963–1986*, no. 402.6.

17. 'Abdu'l-Bahá, *Paris Talks*, no. 50.10; 'Abdu'l-Bahá, in *Women*, no. 12; 'Abdu'l-Bahá, *Promulgation*, p. 76.

18. 'Abdu'l-Bahá, *Promulgation*, p. 283; 'Abdu'l-Bahá, *Paris Talks*, no. 50.14.

19. The Universal House of Justice, letter dated Riḍván 153 [1996] to the followers of Bahá'u'lláh in Australia, the Cook Islands, the Eastern Caroline Islands, the Fiji Islands, French Polynesia, the Hawaiian Islands, Indonesia, Japan, Kiribati, Korea, the Mariana Islands, the Marshall Islands, New Caledonia and the Loyalty Islands, New Zealand, Papua New Guinea, the Philippines, Samoa, the Solomon Islands, Tonga, Tuvalu, Vanuatu, and the Western Caroline Islands, *Four Year Plan*, no. 8.5.

20. The Universal House of Justice, letter dated Riḍván 153 [1996] to the followers of Bahá'u'lláh in the Andaman and Nicobar Islands, Bangladesh, India, Nepal and Sri Lanka, *Four Year Plan*, no. 10.11.

21. The Universal House of Justice, letter dated Naw-Rúz 1979 to the Bahá'ís of the World, *Messages from the Universal House of Justice, 1963–1986*, nos. 221.13j; 394.7.

22. Extract from a letter dated 9 August 1984 written on behalf of the Universal House of Justice to an individual, in *Women*, no. 78.

23. Extract from a letter dated 16 June 1982 written on behalf of the Universal House of Justice to an individual, in *Women*, no. 77.

24. National Spiritual Assembly of the Bahá'ís of the United States, *Two Wings of a Bird: The Equality of Women and Men* (Wilmette, Ill.: Bahá'í Publishing Trust, 1997), pp. 7–8.

25. The Universal House of Justice, letter dated 25 May 1975 to all National Spiritual Assemblies, *Messages from the Universal House of Justice, 1963–1986*, no. 162.32; 'Abdu'l-Bahá, in *Women*, no. 19.

26. 'Abdu'l-Bahá, *Paris Talks*, no. 50.15.

27. 'Abdu'l-Bahá, *Selections*, no. 113.2.

28. Extract from a letter dated 29 February 1984 written on behalf of the Universal House of Justice to the National Spiritual Assembly of the Mariana Islands, in *Women*, no. 124.

29. The Universal House of Justice, letter dated 31 May 1988 to the National Spiritual Assembly of the Bahá'ís of New Zealand, p. 4.

APPENDIX / TWO WINGS OF A BIRD

1. See the Universal House of Justice, *Promise of World Peace*, pp. 26–27.

2. Bahá'u'lláh, in *Women*, no. 54.

3. 'Abdu'l-Bahá, *Promulgation*, p. 175.

4. 'Abdu'l-Bahá, *Secret of Divine Civilization*, p. 39.

5. Bahá'u'lláh, *Hidden Words*, Arabic, no. 68.

6. 'Abdu'l-Bahá, *Promulgation*, p. 375.

7. Bahá'u'lláh, *Tablets*, p. 51.

8. 'Abdu'l-Bahá, *Selections*, no. 114.1.

9. Bahá'u'lláh, in *Women*, no. 2; 'Abdu'l-Bahá, *Promulgation*, p. 300.

10. Ibid., p. 135.

11. 'Abdu'l-Bahá, quoted in Esslemont, *Bahá'u'lláh and the New Era*, p. 149.

12. 'Abdu'l-Bahá, *Paris Talks*, no. 40.33.

13. Ibid., no. 50.14.

14. Shoghi Effendi, *Advent of Divine Justice*, p. 40.

Bibliography

AUTHORITATIVE BAHÁ'Í TEXTS

Bahá'u'lláh. *The Kitáb-i-Aqdas: The Most Holy Book*. Pocket-size ed. Wilmette, Ill.: Bahá'í Publishing Trust, 1993.

Bahá'u'lláh, 'Abdu'l-Bahá, Shoghi Effendi, and Bahíyyih Khánum. *Bahíyyih Khánum: The Greatest Holy Leaf*. Compiled by the Research Department at the Bahá'í World Centre. Haifa: Bahá'í World Centre, 1982.

Messages from the Universal House of Justice, 1963–1986: The Third Epoch of the Formative Age. Compiled by Geoffrey W. Marks. Wilmette, Ill.: Bahá'í Publishing Trust, 1996. Sections 145, 166, 197, 203, 272, 291, 342, 364, 389, 398, 401, 402, 407, 448, 455.

The Universal House of Justice. *Preserving Bahá'í Marriages: A Memorandum and Compilation*. Thornhill, Ont.: Bahá'í Canada Publications, 1991.

The Universal House of Justice. *The Promise of World Peace: To the Peoples of the World*. Wilmette, Ill.: Bahá'í Publishing Trust, 1985.

OTHER WORKS

Arbáb, Furúgh. *Akhtarán-i-Tábán*. New Delhi: Mir'át Publications, 1990.

Bahá'í International Community Office of Public Information. *The Prosperity of Humankind*. Wilmette, Ill.: Bahá'í Publishing Trust, 1995.

Bahá'í International Community. *Turning Point For All Nations: A Statement of the Bahá'í International Community on the Occasion of the 50th Anniversary of the United Nations*. New York: Bahá'í International Community, 1995.

The Greatness Which Might Be Theirs. New York: Bahá'í International Community Office for the Advancement of Women, 1995.

Balyuzi, H. M. *Khadíjih Bagum: The Wife of the Báb*. Oxford: George Ronald, 1981.

Blomfield, Lady (Sitárih Khánum). *The Chosen Highway*. Wilmette, Ill.: Bahá'í Publishing Trust, n.d.; repr. 1975.

Boyles, Ann. "Towards the Goal of Full Equality: 150 Years of the Advancement of Women," in *The Baha'i World, 1993–1994*. Haifa: Bahá'í World Centre, 1994. pp. 237–76.

Bramson-Lerche, Loni. "An Element of Divine Justice, the Bahá'í Principle of the Equality of Women and Men," in Charles O. Lerche (ed.). *Towards the Most Great Justice*. London: Bahá'í Publishing Trust, 1996. Pp. 75–112.

Ellis, Wilma. *Women, Peacemakers, Reformers, Leaders*. Mona Vale: Bahá'í Publications Australia, 1997.

Faizi, Abu'l-Qásim. *Milly, A Tribute to the Hand of the Cause of God Amelia E. Collins*. Oxford: George Ronald, 1977.

Garis, M. R. *Martha Root: Lioness at the Threshold*. Wilmette, Ill: Bahá'í Publishing Trust, 1983.

Ghaznavi, Agnes. *The Family Repairs and Maintenance Manual*. Oxford: George Ronald, 1989.

———. *Sexuality, Relationships and Spiritual Growth*. Oxford: George Ronald, 1995.

Hollinger, Richard, ed. *'Abdu'l-Bahá in America: Agnes Parsons' Diary, April 11, 1912–November 11, 1912, supplemented with episodes from Mahmúd's Diary*. Los Angeles: Kalimát Press, 1996.

Ma'ani, Baharieh Rouhani. *Ásíyih Khánum: The Most Exalted Leaf entitled Navváb*. Oxford: George Ronald, 1993.

Mahmoudi, Hoda. "Shifting the Balance: The Responsibility of Men in Establishing the Equality of Women," in Charles O. Lerche (ed.), *Towards the Most Great Justice*. London: Bahá'í Publishing Trust, 1996. Pp. 113–36.

Marion Jack, Immortal Heroine. Thornhill, Ont.: Bahá'í Canada Publications, 1985.

Metalmann, Velda Piff. *Lua Getsinger: Herald of the Covenant*. Oxford: George Ronald, 1997.

Munirih Khanum memoirs and letters. Translated by Sammireh
     Anwar Smith. Los Angeles: Kalimát Press, 1986.
Nakhjavání, Bahíyyih. *Asking Questions: A Challenge to Fundamen-
     talism.* Oxford: George Ronald, 1990.
Root, Martha. *Ṭáhirih the Pure, Irán's Greatest Woman.* Karachi:
     Martha L. Root, 1938.
Rutstein, Nathan, with Edna M. True. *Corinne True: Faithful
     Handmaid of 'Abdu'l-Bahá.* Oxford: George Ronald, 1987.
Weinberg, Robert. *Ethel Jenner Rosenberg: The Life and Times of
     England's Outstanding Bahá'í Pioneer Worker.* Oxford:
     George Ronald, 1995.
Whitehead, O. Z. *Some Early Bahá'ís of the West.* Oxford: George
     Ronald, 1976.
———. *Some Bahá'ís to Remember.* Oxford: George Ronald, 1983.
———. *Portraits of Some Bahá'í Women.* Oxford: George Ronald,
     1996.
Wilcox, Patricia. *Bahá'í Families, Perspectives, Principles, Practice.*
     Oxford: George Ronald, 1991.
Women: A compilation of extracts from the Bahá'í Writings. Rev. ed.
     Compiled by the Research Department of the Universal
     House of Justice. London: Bahá'í Publishing Trust, 1990.

Index

A

'Abdu'l-Bahá
   appointment of, as successor to
      Bahá'u'lláh, 8
   assigning responsibilities to
      Agnes Alexander, 178–79
      Agnes Parsons, 176–77
      Corinne True, 173–76
      Ella Cooper, 177
      Ethel Rosenberg, 172–73
      Helen Goodall, 177
      Lua Getsinger, 178
      Martha Root, 178–79
   as authoritative interpreter, 162
      on enlarging context, 163–67
      on timelines, 162–63
   on balance of power between
      sexes, 20–21
   on cause of women, 152–53
   on challenging stereotypic
      thinking, 167–71
   on doctrine of original sin,
      30–31
   on education of daughters, 42,
      90, 91, 92
   and equality of sexes, 25, 48,
      67–68
   as exemplar of Bahá'í Faith,
      153–61, 202
   on family, 62–63
   on fostering intellectual
      development, 191–94
   on importance of cooperation
      and reciprocity, 79–80
   on integrity of family bond, 75
   on Manifestation of God, 23
   passing of, 8, 201–02
   on position of women in
      antiquity, 22–23
   on prolongation of warfare, 73
      in promoting enlightenment of
         women, 183–91
      in providing encouragement,
         180–83
   relationship of, with women in
      His daily life, 153
   on role of education in establish-
      ing equality of women,
      41–42
   on selecting prospective marriage
      partners, 87
   on spiritual and social principle,
      38
   and use of analogy, 167
   and use of contemporary
      examples, 171
   and use of direct challenge,
      168–69
   and use of examples from
      history, 169–71
   and use of rhetorical questions,
      167–68
   Will and Testament of, 8
   writings of, 31n
Ablutions, prescriptions for, 104–05
Abu'l-Faḍl, Mírzá, 192
Adam and Eve, account of, 29–31
Administrative Order, 7–10
   distinctions between rank in, 131
   institutions of, 203
   involvement of women in, 122
   role of Shoghi Effendi in
      developing, 205–12
Adultery, 117
Advocates for African Food Security,
   243
Aggression, expression of, 72
Al-Bukhari, 33
   and collection of hadith, 33–34
Alcohol, prohibition of, in Islam, 99

Alexander, Agnes, 178–79, 221
'Alí-Akbar, Mullá, 187
All-Asian Women's Conference, 215
Al Sahih (Al-Bukhari), 33
Amatu'l-Bahá Rúḥíyyih Khánum, 221
Analogy, 'Abdu'l-Bahá's use of, 167
Antiquity, role of women in, 20–23
Apostolic Age
    conclusion of, 201
    principle of equality of men and
        women, 201–02
Ashraf, Ghodsia, 193
Asia, position of women in, 22–23
Ásíyih (daughter of Pharaoh), 170
Ásíyih Khánum, 146–47
Attitudes
    role of parents in changing,
        88–89
    transmission of
        on equality to wider society,
            70–74
        to wider society, 70–74
Attitudinal changes, 258–61

B
Bagum, Zahrá, 149
Bahá'í Administration, fostering
        women's participation in,
        235–39
Bahá'í beliefs
    acceptance of, on faith, 128–29
    on complementarity, 46–49
    devotional practices enjoined in,
        102–05
    on divorce, 117
    on education of daughters, 42–44
    on equality of sexes, 7, 36–49, 283
        within community, 291–94
        at individual level, 283–87

    within marriage and family,
        287–91
    on family dynamics, 61–92
    on group decision-making,
        81–87
    historical perspective, 5–6
    on implementation, 49–53
    on implementing equality,
        49–53
    on importance of educating girls
        and women, 40–44
    Manifestation of God in, 23–27
    and practice, 139–40
    on purpose of religion, 267
    role of faith in, 127–28
    translating into practice,
        268–69
        individual conduct, 271–77
        interaction with society,
            277–83
        spiritual dimension, 269–71
Bahá'í Cause, participation of
        women in work of,
        143–44
Bahá'í community
    consultation in, 82–87
    look to future of, 13
    perpetuation of unity and
        integrity of, 8
Bahá'í Council, 173
Bahá'í Dispensation, 29, 99, 132
    Formative Age of, 201
    termination of Apostolic Age of,
        201–03
Bahá'í Faith
    'Abdu'l-Bahá as Exemplar of,
        153–61
    application of laws and
        principles of, 139–40

enrollment as member of, 269
equality of men and women in,
    5–6
and need for power, 11
on participation of women in
    world at large, 44–46
principles of, 6–7
as religion of change, 11–13
as religion of freedom and
    happiness, 5
Bahá'í holy days, 273–74
Bahá'í institutions, service on, by
    women, 120–34
Bahá'í International Community,
    241, 243
Bahá'í law(s), 97–134
    application of, 134
        to women, 101–02
    devotional practices in, 102–05
    element of faith in acceptance
        of, 98
    and equality, 97
    and financial rights of women,
        118–20
    flexibility of, 99–100
    marriage and divorce in, 111–17
    nature of, 98–102
    of personal conduct for women,
        102–17
    progressive application of, 99
    regulating sexual conduct, 105–10
    and service on Bahá'í institutions,
        120–34
    ultimate aim of, 98
Bahá'í life, devotional practices in,
    6–7
Bahá'í Temple, construction of,
    123–24
Bahá'í Women's Committee, 247

Bahá'í Women's Conference of
    Malaysia, 232
Bahá'í World Center, 205
Bahá'í World Commonwealth, 201n
Bahá'í writings on relationship
    between equality and
    peace, 62
Bahá'u'lláh
    actions of, 140
    claims of, as Manifestation of
        God, 6, 11, 98, 127
    Covenant of, 8, 29, 100, 296
    examples from His personal
        relationships, 145–52
    guidance and encouragement to
        women by, 142–45
    laws prescribed by, 5
    on responsibilities of parents,
        78–79
    teachings of, 6–11, 140–42
    writings of, 31n
Bahá'u'lláh and the New Era
    (Esslemont), 222
Bahá'u'lláh, Revelation of, 202
Bahíyyih Khánum, 148–49, 153,
    154, 155, 156, 157, 159,
    205, 231
Baker, Dorothy, 221
Baker, Effie, 216–17
Banani International Secondary
    School for Girls, 255
Barney, Laura Clifford, 191–92
Baxter, Ian F. G., 118
Betrothal, 113
Bible. See also Christianity
    attitude toward women in,
        29–32
    equality of sexes in, 24, 25–26,
        27–28

Bird, wings of, 48, 299–304
Blomfield, Lady, 156–57, 183
Bombay of Persian Zoroastrian, 215
Burma, Bahá'í women in, 214–16

C

Canavarro, Madame de, 157, 159
Catherine the Great of Russia, 170
Cause of God, 222
Center for Partnership Studies, 70–71
Change
    creating psychological climate for, 49–51
    process of, 11–13
Chase, Thornton, 174
Chastity, 109
Children
    education for, 291
    rights of, in Bahá'í family, 75
    teaching consultation skills to, 90
Christianity, 121. *See also* Bible
    attitude toward women in, 29–32
    and doctrine of original sin, 30
    ecclesiastical functions in, 121
    influence on society, 32
City of God, The (Saint Augus-tine), 30
Cleopatra, 170
Clock, Sarah, 161
Collaboration in Bahá'í family, 79–81
Collins, Amelia E., 221, 223–25
Community, equality of sexes in, 291–94
Complementarity, Bahá'í concept of, 46–49
Constitution of the Universal House of Justice, The, 226

Consultation, teaching skill of, 89–90
Consultative decision-making in family, 82, 288
Continental Boards of Counselors, 122
Cooper, Ella, 177
Cooperation in Bahá'í family, 79–81
Covenant, Book of the, 8
Coy, Genevieve, 183, 185–86
Creation, divine purpose of, 301
Cultural diversity, 10

D

Dawn-Breakers, The (Nabíl-i-A'ẓam), 217
Declaration of Sentiments, 142
Devotional practices, distinction in, for men and women, 102–05
Direct challenge, 'Abdu'l-Bahá's use of, 168–69
Distance learning, 53
Divine Plan, 204n
Division of work in marriage, 289–90
Divorce
    Bahá'í teachings on, 117
    rights of women in initiating, 26
Ḍíyá, 154–55
Domestic pursuits, confinement of women to, 68
Dominance, paternalistic, 66
Dowry, 26, 75, 113–15, 118
Dunn, Clara, 221

E

Education
    for children, 291
    of daughters, 90–92

denial of facilities of, for
  women, 68
of girls and women, 40–44,
  251–55, 293–94
and participation in world at
  large, 46
Effendi, Shoghi, 155, 159, 202
on consultation, 86–87
ministry of, as Guardian, 211–12
on proposal of marriage, 74
role of, 203–04
  in developing Administrative
    Order, 205–12
  in fostering advancement of
    women, 212–16
  in international assignments
    to women, 216–25
  in interpreting teachings of
    Bahá'u'lláh and 'Abdu'l-
    Bahá, 204–05
on role of parents, 76
Eisler, Riane, 72–73
Emancipation of women, 39, 46
Encouragement
'Abdu'l-Bahá's role in providing,
  180–83
in Bahá'í family, 79–81
Engagement, 113
Equality of men and women
Bahá'í approach to achieving, 7,
  52–53
Bahá'í approach to implementing, 50–55
in Bahá'í Faith, 5–6
and Bahá'í law, 97
Bahá'í teachings on, 36–50
Bahá'u'lláh's teachings on,
  140–42
complementarity of, 46–49
denial of, 59

full expression of, 5–6
historical survey of, 19–36
promulgation of, 5–6
relationship of, to world peace,
  62–63
significance of, 19
as spiritual principle, 38–39
transmission of attitudes of, to
  wider society, 70–74
Esslemont, John, 222
European Task Force for
  Women, 247
Evil, women as agents of, 22, 30,
  103, 106–07
Examples
'Abdu'l-Bahá's use of contemporary, 171
power of, 194–95
Extremism, rise in, 55

F

Faizi Vocational Institute for Rural
  Women, 251–54
Family. *See also* Parents
Bahá'í, 74–76
Bahá'í teachings on dynamics of,
  61–92
coequality of husband and wife
  in, 89
collaboration, cooperation, and
  encouragement in, 79–81
contribution of, to creating
  peace, 87–88
distinctiveness of, 74–76
equality and disruption of
  structure in, 61
equality of sexes in, 287–91
as matrix, 61
patriarchal, 63–70
rights of children in, 75

Family (continued)
  role of parents in, 76–79
  socialization roles of, 70–74
Family values
  Bahá'í, and peace, 74–92
  traditional, and warfare, 63–74
Fathers. See also Men; Parents
  benefits from greater involvement
    of, in child rearing, 81
  role of, in Bahá'í Faith, 76–79
Fatimih (daughter of Muḥammad),
    121
Fáṭimih Begum, 149–50
Fáṭimih Khánum, 187
Fazl'u'lláh Khán, Mírzá, 193
Federation of Women's Clubs in
    Chicago, 240
Female infanticide, forbidding of, in
    Qur'án, 26
Fertility, worship of, 21
Financial rights of women, 118–20
Five Year Plan (1974–1979), 230, 231
Formative Age, 201
  inception of, 202
Fourth World Conference on
    Women, 243
Four Year Plan (1946–1950), 209
Fozdar, Shirin, 215, 216, 247
Future, facing, with confidence,
    294–96

G

Gender prejudice, damaging effects
    of, 299–300
Gender-specific language, 31n
Genital mutilation, 109, 246
Getsinger, Lua, 178
Girls. See Women
God, teachings of the Manifesta-
    tions of, 23–27

Golden Age, 201
Goodall, Helen, 177
Greatness Which Might Be Theirs,
    The, 243
Group decision-making, Bahá'í
    approach to, 81–87
Guardianship, 8

H

Hands of the Cause of God, 186,
    187, 211, 216, 218, 220,
    221n, 223, 224
Health Awareness Project, 256
History, 'Abdu'l-Bahá's use of
    examples from, 169–71
Hoagg, Emogene, 192
Homosexual relationships,
    prohibition of, 109
House of Justice, 132
House of Spirituality, 187
Human development, 165–66
Human rights, concept of, 71–72
Human spirit, liberation of, 11
Húr, 35

I

Ibn-i-Abhar, 186, 187
Ideal community, vision of, 51–52
Implementation, Bahá'í approach
    to, 49–55
Incest, 66–67
Independent investigation, Bahá'í
    principle of, 269–70
India, Bahá'í women in, 214–16, 238
Individual conduct, 271–77
Individual development, interactive
    relationship between
    social development and, 7
Individual level, equality of sexes at,
    283–87

Inferior, woman as, 22–23
Inheritance, 118–20
Intellectual development, 'Abdu'l-
Bahá in fostering, 191–94
Intellectual vitality, 10
International Bahá'í Congress,
first, 177
International Bahá'í Congress
Day, 177
International Bahá'í Council,
211–12, 224
International Bahá'í Women's
Conference, 233
International Teaching Center,
women as Counselor
members of, 122
Interpersonal relatedness, underde-
velopment of, 67
Intestacy provisions, 120
Iran, Bahá'í women in, 207–09,
211, 212
Irwin, Beatrice, 194
Isabella (Queen), 170
Ishráqíyyih Dhabíh, 186
Islam, prohibition of alcohol in, 99
Islamic countries
Bahá'í community in, 207–09
ecclesiastical functions in,
121–22

J

Jack, Marion, 184
Jesus Christ
attitude of, toward women, 24,
25–26
and woman from Samaria, 24, 121
Judaism, ecclesiastical functions
in, 121
Justice, need for, within family
unit, 71

K

Kappes, Lillian, 185
Khadijah, 121
Khadíjih Bagum, 149
Kitáb-i-Aqdas. See also Bahá'í law(s)
inheritance in, 119–20
laws of, 98, 101–02
prescriptions for ablutions in,
97, 105

L

Language, question of gender
in, 31n
Lar Linda Tanure Orphanage, 254
Latin America, Bahá'í women in,
213–14
League of Nations, 215
Lerner, Gerda, 66, 169–70
Lewis Institute (Chicago), 193
Literacy training, 252
Local Spiritual Assemblies, women
as members of, 122

M

Madhya Pradesh, India, 252
Manifestation(s) of God, 5–6, 8
Bahá'u'lláh's claim to be, 6, 11,
98, 127
teachings of, 23–27
Marie of Rumania (Queen), 222–23
Marital rape, 66–67
Marriage
attitude and relationship between
husband and wife in, 74
Bahá'í ceremony of, 74–75
Bahá'í teachings on, 111–16
causes of breakdown of, 115–16
consent of both parties for, 113
dowry in, 26, 75, 113–15, 118
equality of sexes in, 287–91

Marriage *(continued)*
  parental consent for, 87
  prohibitions in selection of mate
    for, 101
  rights of women in, 26–27
  selection of partner for, 87
  sexual conduct within, 116–17
  violence in, 116–17
Mary Magdalene, 24, 121, 170
Mary (mother of Jesus), 170
Maulānā Muḥammad 'Alí, 35
Medical compounds, 128
Memorials of the Faithful ('Abdu'l-
    Bahá), 149–50
Men. See also Fathers
  arrogance and preoccupation
    with honor in, 35
  attitudinal change in, 258–61
  complementary relationship be-
    tween women and, 46–49
  devotional practices set out for,
    102–05
  equality of, with women in
    Bahá'í Faith, 5–6
  fostering of aggression of, within
    family setting, 72
  spiritual equality of women and,
    37–40
"Men of Justice," 123
Menstruation, exemption from
    certain devotional
    activities during, 102–03,
    105
Mernissi, Fatima, 33
Mihdí, Mírzá, 146
Military prowess, 72
Miller, Jean Baker, 65
Monogamy, 111–12
Moody, Susan, 161

Moral imperative, 267–68
Mother Nature, association of
    female of species with,
    21–22
Mothers. See also Parents; Women
  function of, 44
  restoration of, to position of
    honor and respect,
    290–91
  reverence for, and protection of,
    302
  role of, in Bahá'í Faith, 76–79
Muḥammad, 121
  attitude of, toward women,
    33–36
Munírih Khánum, 153, 156, 157,
    158, 159, 184, 186, 187
Mutuality, appreciation of, 80

N

Nabíl-i-A'ẓam, 217
National Spiritual Assembly,
    ordination of, 123
National and Unit Conventions, 82
National Women's Progressive
    Committee, 209
New Zealand, Bahá'í women in,
    238
Nineteen Day Feasts, 82, 122,
    236n, 274
Nongovernmental organization
    (NGO), 240
  Forum on Women, 243
Nushúz, 27

O

Okin, Susan Moller, 71
Original sin, Christian doctrine of,
    31–32

P

Panama-Pacific International
    Exposition, 177
Parents. *See also* Fathers; Mothers
    applying Bahá'í consultation to
        decision-making by,
        84–85
    role of, in Bahá'í family, 76–79
    socialization roles of, 70–74
Parsons, Agnes, 176–77
Paternalistic dominance, 66
Patriarchal family, harmful effects
    of, 63–70
Paul's view of women, 29–30
Peace
    Bahá'í family's contribution to
        creating, 87–88
    Bahá'í family values and, 74–92
    inevitability of world, 61–62
    relationship of, to equality,
        62–63
    role of women in universal, 303
    women's contributions to, 46
    and women's participation in
        society, 46
Persian Bahá'ís, and establishing
        schools for girls, 43
Personal conduct
    Bahá'í principles of, 276
    women and laws of, 102–17
Personal transformation, process of,
        272
Persuasion, power of, 11
Pilgrimage, exemptions to women
        from performance of
        Bahá'í, 103–04
Pioneering, 211n
Polygamy, 21, 26, 111, 112–13
Power

of example, 194–95
    use of, 11
Prayer
    devotional practices of, 6
    exemptions from laws of
        obligatory, 103–04, 105
Present day, women in, 53–55
Progressive clarification, 125–26
    Bahá'í approach to, 125–26
Promise of World Peace, The
    (Universal House of
    Justice), 227
Prosperity of Humankind, The
    (Bahá'í International
    Community), 248
Psychological climate for change,
    creating, 49–51

Q

Qur'án
    attitude toward women in, 27–28,
        33–36
    dowry in, 114
    equality of sexes in, 24–25,
        26–29

R

Radical feminism, problems caused
        by, 61
Ransom-Kehler, Mrs. Keith, 216,
        217–21
Rape
    blaming victims of, 22
    marital, 66–67
    prevalence of, 110
    treatment of victims of, 107–08
Religion
    failure of community to preserve
        its pristine purity, 28

Religion *(continued)*
  purpose of, from Bahá'í
    perspective, 267
  rise in fanaticism in, 54
  role of, 5
  role of women in functioning of,
    120–21
  treatment of women by leaders
    in, 28–36
  true purpose of, 10
Rhetorical questions, 'Abdu'l-Bahá's
  use of, 167–68
Ritual impurity, 103, 104–05
Role definition, creation of rigid
  sense of, 68–70
Root, Martha, 132, 178–79, 194,
  221–23, 231
Rosenberg, Ethel, 172–73, 205–06,
  212
Rúhangíz Fath-'Azam, 186
Rutstein, Nathan, 174

S

Saint Augustine, 30
Saint Thomas Aquinas, 32
Samaria, woman of, 24, 121
Sarah (wife of Abraham), 170
Scapegoats, choice of women as, 22
Scheffler, Carl, 174
Secondary House of Justice, 123
Secret of Divine Civilization, The
  ('Abdu'l-Bahá), 140
Self-discipline, 5
Self-expression, legitimate rights of, 10
Seneca Falls Women's Rights
  Convention, 142
Service by women on Bahá'í
  institutions, 120–34
Seven Year Plan (1979–1986), 234
Sex roles

problems created by traditional
    expectations of, 69
  rigid definition of, 72–73
  stereotypic, 166
  traditional, 166
Sexual abuse of women, 107–08,
    116–17
Sexual conduct
  Bahá'í laws regulating, 105–10
  within marriage, 116–17
Sexual harassment
  blaming victims of, 22
  in workplace, 54, 108–09
Sexual objects, tendency to debase
    women into, 35
Shahin Vafai, 272n
Shoghi Effendi, 8
Sin. See Original sin
Social development, interactive rela-
    tionship between individual
    development and, 7
Socialization, role of family in,
    70–74
Society, Christian influence on, 32
Sodomy, 110
Spiritual Assemblies, 123, 124–25
  of the Bahá'ís of India and
    Burma, 214–15
  of Bahá'í Women, 187, 212
  decision-making in, 81
  in Egypt, 210
  election of first woman to,
    237–38
  formation of, 202–03, 205
  role of, in monitoring commu-
    nity, 292–94
  role of, in providing encourage-
    ment, 180–83
  women as members of, 122
Spiritual life, ideal, 6–7

Stewart, Elizabeth, 161
Subordinates, roles of, in patriarchal family, 65
Subordination of women, 67–68
Summa Theologica (Aquinas), 32
Supreme Tribunal, 131n

T

Tarbíyat school for girls, 184, 191
Technological advances and equality of sexes, 53
Telecommuting, 53
Ten Year Plan (1953–1963), goals of, 225
Timeliness, 'Abdu'l-Bahá on, 163–64
True, Corinne, 173–76, 175, 205–06, 212, 221
True, Katherine, 193
Truth, independent investigation of, 127
Túbá Khánum, 160
Turning Point For All Nations (Bahá'í International Community), 249
Two Wings of a Bird (National Spiritual Assembly of the Bahá'ís of the United States), 261

U

United Nations
  Children's Fund (UNICEF), 240
  Commission on Human Rights, 244
  Commission on the Status of Women, 243–44
  Decade for Women (1976–1985), 240–41
  Development Fund for Women (UNIFEM), 243, 258

Economic and Social Council (ECOSOC), 240
Universal Declaration of Women's Rights, 216
Universal House of Justice, 8–9, 10
  on adultery, 117
  Bahá'í teachings on membership of, 130
  confinement of membership of, to men, 122–23
  on consultation, 83–84
  decision-making of, 100
  election of members of, 124–25
  on emancipation of women, 46
  on equality of men and women, 47
  exclusion of women from membership of, 124–27
  on father's responsibilities, 78
  formation of, 202–03
  functions of, 133
  on mother's responsibilities, 77
  on peace, 42
  role of, 225–26

V

Violence
  in marriage, 116–17
  against women, 244–46
Virginity, 115
Voices and Choices: The Women's Movement in Singapore, 247

W

War
  and traditional family values, 63–74
  women's opposition to, 73
Will, writing of, 118–20

Williams, Juanita, 21
"Woman's Society of Progress," 193
Woman's Suffrage meeting, 240
Women. *See also* Mothers
  'Abdu'l-Bahá in promoting
    enlightenment of, 183–91
  as agents of evil, 22, 30, 103,
    106–07
  in antiquity, 20–23
  application of Bahá'í law to,
    101–02
  association of, with Mother
    Nature, 21–22
  attitude of Jesus Christ toward,
    25–26
  attitudinal change in, 258–61
  Bahá'u'lláh's guidance and
    encouragement to,
    142–45
  choice of, as scapegoats, 22
  Christian attitude toward, 29–32
  complementary relationship
    between men and, 46–49
  confinement of, to domestic
    pursuits, 68
  confinement of, to service
    positions in employ-
    ment, 73
  contributions of, to peace, 46
  denial of education facilities
    for, 68
  denial of full social equality of,
    with men, 63–70
  devotional practices set out for,
    102–05
  education of, 40–44, 251–55,
    293–94
    and participation of, in world
      at large, 46

  emancipation of, 39, 46
  equality of, with men in Bahá'í
    Faith, 5–6
  financial rights of, 118–20
  fostering development and
    participation of, 90–92
  fostering participation by, in
    Bahá'í administration,
    235–39
  improving health care of,
    255–58
  income-earning capacity of, 254
  as inferior, 22–23
  intelligence of, 32
  international assignments to,
    216–25
  as intrinsically unclean, 21–22
  and laws of personal conduct,
    102–17
  Muslim attitude toward, 33–36
  Office for the Advancement of,
    240–49
  participation of, in world at
    large, 44–49
  in present day, 53–55
  promoting social and economic
    development of, 249–50
  rights of, 141–42
  in Asia, 247–48
  in marriage, 26
  role of Shoghi Effendi in
    fostering advancement of,
    212–16
  and service on Bahá'í institu-
    tions, 120–34
  sexual abuse of, 107–08
  social position of, 25–26
  spiritual equality of men and,
    38–40

subordination of, 67–68
systematic oppression of, 299
tendency to debase, into sexual
    objects, 35–36
treatment of, in religious
    practice, 27–36
veiling of, 34
violence against, 244–46
Women's Assembly of Teaching, 187
Women's rights movement in Amer-
    ica, founding of, 300

Workplace, sexual harassment in,
    54, 108–09
World Conference on Human
    Rights in Vienna,
    244
World Conference on Religion and
    Peace, 246
World peace. *See* Peace

Z

Zenobia, 170